Herman Melville's *Clarel*

A Spiritual Autobiography

Herman Melville's *Clarel*

A Spiritual Autobiography

VINCENT KENNY

Archon Books
1973

Library of Congress Cataloging in Publication Data

Kenny, Vincent S.
Herman Melville's Clarel.

Bibliography:
1. Melville, Herman, 1819-1891. Clarel. I. Title.
PS2384.C53K4 1973 811'.3 73-3074
ISBN 0-208-01226-5

FIRST PUBLISHED 1973 AS AN ARCHON BOOK
BY THE SHOE STRING PRESS, INC.,
HAMDEN, CONNECTICUT

Printed in the United States of America

To Gloria
who if the truth were known is co-author of this book

Contents

Foreword

For some years I taught two graduate seminars at New York University, one devoted to Walt Whitman and the other to Herman Melville. Though most of my publications were in the field of Whitman studies, I often found the Melville seminar more stimulating, both to the students and myself. Because *Moby-Dick* alone provided more than enough problems for a semester of intensive study, I usually neglected Melville's late, 18,000-word poem, *Clarel*. One of my most competent students, Vincent Kenny, thought this long poem too important to be neglected. The poet's apparently compulsive quest for religious faith through the minds of his many characters in *Clarel* seemed to him not only of intrinsic value itself, with its search for answers to questions which the twentieth century has inherited from the nineteenth, but also, he maintained, *Clarel* was of crucial importance in understanding the mind and literary career of Herman Melville. Except for *Billy Budd*, this was Melville's final effort to expiate the tragic guilt of Taji, Ahab, and Pierre.

Of course I encouraged Mr. Kenny to undertake an exhaustive study of *Clarel*, and the doctoral dissertation which he submitted in 1965 was both thorough and illuminating. In reading it again, I wonder why I did not encourage him to publish it without delay, but I remember that he had recently recovered from a long illness, and I thought at the time that he should rest before undertaking some minor revisions which the manuscript needed before being published—as nearly every doctoral dissertation does. Having other theses to supervise, my attention was diverted from Mr. Kenny's work. Fortunately, his essay on "Clarel's Rejection of the Titans," recently published in *The American Transcendental Quarterly* (7: 76-81) aroused interest in his neglected dissertation, and led to this present volume. Professor Kenny has meanwhile revised the manuscript which he submitted for his thesis, thus removing my only reservation; and now I am trying to atone for my negligence by writing this foreword.

In recent years *Clarel* has begun to attract more attention, partly through the efforts of several critics to evaluate Melville's increasing sympathy in his old age for Catholicism, though Kenny finds more tolerance than sympathy in *Clarel.* For Clarel, whose religious quest resembles Melville's (though he is not entirely the author's alter ego), none of his host of companions finds a solution "adequate for him." Thus, "when last seen, Clarel 'Vanishes in the obscurer town,' alone since the reluctant departure of Rolfe, Vine and Derwent, and close to despair. . . . He walks alone but resolutely behind the crowd." Thus Kenny agrees with those critics (who are in the majority), who regard *Clarel* as Melville's spiritual autobiography, though he does not, like Lewis Mumford, see the poem as an intellectual dramatization of Melville's trip to Palestine in 1856-1857. The trip provided impressions and imagery for the poem, but the debates were those the author had been holding with himself both before and after his trip, and were as agonizing for him in 1876, when he published the poem, as during the time he was being devoured by fleas and bedbugs at night and stifled by the dust of ruins by day as he retraced the steps of Jesus and His Disciples across what Melville called in his diary the "diabolical landscape of Judea," which "must have suggested to the Jewish prophets their ghastly theology."

Rereading Kenny's study of *Clarel* leads me to suggest that the poem ought to be approached by three routes. There is, first of all, Melville's life-long search through primitive cultures, the dreamworld of mythology, the history and literature of civilization, and his own spiritual quest for the meaning of existence. Professor Kenny has outlined this route to *Clarel* and shown the continuity of the agonizing journey.

Then there is the influence of Melville's actual trip to Palestine and adjacent lands, as recorded in his *Journal/Up the Straits/1856*. He visited Jerusalem at a time when it was under Moslem control and the places sacred in Christian memory had been abused, exploited, and abandoned to filth, decay, and every kind of contempt. He met a few half-demented Americans who had gone there to convert the infidel or teach the Jews how to farm. Unlike the missionaries Melville had satirized in *Typee* and *Omoo*, they were doing little if any harm, and as little good. But they helped to confirm Melville's suspicion that the Holy Land was a hoax on his credulity. Possibly in his youthful innocence, like Wellingborough Redburn on his trip to Liverpool, he might have felt compassion for the ragged Arabs and the homeless Jews, but in 1856-1857 they only intensified his pessimistic view of human destiny.

The third approach to *Clarel* is well prepared for in this book, which can serve as a guide for further study. Professor Kenny is acutely aware of the influence of Melville's misfortunes on his psychology and philosophy, but he points out that his sciatica was not entirely (if at all) psychosomatic. In 1854, one of the happier years of his life, he suffered severe pains in his back. Similarly, his tragic views of man were not simply reflex reaction to pain, or the half-baked ideas of a poorly educated man. When Van Wyck Brooks declared that an elementary course in philosophy might have saved Melville from his intellectual floundering, it was he who was the superficial one. Melville anticipated the "scientific" pessimism of Arthur James Balfour in *The Foundations of Belief* (1895):

> The energies of our system will decay, the glory of the sun will be dimmed, and the earth, tideless and inert, will no longer tolerate the race which has for a moment disturbed its solitude. Man will go down into the pit, and all his thoughts will perish. The uneasy consciousness which in this obscure corner has for a brief space broken the contented silence of the universe, will be at rest. Matter will know itself no longer. 'Imperishable monuments' and

> 'immortal deeds,' death itself, and love stronger than death, will be as if they had not been. Nor will anything that is, be better or worse for all that the labor, genius, devotion and suffering of man have striven through countless ages to effect.

William James declared that he could not live in such a world. Mark Twain also rebelled against it in his own sardonic way, and Henry Adams was driven into ironic solipsism. In the twentieth century Wallace Stevens did learn to live in the "old chaos of the sun," with all the fatal implications of Balfour's description, finding compensation in pure sensation for the loss of faith in everything transcending the senses. But such consolation was not possible for Herman Melville, and existential man in the atomic age still walks in the shadow of Clarel's solitude. The dense poem *Clarel*, long thought to be unreadable—even by its author—now has something to say to twentieth-century readers.

There still remains, however, the difficulty of what Professor Kenny calls the "constricted lines," which he admits to being an aesthetic hurdle. Granting that the "arid style" fits the tone and theme of the poem, the rhymes are still a blemish. The 18,000 verses of rhymed octosyllabics require an inordinate quantity of rhymewords, and Melville often had to sacrifice precision of meaning for a vain tinkling of sound. The awkward inversions for the sake of rhyme could be endured, as they have to be in reading Whittier, but wrenching semantics for the game of rhyme is less pardonable. For example, in the passage quoted on p. 76 the complusion under which Mortmain travels is more like a curse or a spell (enchantment) than a "ban," and "dearth" in the line following is even more inappropriate—trite, inaccurate, and feeble. A prosodic form such as Milton used in *Sampson Agonistes*, which Melville certainly knew, might have saved him such shoddy compromises. But it is needless to quarrel with the poet—if Melville can be called a poet, and he certainly had been, perhaps unconsciously, in many passages of his earlier prose—for he deliberately hobbled his muse in writing *Clarel*, and the reader must be patient with his stumbling gait for the sake of his companionship and "deep diving" thoughts. For travel guide, I recommend Vincent Kenny's *Herman Melville's* CLAREL.

GAY WILSON ALLEN
Emeritus Professor of English

NEW YORK UNIVERSITY

Preface

I remember the response of Professor Oscar Cargill when he heard of my interest in a closer look at Melville's *Clarel*: "Kenny, I believe you have greater fortitude than intelligence." After countless readings of this leviathan poem, I know what he meant in part, for it was designed by Melville for the brave of heart. But this is only half the truth, as Cargill in sly fashion knew. John Hoadley—Melville's brother-in-law—observed that "thoughtful reading" will reward the person who stays with the poem to the end and will introduce him to one of the most profound poets of the nineteenth century. I do not see this poem ever as a best-seller in paperback circulation, nor as assigned reading in collegiate or graduate courses in American literature. But there will be a greater number of readers following Hoadley's advice, because the development of thought in the western world during the twentieth century corresponds to the rebellious ideas, debilitating anxieties, and moral postures that Melville incorporated in *Clarel* and the other poems after the Civil War. Melville, it is becoming clear, is more of our age than he was of his own. Camus saw this clearly when he recognized his literary relationship with the older Melville; and contemporary critics find the twentieth-century problems of alienation, rebellion, Godlessness and the need for inner journies thoroughly explored by an author who was never able to get outside his own existential concerns. Indeed, anxiety over faith-doubt; anticipation of a Pentecostal resurgence of religion in a triumph of heart over head; and interest in a naked form reflecting stripped ideas stamped Melville—and *Clarel* in particular—as current in our time

Despite the title of the book, this is not a biography in the usual sense of the word. This is why, in the many areas where the facts of Melville's life are involved, I have relied heavily on *The Letters of Herman Melville* and *The Melville Log*. For critical reference to the author's writings, I have used *The Works of Herman Melville* (The Standard Edition of Constable reissued in 1963 by Russell and Russell) with two exceptions: the Northwestern-Newberry edition of *Mardi* and the Hendricks House edition of *Clarel*.

Professor Gay Wilson Allen's gentle and thoughtful persuasion managed me through the early and difficult reading of *Clarel* until Melville's own controlled excitement forced me to return many times thereafter. I am grateful to Professor Allen, as I am to the behind-the-scenes persons: Alan Meckler, the mystery readers of my work, and the committee at my college who granted me leave to finish this book. The librarians at Marymount College are once again in my debt for their ready assistance. Ann Daly, Marian Downey, and Dr. Helen Hayes performed tasks which literally brought my work to a finished state. All of them constituted for me the "joint stock-company" that Ishmael looked for on the *Pequod*.

Herman Melville's *Clarel*

A Spiritual Autobiography

I

Introduction

> With the few who were permitted to know him he was the man of culture, the congenial companion, and the honestest and manliest of all earthly friends.
> O. G. Hillard, *New York Times* (October 6, 1891)

The overnight success that Herman Melville enjoyed with *Typee* and *Omoo* hardly prepared him for the rude reception he received for his more serious efforts. Thus the execration of *Mardi and a Voyage Thither* by the critics and the general indifference to or violent dislike for *Moby-Dick* and *Pierre* infuriated and saddened him. Instead of fighting back openly, however, he withdrew from a society he believed incapable of understanding his work.[1] With *Typee* and *Omoo* he had won a vast audience as a storyteller; he had become "the man who lived among the cannibals" to a reading public that relished the exotic, lush, South Sea episodes as much as they abhorred the didactic in fiction. He had demonstrated to them again a command of this narrative formula with *Redburn* and *White-Jacket* immediately after *Mardi*, but they left him frustrated with himself as an artist:

> I am so pulled hither and thither by circumstance. The calm, the coolness, the silent grass-growing mood in which a man *ought* always to compose,—that, I fear, can seldom be mine. Dollars damn me; and the malicious Devil is forever grinning in upon me, holding the door ajar . . . What I feel most moved to write, that is banned,—it will not pay. Yet, altogether, write the *other* way I cannot. So the product is a final hash, and all my books are botches.[2]

The little happiness Melville enjoyed at his Berkshire farm through his friendship with the Hawthornes and Morewoods in 1850-1851 was dissipated thereafter in the aftereffects of *Moby-Dick* and *Pierre*. One biographer, overstating the case, believes that any glimpse we have of him after this time is of a tired, middle-aged man, silent, morose, and only a shadow of the early South Sea adventurer.[3]

The modest but brief prosperity Melville earned from farming "Arrowhead," and the themes of patience, endurance, and nonaggression evident in the much-discussed Agatha story, as well as in *Israel Potter*, "The Encantadas," and in the other *Piazza Tales*, express a comparative contentment or acceptance during this time in Pittsfield which suggests that he did discover the grass-growing mood requisite for art. This was only occasional, however, for the patience too often gave way to a conviction and fear of evil as the dominant reality in life: this fear became the source and power of the short story "Benito Cereno." Like Pierre and Benito, Melville constantly examined his interior life, and at no time more so than during this period between 1852 and 1856, when he moved from periods of peace to ones of dissatisfaction with himself as a man, a farmer, and a writer. Every work he produced in Pittsfield reflects this tortured condition, in one way or another.

The decision by Elizabeth Melville to call in Dr. Holmes for advice on her husband's health makes good sense in the light of these mixed moods. The romantic aura Melville had earlier carried with him apparently was gone, for Elizabeth saw now only a man who had failed financially as a writer and a farmer, who suffered from backache, chronic sciatica, and weak eyes, who had already seen the glamour of marriage disappear, and who felt compelled to plumb the causes of his own melancholy. Frequent nervous fits of temper and ramblings of a perverse conscience led to "the family's decision to send Herman abroad for his health."[4] Dr. Holmes's concurrence and Lemuel Shaw's gracious loan to cover expenses completed the plan and enabled Melville to go abroad for seven months.

He traveled to England in October of 1856. There for a few days, he renewed his acquaintanceship with Hawthorne, then the American Consul at Liverpool. The older friend's fear for Melville's mental health, expressed after the first day together, argues against Evert Duyckinck's diary entry, indicating that at the time of his sailing from New York Melville seemed in excellent spirits.[5] The good spirits must have been euphoria, for Hawthorne saw clearly the same morbidity and nervousness that had characterized Melville's conversations earlier in Lenox now manifest in a more advanced condition.[6]

Melville continued his trip, leaving Liverpool directly for Constantinople on November 19, 1856. The remaining months constituted a pilgrimage for him, unlike any of the earlier trips of adventure. He visited Constantinople and Alexandria, the Greek mainland and a few of the Isles, other villages and cities in the Middle East, but during this phase of the trip he concentrated his time and attention on the Holy Land. He landed at Jaffa on January 6 and remained in the Palestine area until January 27. His return home was a leisurely one: it included another visit to Greece, a prolonged tour of Italy—Naples and Rome in particular—a sail up the Rhine, a "waterlogged" stay in London and a romantic visit to Oxford, and final embarkation from Liverpool on May 6, 1857. He arrived in New York on May 19.

The seven-month vacation was sporadically recorded by Melville in three slim volumes of cryptic observations. He considered the work as little more than a series of jottings, or so the quality of the writing and the careless title he gave it on the cover of the second volume would indicate—*Journal/Up the Straits/1856*.[7] It is also significant that this long and emotional experience was not immediately worked into a novel or a story, contrary to the literary practice Melville adopted after the earlier experiences away from home.[8] The seven-months period was not altogether lost, however, for he delivered a lecture on "Roman Statuary" wherever and whenever he was invited to speak after his return in 1857. Even more important than this topic for the first lecture series, the Holy Land episode ultimately inspired the most ambitious work of his life, the poem *Clarel*, which was written on and off over the next fifteen years.

It is this extraordinary and different composition of Melville's that will be examined in this book, both as a poem qua poetry and as a clear reflection of the author's life and work. Such a lengthy study is necessary, first, because this important aspect of Melville has drawn little interest from the critics; and second, because the poem is a culmination of the author's philosophical, political, social, and religious views. Any reading of the voluminous writings of Melville that does not include *Clarel* leaves the author only half-discovered at best; for this poem more than any other single composition forcefully demonstrates how Melville could not and would not write "the other way."

Clarel is longer than *Paradise Lost* and more ambitious than *The Prelude*. It is written in a fairly consistent iambic tetrameter pattern of irregular, hooked rhymes. The subject matter circles almost endlessly around a modern pilgrim's search for truth and blisters all of the popular nineteenth-century notions of progress, optimism, and meliorism. Such form and subject matter precluded all possibilities for popular success. Indeed, aside from the critics who were obligated to read the poem and Melville's immediate family and friends—some of whom admitted they could not get through it—the poem remained a private affair. Buffeted by the critics for twenty years before, however, Melville was serenely indifferent to positive or negative reactions from the reading public: his primary purpose was to record his own spiritual and psychological inventory. This accounts for the wry statement he placed at the beginning of the poem:

> If during the period in which this work has remained unpublished, though not undivulged, any of its properties have by a natural process exhaled; it yet retains, I trust, enough of the original life to redeem it at least from vapidity. Be that as it may, I here dismiss the book—content beforehand with whatever future awaits it.[9]

In *Clarel* Melville examined the nineteenth century, in which the high promises of the Transcendentalists had borne only the fruit of "The Great Barbecue," one in which the scientific investigations and conclusions of German higher criticism produced a spiritual vacuum, an age altogether that repelled him. Nothing in history and his own experiences could persuade him to accept even in part the Emersonian formulas that argued away the force of evil. The Lutheran Protestantism that held such promise for democracy was equally meaningless to him. It had splintered itself into a thousand pieces, each piece divisible again. For him, the pieces could never be fitted into a whole, convincing, enduring body of religious belief. What was left was only a stale, flat meliorism to a man who "wildly longed" for unity and for resolution in a fixed set of values. Thus the "loss of faith is the basic assumed fact of the poem, and its largest problem is how to endure the overwhelming sense of a shattered vision."[10]

In his assessment of the age and man's ciphered condition, Melville was not unmindful of the solutions offered by the Darwins, Spencers, and Fiskes. They presented a cheerful and seemingly plausible explanation of mankind's evolution out of a slimed existence to a paradise of its own making. These social scientists argued that God had no part in this creativeness, that belief in His existence only admits of an intellectual deficiency, and that other consequent illusions would be dispelled through newer and greater scientific discoveries. To all of these claims and to the others in natural science and the political sphere, Melville's answer was simple: "the greater the light, the more the shadow."

Conversely, Melville judged as quixotic the social thrust of rebels and anarchists who would create a democratic state through violence; such action to him was as unrealistic as the perfective views of the Transcendentalists and the scientists. In *Redburn* and *White-Jacket*, of course, he had argued for an end to brutality: both books were vehement in their attacks on poverty and flogging. But neither in them nor in any other work did Melville support a plan for leveling *en masse*. He applauded the hero who labored to help his neighbor but he insisted that all men must assert their own heroism too. He believed that ready-made plans for the ensurance of human equality contradict the facts of history and thwart the instincts of human nature. Man is not intended for the paradise on earth the social rebels insisted must come. Melville abhorred the persecution of any man, but he could not accept utopian theories that would blot out the awful fact of tragic human existence. Each man must face up to the forces working against him, according to the degree of his fortitude. No one can legislate away this responsibility or remove it through acts of charity.

Melville realized that in the buoyant nineteenth century such assessments would be construed as indifference to the human race or as outright misanthropy. He also knew that a catalog of cautions and negations in his long poem would antagonize most readers who were ready to reject any hints of nihilism. Their reaction was of no real interest to him. What did concern him was a failure to find a center in his own moral sphere by which he could judge human action free from ambiguity. As far back as *Redburn* he had presented to his young hero a moral problem in the discovery of the mother and her children dying of hunger in Launcelott's-Hey: should Redburn be filled with compassion over this suffering, or should his heart be murderously angry with society for ignoring these helpless people? It was not clear to Melville, in the 1840s or the 1870s, whether his pity or love for man and his impatience with their dreams, inevitable failures, and villanies could be reconciled in any ethic or in any system of values. Despite all of his past failures to find such a system or norm for moral judgment, Melville obviously persisted right up to the composition of his long poem, and probably to the end of his life. This endless inquiry literally became the form of *Clarel*, as the young hero moves through a series of experiences, relationships, and options. One of the choices offered him is the teaching of the Roman Catholic Church. This accounts for the unusual and highly unlikely examination of the Church, an institution that on the surface, at least, struck Melville as one that demands heroism of its members at the same time it embraces them as failures.

In the poem, Clarel is in awe of the Church's longevity and of her ready response to man's emotional needs. He is impressed by her lineage of grandeur, emanating from the Hebrew patriarchs and culminating in the great humanitarian, Jesus; by her set of beliefs which reach a human apotheosis in the Sermon on the Mount, and which suggest an absolute quality vitally needed in a world of constantly shifting values. He sees as exemplary the Church's insistence upon the dignity of a man despite his weaknesses, symbolized in ritual and practiced in compassionate actions; and this in sharp contrast to the indecorum of the gilded age and the disregard held for the person in the barbarous nineteenth century. Even with such awe for the Church, however, Clarel knows that she cannot finally remove the gnawing doubts, loneliness, and pain. Her glossing over the fact of tragedy through prayer, sacrifice, and the sacraments is as unacceptable to him as are the legends of the resurrection and ascension of Christ. Through Clarel and others as spokesmen in the poem, sympathy in Melville for the Catholic Church included a wonder over her centuries-old existence and approval of her psychological approach to suffering. But in no way could he accept the Church's dogma or institutional character.

Melville's interests lay in another similar explanation of man's sorrowful condition: the one expressed by Henry James, Sr., and many others, as the "Fortunate Fall." Like Melville, James scorned the optimism of the nineteenth century. He insisted that the nature of man is imperfect as a consequence of his fall from grace, which left him a tragic figure. Melville never doubted this view of alienated man. He also believed in James's principle of universal brotherhood as the foundation of society and the way to amelioration. Ishmael's "joint stock-company" appears throughout his writings as a correct social offset to individual selfishness. Although he saw it as an oversimplification, Melville believed that the "selfish principle or proprium" did corrupt civilization and render harmonious relationships impossible to achieve. This was the dilemma he created in Ahab's admirable ambition and the inevitable destruction it effected. But the preachment of the "Fortunate Fall" concluded that this tragic figure has a heroic potential for regeneration which can carry him to paradise; and that knowledge of this perfectibility of human nature leads man logically to the acceptance of Christ's True Church as coextensive with the human race.[11] It was in this conclusion that Melville parted company with the advocates of the "Fortunate Fall" position. Like them he believed in the resiliency of man when faced with the most awful odds; but he never saw evidence of any progress toward the perfection these optimists looked for. Accordingly, in the poem Melville does have Clarel experience tragedy and discover the fact of pervasive evil. But unlike James, he precludes any salvation for Clarel: the future holds for his character only a continuation of sorrow that must be faced heroically and alone.

In *Clarel*, then, Melville evaluates the fall of man and consequent redemption as taught by the Catholic Church and, in a different way, as demonstrated by James and other religious enthusiasts of his day. He finds both views psychologically sound because they recommend individual responsibility as the prerequisite for ethics. But he rejects any extension into philosophic truth which discounts the need for faith, or, conversely, into a theological system in which faith alone attests to the truths of humanity and the universe. To phrase it differently, he wished to accept programs of certainty at the same time that he knew none were possible; he longed for an end to his skepticism even as he doubted that a man could exist free from uncertainty. Thus he expressed in the 1870s the same Babbalanja-Taji conflict, but with no resolution more available than in the 1840s. He still saw man as homeless, a wanderer cut off from all other men and things of meaning, and further burdened in the awful discovery of his condition. Nor could he find any relief in the solutions he saw in practice all around him: erotic or romantic love, membership in formal religion, establishment of friendship or postures of misanthropy and violence, dedication to business. A man in this predicament, Melville believed, knows that God exists, or he thinks that God exists, or he wishes to believe that God exists, at the very time when the awful fact of His aloofness from him and the finite world crushes any hope for transcendence.

The following chapters will explore the poem for evidence of this dilemma over faith and despair and for any signs of a solution. Melville's earlier writings and significant events of his life will be examined first to demonstrate how the poem in this respect is also the culminating statement in the later years of the author's life. Equally important, *Clarel* will be viewed as it ought to be seen, as a work of art. It would appear from the outset that the content and the form are one.

II

The Strain of Rebellion

> Captain Gardiner, I will not do it. Even now I lose time. Good bye, good bye. God bless ye man, and may I forgive myself, but I must go.
>
> *Moby-Dick*

In the 1840s *Typee* and *Omoo* carried thousands of readers into an exotic South Sea setting. Through the two novels Melville's reputation as a storyteller was established at once. The books, in fact, were read as documentary travelogues by men and women who could never leave their own dull, sedentary jobs in America and England. Toby Greene's later verification of the factual basis of *Typee* stamped the novel as genuine and thereby elevated the author's literary position with the suspicious professional critics who were unreceptive to romantic fiction. More recent discoveries disclose the elements of the two novels that are authentic; moreover, they demonstrate the creative imagination that shaped these facts into romance.[1] The effect thereafter of *Mardi*, *Moby-Dick*, and *Pierre* on the same reading public that had joyously accepted *Typee* and *Omoo*, however, was one of disenchantment with an author who obviously hated society, who cared nothing for traditional behavior, art, and logic, and who implicitly announced through his three rebels that he was resigning from the human race. A note from Melville to Richard Bentley, his English publisher, informing him that *Pierre* contained the stuff of art the people wanted,[2] suggests that Melville actually worked to achieve the aesthetic distance art demands; it implies that he believed the imaginative power that successfully translated the actual happenings of his South Sea adventures had also operated in the three later novels. A century later, the modern reader agrees with him and sees in these romances much more than the cries of a confused misanthrope: the distance of time provides for this kind of fairer criticism. But in the two decades between 1840 and 1860, Melville's fiction was denied this kind of reading and, with certain exceptions, was taken as the ravings of a man who covered up his distorted views of the world with congeries of abstract characters, half-truths, rambling sentences and lost metaphors, and tasteless protests.[3]

The twentieth-century judgment of a more critical reading public has served Melville well. Thus all five novels have been praised for their individual merits; the necessary separation between the author and his material has been noted so that Melville, the man in society, and Melville, the novelist, have distinct entities. Nevertheless, the earlier judgments that scored Melville's involvement in the action and ideas of his work were not altogether misplaced. To read all of Melville's writings carefully now is to discover a consistent personal theme and pattern: the mission of a seeker to find identity with something beyond himself, his initiation and reaction to terrifying reality, and his final acceptance or rejection of an enigmatic world. Read in this light, *Typee* and *Omoo* are the idyllic wanderings of a man who hopes that geographic isolation will return him to a permanent state of bliss. *Mardi*, *Moby-Dick*, and *Pierre* inform the world that its mediocrity kills off those with heroic aspirations of virtue. *Clarel* and *Billy Budd* summarize the enthusiasm of the youthful quester and the disillusionment of his discovery, and recommend that man resign himself to the workings of fate. *Clarel*, more than any other work, rehearses all of this joy and disillusion, rebellion and defeat, and final resignation of Melville's life and literary expression. Written over a period of twenty years, it emerged out of painful experience and thought, and constitutes a spiritual autobiography. How accurately the poem does reflect the author's life can be determined by a review of the significant events, actions, and works in the years prior to the publication of *Clarel* in 1876. The following pages of this chapter will sketch these earlier years as prologue to a closer study of the poem.

The two main characters in *Mardi* give a clue to Melville's thought at the end of the 1840s. The novel contains many other areas for study as well. But in the characters of Babbalanja and Taji Melville presented spokesmen of the major theme in the book and in his life: the dilemma over faith and doubt.

Towards the end of *Mardi*, Babbalanja falls into a fit of madness. As the unfolding events disclose, the madness seems to answer his own earlier demand, made significantly in the dead of night.

> . . . Yoomy, we are men, we are angels. And in his high faculties, high Oro is but what a man should be, infinitely magnified. Let us aspire to all things. Are we babes in the woods, to be scared by the shadows of the trees? What shall appall us? If eagles gaze at the sun, may not men at the gods?[4]

The madness is actually a purgation necessary for conversion in that he has already pruned his mind of error down to the standard of what is unchangeably true,[5] so that he can discover the absolute truths hinted to him in the revelations of Bardianna. Shortly after, the searchers arrive at Serenia. Babbalanja sees Alma's message put into practice there: charitable living supplants religious theory, and equal benefits come to all, according to one's nature and needs. All is love. There are no churches, yet Alma is adored everywhere, joyously. There are no priests, no precepts, for the dictates of the heart are one with right reason and with Alma.

Babbalanja is converted ecstatically, and thereupon renounces his determined search for the ultimate:

> Some things there are, we must not think of. Beyond one obvious mark, all human lore is vain. Where have I lived till now? Had dark Maramma's zealot tribe but murmured to me as this old man, long since had I been wise! Reason

> no longer domineers; but still doth speak. All I have said ere this, that wars with Alma's precepts, I here recant. Here I kneel, and own great Oro and his sovereign son.[6]

Babbalanja does not expunge his intellect, for even after the vision which leads to the conversion he asks why man is created to sin and suffer. The answer satisfies him now. This seeming malice must be accepted as a mystery of life; to know more is to presume equality with God; the only happiness that man can expect is in the exemption from great woe:

> Great love is sad; and heaven is Love. Sadness makes the silence throughout the realms of space; sadness is universal and eternal; but sadness is tranquillity; tranquillity the uttermost that souls may hope for.[7]

Out of this new faith he tells Taji that Yillah will never be found, that she is only a phantom for nothing in this world can be apprehended externally: truth as an absolute hides only in the heart. He will settle for Serenia, therefore, a place and a way of life which present a "more fitting truth for man to learn."[8] Serenia for him is a triumph of the heart and an escape from the destruction that awaits all uncompromising men of the intellect.

The resolution of Taji becomes stronger in the face of Babbalanja's defection: "But I was fixed as fate." There can be no half way for him in "the endless sea." He will find absolute good in "that outer ocean" and live thereafter in perfection. If it be unattainable, or non-existent, he will accept that for what it is worth: "And why put back? is a life of dying worth living o'er again?—Let *me*, then, be the unreturning wanderer. The helm: By Oro, I will steer my own fate, old man.—Mardi, farewell."[9] Taji will prove Media's words a lie: "final, last thoughts you mortals have none; nor can have . . . you mortals dwell in Mardi, and it is impossible to get elsewhere."[10] Only the ultimate can satisfy him. Yillah's death does not deter him either. By then he has abandoned all civilized connections, friends, philosophies, and normal hopes. He will trust himself in a war against the elements' impersonal ferocity and the malevolence of his pursuers.[11]

Melville erred artistically when he dropped Taji out of sight after the group set out in pursuit of Yillah. This becomes more obvious at the end of the novel. By then Taji resolves to pursue the more dangerous course, at a point where he has not participated in the action and dialogue, and at a time when the reader has almost forgotten him. But Taji was probably removed because Melville knew that Babbalanja's separate quest and discovery are the only ones available as a practical reality. A determination by Babbalanja to remove all illusions, traditions, and habits so that he can grasp essential truth was Melville's own attempt in the writing of the novel itself. In addition, the philosopher's inspirational demon which provokes irrational outbursts lurked deep in Melville as well, bringing them that much closer together. Of greater appeal to Melville was the large nature of Babbalanja which has him realize the impossibility of his quest and then change course for a more serene port. This was the direction Melville himself would follow, if he could. But though he saw Babbalanja's actions as prudentially sound, and Taji's as fruitless and possibly foolish, he was himself too much like Taji, "fixed as fate." For him there were no magical solutions, such as Serenia's life-principle and implementation of love.[12] Life is a tragedy which must be worked out to the end. The chartless seas must be sailed if they are to yield their enigmatic truths. At this time of his life Melville defied all who diverted him or stayed his way, God included. Taji might have been removed from the scene of *Mardi* too long a time for artistic consistency,[13] but he is the triumphant figure of the novel. It is his final act of defiance that the author himself must admire and imitate.

In the following year, Melville resumed the subject of an endless search by the free soul in a world of limited freedom. In what he considered his second serious effort, however, the author's sympathies are more difficult to locate: in *Moby-Dick* ambivalency is a constituent of the form.

In addition to the author's obvious awe of Taji's impractical but heroic determination, a major consideration of *Mardi* is the measure of peace Babbalanja finds in Serenia. He had hoped for more but he settles for less. Ishmael, similarly, acquires a wisdom which will enable him to live in this life, however lonely the existence will be. His original misanthropy, as seen in his fondness for funeral corteges and a need to knock off people's hats, undergoes the sweet change of friendship through love for a savage saint. His conversion at the beginning of the book, however, has shallower roots than Babbalanja's, for his return to the magnetic chain of humanity shifts and turns to the degree that Ahab's hatred of the white whale engenders the same deep hatred in him. The Captain's titanism directly influences the more malleable Ishmael, whereas Taji's cannot touch Babbalanja. Thus the essay on whiteness as an ultimate expression of the terrifying indifference or malevolence of the universe is, appropriately, Ishmael's rumination and indicates how deeply the young seeker has shared Ahab's monomania.

Probings by Ishmael aboard the *Pequod* for the essential meaning of life, complemented by his original distrust for society, bring him to the brink of Ahab's madness:

> Chief among these motives was the overwhelming idea of the great whale himself. Such a portentous and mysterious monster roused all my curiosity. Then the wild and distant seas where he rolled his island bulk; the undeliverable, nameless perils of the sea.[14]

His course steers in these perilous waters for as long as Ahab's influence commands obedience, but a dramatic response to his own instincts for humanity saves him from destruction:

> Look not too long in the face of fire, O man! Never dream with thy hand on the helm: Turn not thy back to the compass; accept the first hint of the hitching tiller; believe not the artificial fire, when its redness makes all things look ghastly. Tomorrow, in the natural sun, the skies will be bright; those who glared like devils in the forking flames,

> the morn will show in far other, at least gentler, relief; the glorious, golden, glad sun, the only true lamp—all others but liars![15]

At this point of the voyage, Ishmael forswears the pledge he made to Ahab during the baptism rite and thereby resumes the human values he had rejected at the outset. Like Babbalanja, short of his original goal to see the giant fish, he achieves his vision, or at least settles for the reality of human possibilities: "There is a wisdom that is woe; but there is a woe that is madness." His conversion is complete.[16]

Ishmael portrays only one side of Melville, and perhaps the least important. It is Ahab who commands Melville's attention, respect, pity, and awe. His promethean challenge, like Taji's, must end in defeat, but only when it is viewed from Ishmael's angle. Father Mapple's orthodox homily has no meaning for this ungodly godlike man: "There is salvation in repentance and in acknowledgment of the will of God." Nor can Starbuck's appeal to the green homeland, the warmth of loved ones, adherence to duty, and fear of the impending disaster dissuade Ahab. Land persuasions are meaningless for him at sea; Christian ethics or ordinary mores are foolish to a man whose egocentric values cancel outside forces:

> . . . look there,—three peaks as proud as Lucifer. The firm tower, that is Ahab; the volcano, that is Ahab; the courageous, the undaunted, and victorious fowl, that, too, is Ahab; all are Ahab; and this round gold is but the image of the rounder globe, which, like a magician's glass, to each and every man in turn but mirrors back his own mysterious self. . . . From storm to storm! So be it, then. Born in throes, 'tis fit that man should live in pains and die in pangs! So be it, then! Here's stout stuff for woe to work on. So be it, then.[17]

This solipsism springs from a source beyond his knowledge and control: "Swerve me? The path of my fixed purpose is laid with iron rails, whereon my soul is grooved to run." If he discovers along the way that the covenant between God and man no longer exists, then so be it.[18] Ahab will also discard all appurtenances of civilization—hat, pipe, quadrant—for he renounces all interrelatedness and dependence on things. His actions will strike away the mask of appearances to discover elemental truth. He has no doubt that a tragic ending lies in this path. But in its working out, Ahab insists that he will learn the true meaning of himself in the universe: "There's a riddle now might baffle all the lawyers backed by the ghosts of the whole line of judges:—like a hawk's beak it pecks my brain. *I'll, I'll* solve it, though." He may go down in defeat, but his soul will remain his own:

> Ho, ho! from all your furthest bounds, pour ye now in, ye bold billows of my whole foregone life, and top this one piled comber of my death! Towards thee I roll, thou all-destroying but unconquering whale; to the last I grapple with thee; from hell's heart I stab at thee; for hate's sake I spit my last breath at thee. Sink all coffins and all hearses to one common pool! and since neither can be mine, let me then tow to pieces, while still chasing thee, though tied to thee, thou damned whale! Thus, I give up the spear.[19]

Moby-Dick begins and ends with Ishmael cut off from the world. The coffin of the funerals he follows in the beginning externalizes the November drizzle in his soul and augurs the death he seems determined to achieve by signing as a hand on the doomed *Pequod*.[20] Queequeg's coffin at the end, conversely, rescues Ishmael literally when it lifts him like a resurrected Lazarus from the dead. Despite the terrifying loneliness Ishmael suffers in the great rolling ocean, and notwithstanding the pervasive coffin symbol that reflects and substitutes for the sinking *Pequod*, Ishmael's deliverance hints at a mild exultation in the author. Ishmael passes into a kind of Serenia, but not one as clearly limned as Babbalanja's; and his itchiness for things remote will probably never again get the upper hand to overwhelm his newly won land sense. He has come to a wisdom that Melville admired and would share, if he could. Like

Babbalanja and Ishmael, Melville did try friendship deliberately as his own cure for an unusual concern for evil and an anxiety over certitude. The warm relations he enjoyed with the Hawthornes and Morewoods in the Berkshires presented community as a possibility to him, but one he seemed constitutionally unable to choose, except on a temporary basis.[21] He applauds Ishmael's passage into maturity through friendship and commitment, but he judges the young man's outright rejection of Ahab and passionate dedication to Queequeeg as simplistic. At this time of his life, Melville could not live in Ishmael's state, where mystery and antagonisms are to be lived with as natural conditions of life. He insisted upon knowing who or what the whale is; if its apprehension is the paradox of death and nothingness, then he would accept the consequences. He and Ahab were close in spirit at this time, for Melville's self-reliance exceeded Emerson's in his trading blows with the universe and its ministers.[22] As he did before in *Mardi*, Melville plotted the common-sense course a wise man could follow without the slightest loss of dignity. Thus the desertion by Ishmael provided peace and a measure of happiness for him. But like Ahab's, the "bold billows of [his] whole foregone life" forced the author beyond Ishmael's rejection of hell-fire into an assault on ultimate truth, a breach which could result only in "predestinated" madness or death.[23]

The third and last inquiry during this period into the meaning of man, society, nature, and God appeared in *Pierre*.[24] In *Mardi* and *Moby-Dick*, Melville maintained an aesthetic distance sufficient to offer a dual vision of good and evil. In them the heroes were afforded the opportunity to achieve one or the other. When they did not choose the "good" it was their own fault partially, and their tragedies resulted directly from their own actions. But *Pierre* contained a one-dimensional view of evil and failure. In the novel, an inability by Melville to remove his own anguish from Pierre's foolish mission destroyed whatever merits the work might otherwise have possessed. One critic noted in this connection:

> Something was wrong psychologically with the distance between Melville and his material: he could not remove himself far enough from it to be its master rather than its victim. . . . The stuff of *Pierre* was the stuff of Melville's daily sufferings as he wrote it—his rock of Sisyphus, which he could not have attempted both to roll uphill and to describe.[25]

At the beginning of the novel, Pierre Glendinning appears as an innocent. In a short time, introduction to evil in his own family prepares him for the possibility that life's bright side of Christian virtue might be only an illusion. He examines thereafter the imaginary and real causes and circumstances that committed him to Isabel's salvation and to the protection of his father's reputation. The examination produces a second shock, informing him that evil is a necessary and dominant part of his own nature. From these early revelations to the final calamity in jail, illusion after illusion disappears, and his high moral aspirations go down to defeat. As they do, he recognizes the absurdity of his Christian ethics and exults as they collapse:

> Here, then, is the untimely, timely end; Life's last chapter well stitched into the middle! Nor book, nor author of the book, hath any sequel, though each hath its last lettering! It is ambiguous still. Had I been heartless now, disowned, and spurningly portioned off the girl at Saddle Meadows, then had I been happy through a long eternity in heaven: Now 'tis merely hell in both worlds. Well, be it hell. I will mould a trumpet of the flames, and with my breath of flame, breathe back my defiance! But give me first another body! I long and long to die, to be rid of this dishonored cheek. *Hung by the neck till thou be dead.*—Not if I forestall you, though!— Oh now to live is death, and to die is life; now, to my soul, were a sword my midwife![26]

Before this suicidal resolution, Lucy's flight to Pierre serves, to a lesser degree, the same function as Babbalanja's appeal to Taji and Starbuck's entreaty to Ahab. Like Taji and Ahab,

Pierre cannot return to what he was before and so rejects the counsel of his former fiancée as childish. His monomaniacal pursuit demands full expression of his manifold nature and of the world about him.[27] There can be no recantation, no compromise. Nor can Pierre accept the doctrinal message of love, prudence, and human limitations—the land sense in essence—implicit in Plinlimmon's philosophy. In his virtuous mission of charity, and in his determination to know absolute truths, Pierre insists upon complete independence and final achievement. The irony of his solitary death—like Young Goodman Brown's—underscores the foolishness of a misdirected altruism.

Pierre was ready for publication in February, 1852. *Mardi* had been completed in May, 1848, and *Moby-Dick* in September, 1851. From late 1847 through the completion of *Pierre* then, Melville's agitated mental state was explored in these three books of quarrel and rebellion. With *Pierre* he was at the nadir of despondency, which probably accounts for the dedication of the book to a thing rather than a person. Like his hero, he had "fled the sweet fields of Saddle Meadows" and descended to levels of existence which attracted and repelled him:

> Deep, deep, and still deep and deeper we must go, if we would out the heart of a man; descending into which is as descending a spiral stair in a shaft, without any end, and where that endlessness is only concealed by the spiralness of the stair, and the blackness of the shaft.[28]

His experiences taught him that the ideal principles of the Sermon on the Mount have no practical application in society.[29] Distinctions between virtue and vice were blurred or meaningless for him. Like Taji, Ahab, and Pierre, he had struck through the mask and found nothing; he had listened for the voice of God and heard only silence; he had gone to the tomb and found only an empty sarcophagus. In 1852, Pierre's anguish reflected Melville's: "That a nothing should torment a nothing; for I am a nothing. It is all a dream—we dream that we dreamed a dream."[30]

Many readers have speculated on what happened to Melville after this frenetic period of writing. Sedgwick, for one, believes that Melville's self-control enabled him to retreat from active life until he could regain the balance of faith and reason he had obviously lost. The subdued tone of the stories written before the Palestine journey, and the choice a few years after his return to work as a cloistered inspector in the Custom House, indicate to him Melville's awareness of the need for such self-therapy.[31] Arvin concurs generally, reading *Pierre* as a theme of "suicidal nihilism," which expressed Melville's despondency at the time. The stories written from 1852 through 1856, he concludes, were evidence of Melville's attempt to recover the dual vision of *Moby-Dick*, to find in man the slightest spark of heroism.[32] Leon Howard questions whether Melville really went through such an agonizing period. He agrees that the publication of *Pierre* set Melville back considerably, particularly after the poor showing of *Moby-Dick*. The vehemence of the critics attacking *Pierre* and the sale of only 238 copies in the first ten months did evidence another artistic and financial failure. This was painful for the reason mentioned earlier: Melville had informed his English publisher, Bentley, that *Pierre* contained genuine romantic material of elevated American life guaranteed to contain a more universal appeal than his previous books had.[33] Notwithstanding this major reversal, Howard argues, Melville recouped his losses, went on with two comparatively successful years of farming, enjoyed a rare and satisfying facility for turning out salable short stories, and, up through the publication of *The Confidence-Man* in 1857, worried decreasingly about his health.[34]

Such judgments continue to come from many and different quarters. For purposes of this study of *Clarel* as a continuing statement on the earlier events and writings, however, Melville's state of mind during the Pittsfield period can perhaps best be discerned by yet another look at the writings to see if any patterns emerge.

One that does appear is the author's dissatisfaction with himself as an artist and an awareness that he has been passed over. This can be found in most of the stories and sketches, but particularly in the dereliction theme of "Jimmy Rose," "The Happy Failure," "The Fiddler," and *Israel Potter*, and in the destruction warnings of "The Bell Tower." "The Fiddler" is particularly revealing in the way Hautboy appears to be Melville himself, and in the bitter comments on the bastard role the artist must play for a crass society that suppresses genius. Earlier letters from Melville to Hawthorne and Evert Duyckinck anticipated the vulgar tyranny of the reading public, but at the time he insisted he would not be trapped. His own pejorative judgments of *Redburn* and *White-Jacket* thereafter, acknowledged his capitulation, as does his description of Jimmy Rose, who was forced to beg for survival: ". . . charity not sent to him, either, but charity for which he had to trudge round to their doors." The projected self-image of the successful commercial author of *Typee* and *Omoo* begging is its own comment; an image that is hardly offset by the obvious cognitive dissonance of "The Happy Failure," a story much closer to the poet of *Moby-Dick*. Melville, in fact, had lost his reputation as a great writer, or as a good risk for the publishers. One of them observed in practical terms: "I don't think Melville's book [*The Piazza Tales*] will sell a great deal, but he is a good name on your list. He has lost his prestige-& I don't believe the Putnam stories will bring it up."[35] As a contributor and subscriber to *Putnam's Monthly*, Melville must have read with anger and sadness the patronizing warnings of Fitz-James O'Brien in that magazine: "Let Mr. Melville stay his step in time. He totters on the edge of a precipice, over which all his hard-earned fame may tumble with such another weight as *Pierre* attached to it."[36] To an author who had bypassed apprenticeship when he wrote two instant successes, such eulogies over a dying or dead career deepened his contempt for an insensitive society. But they also verbalized what he was only hinting to himself concerning his bewildering failure as an artist.[37]

A second attitude that appears at this time concerns the problem of evil. Marius Bewley observes that the evil of the world filled Melville with horror early in his life so that the element of Manicheanism became a permanent part of his sensibility.[38] There is a degree of truth to this, but at no stage of his life, not even in the immediate weeks before the Palestine trip, did Melville ever fall into such a league with Jackson, Fedallah, Claggart, and the other demonics. His difficulty lay always in the conflict between good and evil, an endless struggle he saw as natural to humanity. Or, in less of a medieval dichotomy, he regarded good and evil as intertwined and operative at the same time, with the sensitive person hard pressed to know precisely his real motivation in a given act.[39] In this time after *Pierre*, however, he came across very few signs of good emerging victor, a glum observation of blackness that pervades the short story "Benito Cereno." In it, a domination of black, symbolized in the perverse Babo, is the awful fact of life. At first glance, the story insists that neither ingenuousness nor fortitude counts in the presence of evil. Thus Don Benito, although seemingly rescued by Captain Delano, has been overshadowed; his resources have been sucked away by Babo and the other rebels aboard his ship. The whole story, in fact, anticipates the final paragraph, which sums up the inevitable consequences of the meeting of good and evil:

> Some months after, dragged to the gibbet at the tail of a mule, the black met his voiceless end. The body was burned to ashes; but for many days, the head, that hive of subtlety, fixed on a pole in the Plaza, met, unabashed, the gaze of the whites; and across the Plaza looked towards St. Bartholomew's church; in whose vaults slept then, as now, the recovered bones of Aranda; and across the Rimac bridge looked towards the monastery, on Mount Agonia without; where, three months after being dismissed by the court, Benito Cereno, borne on the bier, did, indeed, follow his leader.[40]

But as pointed as this passage is in its description of evil's pervasive hold, the story itself does continue the dual vision of *Mardi* and *Moby-Dick*, in a less obvious way. Even though Benito succumbs to Babo's influence, and Delano remains too long in sophomoric ignorance of the diabolic struggle, there is a place in the action for goodness asserted. Delano fails to save Benito from the assault on his soul, but he risks his own life in the attempted rescue. Unlike the catastrophic waste he gave to Pierre's life, the author smiles indulgently at the innocence of Delano; but he includes his altruism as a continuing factor of human behavior, even when transcendent redemption is impossible. Except for the one-dimensional conclusions of *Pierre*, and possibly of "Bartleby, the Scrivener," Melville's deep concern for evil during this period was very real but it was offset by a refusal to believe outright that the Babos would overcome the human spirit.

Dissatisfaction with himself as an artist, and an unhealthy concern for evil, were fortunately compensated by a third factor during this time: a continued compassion for the downtrodden. The empathy Melville shared for all men in misery had comprised the most poetic effects of *Redburn* and *White-Jacket*. The same humanitarianism filled out the stories and the spate of sketches on social problems written after 1852. Whatever other meanings they have, and some of them contain Melville's best writing, these short pieces generally indicate Melville's conscious attempts to "return to society" after the bitterness of *Pierre*. The "Paradise of Bachelors and the Tartarus of Maids" as typical, expresses the author's abhorrence of anything that robs a man of his dignity, turns him into a machine, or deprives him of the rights justly due him. The same comment is made, from a slightly different angle, in two sketches in "Poor Man's Pudding and Rich Man's Crumbs." In the second sketch, a hatred for the insensitive rich exaggerates the bestial elements of the Guild Hall charity so that the Inferno quality Melville obviously had in mind is lost. But the first sketch, despite its sentimentality, ends effectively in the reader's shared love with the author for the poor, who struggle to preserve a degree of love and pride in their lives against great opposition from nature and the rich: "The native American poor never lose their delicacy or pride; hence, though unreduced to the physical degradation of the European pauper, they yet suffer more in mind than the poor of any other people in the world."[41] An obvious contempt for the two guides in these sketches—Blandmour and the "civic subordinate"—springs from a distaste in Melville for any incident of class or economic disparity; from a social view that he expresses also in "The Two Temples," and in the satirical catalogue of "The 'Gees." It is clear that throughout his life Melville hovered between acceptance of the traditional verities and renunciation of all respected truths. Hawthorne's account of his friend's desire for "annihilation" and a longing for religious belief underscores this ambivalence. But never was Melville in doubt concerning mankind's endurance and resiliency in the face of tragedy. This paradox was particularly evident during the Pittsfield period. Fortunately, it was this deep compassion expressed then and shortly after, during the Civil War, that provided a balance for him when his whole personality was threatened with collapse.

A fourth aspect of his condition of mind after 1852 rests in an admiration that Melville held for man's patient resignation to an indifferent or malevolent universe. Perhaps in this he consciously put to rest the impulses of Taji, Ahab, and Pierre because their infinite demands were contradictory in a finite world; but it also suggests that he believed there are men and women whose heroic characters emerge at the very time when their defeat is inevitable. Hunilla, the Chola Widow in "The Encantadas," is a prime example. Witness to the drownings of her newly wedded husband and her lone brother, she survives on Norfolk Isle with dogs as her only companions. Subjected to the terror of solitude and the memory of the beloved dead before her eyes, she faces each endless day with courage, if not hope. Accordingly, at the end of the sketch Melville accords her the dignity of an emperor as she rides off on an ass:

> . . . she never looked behind her; but sat motionless, till we turned a promontory of the coast and lost all sights and sounds astern. She seemed as one who, having experienced the sharpest pangs, was henceforth content to have all lesser heart-strings riven, one by one. To Hunilla, pain seemed so necessary, that pain in other human beings—though by love and sympathy made her own—was

> unrepiningly to be borne. A heart of yearning in a frame of steel. A heart of earthly yearning, frozen by the frost which falleth from the sky.[42]

All human misery is summed up in Hunilla whose life has known "no shower from heaven" and whose days are measured as "misery's mathematics." Melville twice signifies her sorrowful state through the same ironic symbol: first, when she places on her husband's grave two old pieces of wood resembling her own worn, featureless crucifix; and second, at the end when she is seen, "passing into Payta town, riding upon a small gray ass; and before her on the ass's shoulders, she eyed the jointed workings of the beast's armorial cross." Her faith in the cross, actually nothing more than peasant superstition, comments further on the sorrowful human condition, for neither in her nor in the narrator is there the faintest hint of its transcendent nature. Her humanity binds her to a "heart of earthly yearning." Like Sisyphus, she has nowhere to go; like him, she continues in her mysterious completion of self: ". . . nature's pride subduing nature's torture."

Although he seems an altogether different person than Hunilla, Israel Potter faces a succession of failures with the same modest, heroic resignation. After long years of meaningless adventure and trial, he escapes from the City of Dis to return to America where he can die in peace: ". . . and back to New England our exile was called in his soul." His home has been changed and his name forgotten, leaving him the cipher he was in the beginning, a victim of life's indifference. But his refusal to quit at any stage, and his recognition of absurdity all about him, won him over to Melville as a paradigm of human resiliency. Indeed, Israel Potter is to be found in all of Melville's life and work:

> Though henceforth elbowed out of many a chance threepenny job by the added thousands who contended with him against starvation, as those tough old oaks of the cliffs, which, though hacked at by hail-stones of tempests, and even wantonly maimed by the passing woodsman, still,

> however cramped by rival trees and fettered by rocks, succeed, against all odds, in keeping the vital nerve of the tap-root alive.[43]

Israel fits into a pattern of quiet, patient, and noble resignation that partially marked this period after *Pierre*. So does Merrymusk, in "Cock-A-Doodle-Do," who finds life endurable so long as Trumpet calls out the hours to him. Merrymusk's steadfastness, a quality Melville came to admire in all little men of courage, depends on the most fragile support: in fact, the cock's crowing alone is the "stuff against despair" and the means for the obscure hero and his family to triumph over their ill fortune. Melville saw the true account of Agatha Hatch Robinson of Nantucket working out this same noble theme of patience. Like Hunilla and Israel, her extraordinary acceptance of a fated life struck him as exemplary.[44] This abiding interest in endurance and patience with nobility suggests that Melville discovered in it a major literary theme to replace the discarded one of titanism.

By far the most important and dominant consideration of Melville's thought at this time was an insistence that patience like Hunilla's, in the face of grinding pain, constitutes a practical virtue for survival and a means for preserving sanity, but in no way does it preclude a continued if subdued rebellion against the inscrutable laws of God, the universe, and society. This preoccupation with passive resistance is seen in two of the best stories Melville wrote over this period—"Bartleby, the Scrivener," and "I and My Chimney."

Despite its pervasiveness throughout the novels, stories, and poems, Melville never explains evil: it is a fact in the world with chance doling out uneven portions. Claggart, in *Billy Budd*, more so than any of his other haunted men, puzzled the author with his abnormal share; or so it would seem from the many changes made in bringing the character to life. Claggart is left finally as one familiar with evil and therefore beyond reasonable explanation for his actions: "To pass from a normal nature to him one must cross 'The deadly space between,' and this is done by indirection."[45] The same mystery shrouds Fedallah and Ahab himself, Redburn's Jackson, and Babo in "Benito Cereno." This familiarity with the infernal leaves a wound in these harrowed men rendering them unfit for society.

Bartleby is one of these wounded victims, beyond reclamation in his exile. Melville does not disclose what experience Bartleby suffered in the Dead Letter Office before he assumed his position on Wall Street, but it destroyed his social instincts, leaving him unable or unwilling to communicate. It brought him face to face with a reality of life never known by the ordinary man, probably the same one that Pip saw deep in the ocean, and that Pierre discovered in the examination of his own soul. Unlike Pierre, in his new role in the lawyer's office Bartleby refuses to react for reaction is a social gesture. He prefers not to involve himself in a futile struggle. Instead, he eats nuts, faces blank walls, and willfully shapes himself as an embryo before a prison wall and dies. An exemplar of passive resistance, he completes ironically the mastery of self that Taji, Ahab, and Pierre sought through a dominance of the external world.

"I and My Chimney" works out the same resolution of passive resistance in a threatening situation, but within the walls of society. The struggle of a central character with evil plays no part in the story, and yet the issue seems no less important, for it concerns the basic rights of the narrator. His assertion of integrity emphasizes an unwillingness to be pawned off by forces greater than his own and a refusal to occupy his days with the meaningless busy things of life:

> Content with the years that are gone, taking no thought for the morrow, and looking for no new thing from any person or quarter whatever, I have not a single scheme or expectation on earth, save in unequal resistance of the due encroachment of hers.[46]

The campaign waged by his wife, daughter, and the consulting Master Mason Scribe to "abolish the chimney," forces the narrator into an indefensible position until his only argument is the Bartleby assertion: "I do not prefer to." Both stories restate

Melville's solipsism, but they indicate forcefully a basic difference in approach from the one that produced Taji, Ahab, and Pierre. In the defense of his chimney the narrator will not yield to the pressures of civil or natural law, but neither will he rail against them. He will maintain a firm, independent spirit: he prefers not to have his chimney-backbone shattered by any force. Not that he regards himself as perfect and impregnable; on the contrary, he knows that his deepest self contains an irreparable universal crack, like the flaw in his chimney. This accounts for his frequent trips to the basement where he digs around the massive foundation "prompted by dreams of striking upon some old, earthen-worn memorial of that by-gone day when, into all this gloom, the light of heaven entered. . . ."[47] Although the issue is more important than the renovation of a house, Melville sees the humor in such a mock-heroic defense and continues the incongruity by giving to an insensitive Scribe the key words of recognition:

> . . . it is my solemn duty to warn you sir, that there is architectural cause to conjecture that somewhere concealed in your chimney is a reserved space, hermetically closed, in short, a secret chamber, or rather closet. . . . What it contains is hid, within itself, in darkness.[48]

The final line can by interchanged with "Bartleby" without any loss of meaning: a summary statement of the inner man who has passed into a secret chamber for his resting place, a place beyond sound, light, and meaning. Both stories, in fact, intimate that Melville was also determined to keep his secret self hermetically sealed, except to his own probings, which were these introspective stories he was writing at the time. The imprisoned characters he created in them reflect himself, fully aware of limited human possibilities, resolute and lonely, like God's few singled out for torment.

In a letter to Hawthorne on June 29, 1851, Melville wrote of the exquisite loneliness of these independent souls:

> This most persuasive season has now for weeks recalled me from certain crotchety and over-doleful chimeras, the like of which men like you and me, and some others, forming a chain of God's posts round the world, must be content to encounter now and then, and fight them the best way we can. But come they will,—for in the boundless, trackless, but still glorious wild wilderness through which these outposts run, the Indians do sorely abound, as well as the insignificant but still stinging mosquitoes.[49]

The banter of Indians and mosquitoes intensifies the self-analysis of melancholy here and discloses the author's attempts to dissipate the "over-doleful chimeras." The jesting and the confession of pain to his friend are balanced by the assertion of glory in the "wild wilderness," like an echo of Milton's hero who would reign in hell sooner than serve in heaven. Melville persisted throughout the period after *Pierre* in this intellectual search for absolutes and relief when all signs indicated the absurdity of such an inquiry that can lead only to nothing. This persistence and discovery are the emphasis of an earlier letter to Hawthorne:

> We think that into no recorded mind has the intense feeling of the visible truth entered more deeply than into this man's [Hawthorne's]. By visible truth, we mean the apprehension of the absolute condition of present things as they strike the eye of the man who fears them not, though they do their worst to him,—the man who, like Russia or the British Empire, declares himself a sovereign nature [in himself] amid the powers of heaven, hell and earth. He may perish; but so long as he exists he insists upon treatment with all Powers upon an equal basis. If any of those other Powers choose to withhold certain secrets, let them; that does not impair my sovereignty in myself; that does not make me tributary. And perhaps, after all, there is *no* secret. We incline to think that the Problem of the Universe is like the Freemason's mighty secret, so terrible to all children. It turns out, at last, to

> consist in a triangle, a mallet, and an apron,—nothing more! We incline to think that God cannot explain His own secrets.[50]

Finally, as this letter indicates, there was a complex overall state of mind that pervaded all the other conditions of Melville's being during this period—a continuing uncertainty. The other attitudes were revealed in his work, as noted: dissatisfaction with himself as an artist, oversensitivity to the problem of evil, compassion for the downtrodden, admiration for those heroic few patiently resigned to an unfriendly world, and resolution to persist in quiet rebellion against the forces of the universe. But these were only incidental to the greater anxiety Melville suffered at this time: an incapacity to live with any single attitude or in any one posture, and a vital need to believe in something of value. This dilemma marks the last two works Melville wrote before the Palestine trip—*The Confidence-Man* and "The Piazza."[51]

Both express sadness over the ineffective efforts of any man to console his neighbor or relieve his burden, but they also indicate satisfaction with his willingness to try. Even in a work as patently bitter as *The Confidence-Man*, Melville echoes Redburn's concern for the lonely man, the "poor drifting sea-weed of the universe," and implicitly calls for a new society ruled by the heart, no matter how many examples of murder, rape, and treason history has recorded. More obviously, it laments a universal loss of faith and consequent spiritual and social chaos. The final scene of the cosmopolitan assisting the old man, who has by then safeguarded himself against all thieves with a Counterfeit-Detector, money-belt, and traveller's locks for door and window, gathers together all of the mistrust and loss of connection on this ship of fools. The one light is extinguished as a final symbol of faith and trust destroyed, for the events throughout conspired to bring about this blackness. And yet the old man is not alone in the darkness; he also has an arm supporting him. This hardly registers Melville's unqualified confidence in humanity ultimately righting itself: the support is given ironically by the cynic who has already exposed all of the charlatans and fools. But there is a genuine quality in this last Confidence-Man, despite the cynicism: instead of taking money from his dupes he gives it away; his actions do not trap the innocent as much as they uncover the frauds like Mark Winsome and Charles Noble; he speaks the truth in a world of liars; and he has compassion in an unfeeling world.[52] In this role Frank Goodman appears to belie his name as he moves about on the boat; but his direction is toward this point of final relationship, properly called by Melville "The Cosmopolitan Increases in Seriousness."

Through Goodman, and all the other disguises of the Confidence-Man, Melville exposes human foibles in harsh satire. But there is no total rejection or despair in the exposure, as there is in the accounts of Taji, Ahab, and Pierre. In the Indian-Hater episode, in this connection, Melville apparently had the difference in mind in the character of Colonel Moredock: "Other youngsters might have turned mourners; he turned avenger." Whereas he had Ahab and the other two move inexplicably to "the outer barrier," Melville, in the judge's words, explains the backwoodsman's hate with hints of environment, heredity, and other psychological factors, and thereby dilutes the hate. Aside from the simple instinct of an eye for an eye, a drive in man not to be eradicated, Melville wonders, in twentieth-century fashion, if Moredock's genius might not have been utilized instead in the amelioration of society. This does not mean that Moredock, given different circumstances, and Frank Goodman, as an ingenuous aid to old men, offer a sanguine hope for the human race. It does mean that in this period of intellectual and spiritual uncertainty shortly before the Palestine "vacation" trip, Melville was less impressed by a titan's disdain for ethical order than he was appalled by the possibility that there was in fact nothing finally to believe in. As Hawthorne observed shortly thereafter, "He can neither believe, nor be uncomfortable in his unbelief."

"The Piazza" more explicitly develops this ambivalence of disbelief and hope. In the short story, the narrator leaves the comfort of his house and piazza in the valley to locate the golden light of a rainbow in a distant mountain. Convinced by the presence of his frolicking yellow bird guides, he believes the fairy land that beckons will fulfill the faith that prompted his journey. But he finds no gold or fairies. Instead, he sees "a pale-cheeked girl, and fly-specked windows, with wasps about the mended upper panes," a "fairy queen" imprisoned in a broken shack surviving each day by illusions of gold lying in the valley below. He returns to his cottage with a clear lesson learned: any certitude based on perception is ephemeral because things are never what they seem to be; therefore, one should rest in peace on his own piazza, content with the knowledge that there is no ring of fairies in the far-off mountains, nor anywhere. But not quite, for Melville in 1856 could not accept the logical conclusion of his story. Accordingly, he wrote one last, short paragraph to underscore his own "haunted" uncertainty and the foolishness of holding tight to any absolute belief:

> But, every night, when the curtain falls, truth comes in with darkness. No light shows from the mountain. To and fro I walk the piazza deck, haunted by Marianna's face, and many as real a story.[53]

Melville seems to say in these two laments, I cannot believe; O Lord, help me in my unbelief. Tortured by agnosticism, in "The Piazza" he scorns the vulgar, inadequate modern substitutes for genuine religion: "—yet, in these times of failing faith; and feeble knees, we have the piazza and the pew." At the same time, he mocks his own inveterate seriousness, citing another one who searched for the grail: "Don Quixote, that sagest sage that ever lived." A chapter in *The Confidence-Man* carries on this self-ridicule, appropriately called, "A Philanthropist Undertakes to Convert a Misanthrope but Does Not Get Beyond Confuting Him." The satire here points to another direction, but Melville had himself in mind as well:

> "Talking of piemen, humble-pie before proud-cake for me. This notion of being lone and lofty is a sad mistake. Men I hold in this respect to be like roosters; the one that

betakes himself to a lone and lofty perch is the hen-pecked one, or the one that has the pip."[54]

The ironies and shifting point of view of *The Confidence-Man* prevent accurate reading of individual passages and of the novel itself as sure evidence of the author's frame of mind at the time of composition. But such a passage as the one cited, with its caution against one's becoming a Bartleby or an Emerson, coupled with others appealing for love, confidence, and faith in something other than one's self, manifest a struggle by Melville during 1856 to return to a belief in something of worth. The fact that he could write on the knavery and gullibility of mankind demonstrates a social sense which was missing in the three novels of rebellion; to anatomize the follies of society he had to leave his "chained post" at the edge of the world to prescribe a cure for the personal and corporate malady. The therapy consisted of a restoration of faith in self, or in fellow man, or, perhaps implicitly, in God.[55] The first one to try the cure would be Melville himself, literally, through a voyage back in time, and away from the West, to Christ's native land. There he would possibly rediscover the tranquility he had known for a few idyllic months in the Marquesas many years before, or, with greater success, return with a belief in God and confidence in man.

III

Flight and Return

Secluded now would pass his life,
And leave to time the sequel of the strife.
"Lee in the Capitol"

Melville did not write exclusively from immediate experience so that his compositions are a vast autobiography. This was a limit that the earliest biographers set upon his creativeness and that his contemporary readers expected of him as a writer of true narratives. In the way of all great artists, his remembrance of things past fused with a keen observation and a productive imagination to reveal a point of view that he expressed continuously in varied forms. The comments in the previous chapter were not intended to contradict this, nor to follow the lead of Mumford and Freeman, seeing in each novel or short story a verification of precise thought, mood, or event, at any given time. However, in these earlier years, that is, before the Civil War poems, Melville was more the prophet of spontaneous expression than he was the careful craftsman. He was convinced of his own genius and spoke as a truth-sayer with evidence discovered in highly charged encounters of his life. It is, therefore, comparatively safe to connect who or what Melville was with what he wrote during this Pittsfield period, or, at least, to infer certain attitudes from his books. If the remarks did provide any understanding of Melville as reflected in the writings, a survey of certain events and conditions during the same time will shed further light on such a formation.

Ostensibly, money worries, an overall sense of failure, and chronic bad health preoccupied Melville from 1851 through 1856. In March, 1855, Elizabeth Melville gave birth to her fourth child, Frances. The burgeoning family compounded the family's financial problems, which had existed since 1849, so that the years 1855, and 1856, in contrast to the comparatively good one of 1854, became ones of deep anxiety and grave decision. In addition, everyone in the Melville-Gansevoort clan knew that Melville was tired of Pittsfield and wished to return to New York.[1] In August, 1855, he was pleased to have inspectors for a proposed asylum examine "Arrowhead" as a possible site. His disappointment with their negative decision was somewhat assuaged by the sale of half the property in April, 1856, for $5,500, money sorely needed at the time. Worsening financial conditions were paramount in his mind, as can be seen in the unusual bickering with Dix and Edwards over royalty rights on the proposed volume, *The Piazza Tales*.[2] The unsuccessful attempts by his family and friends to secure him a government appointment earlier in 1853, and his failure to farm his land profitably forced him to demand higher royalties for any writing he could market. It appears now that his nervousness became more marked to his family and friends in proportion to a dwindling income from his books and the farm.

These very real money troubles, in turn, worsened the periodic bad health that Melville suffered. Those close to him knew of his poor condition in late 1854, when money was not a major problem. Elizabeth, for example, noted in her memoir: "In Feb. 1855 he had his first attack of severe rheumatism in his back—so that he was helpless."[3] The ailment prevented him from working the farm at all in the spring, or so another of her entries would suggest: ". . . and in the following June an attack of Sciatica. Our neighbor in Pittsfield Dr. O. W. Holmes attended and prescribed for him."[4]

The rheumatism, sciatica, and blurred vision were very real and very painful. But they were undoubtedly aggravated by all of the other difficulties. The money problems were coupled with a total dissatisfaction with himself as an artist. Dollars, in fact, did plague Melville so that he was writing the trite material he had earlier told Hawthorne he could not do. His problem, however, had its source far deeper than the prostitution of talent to commercial demand. It was anchored more in an incapacity to work the material he had given form to in his earlier books. One critic saw this inability as conclusive evidence of a debilitation of his powers:

> The first certain place to look for signs of exhaustion in Melville's vitality is in his own creative work; and the structure of both *Israel Potter* and *The Confidence-Man* shows them to have been produced by a man not at all able to write the kind of books he wanted to, but under a miserable compulsion. In the former he started out to portray the tragedy of exile, but when he came to the ex-soldier's destitution in London, his own sense of suffering was so great that he could not bear to dwell on Potter's, and slurred over what was to have been his main subject in a couple of short chapters.[5]

Unsure of his powers as an author, the 1853 fire at Harper's which destroyed many of his books probably symbolized for Melville his own seemingly burned-out energies. He also had strong intimations of the family's lack of confidence in him as a writer, a skepticism that was evidenced in the lines of a letter from Lemuel Shaw, Jr., to his brother:

> . . . I believe he is now preparing another book for the press *(The Confidence-Man)* for which Augusta is making a fair copy for the printer & which will be published before long—I know nothing about it; but I have no great confidence in the success of his productions—.[6]

Young Shaw's mistrust in Melville can be found in other places, for the two were not particularly good friends. However, it seemed to represent the overall family judgment: the failure by Melville to provide for his family through the farm or with his books, and his refusal to work for a lucrative income from business, demonstrated irresponsibility and downright foolishness. In the practical nineteenth century, and especially for two families of Dutch and Yankee backgrounds, such waste was intolerable.[7]

All of these factors combined to provoke a morbid condition that was the greatest source of worry to Melville's family and relatives. Judge Shaw expressed this concern in a letter to his son Samuel:

> I suppose you have been informed by some of the family, how very ill, Herman has been. It is manifest to me by Elizabeth's letters, that she has felt great anxiety about him. When he is deeply engaged in one of his literary works, he confines himself to hard study many hours in the day, with little or no exercise, & this especially in winter for a great many days together. He probably thus overworks himself & brings on severe nervous affections.[8]

The madness hinted at here was always a fear to Melville himself. His father's death after "an alienation of mind" left a deep impression on him as a young boy; as did the mysterious death of his brother in 1846, shortly after a sudden loss of sight: "From his physician, however, I learn that his sight is not materially affected, & that his disorder is in some degree connected with the brain, and a state of nervous derangement, which if it should come now would not surprise me."[9] Melville wrote a letter to Evert Duyckinck in 1849, expressing regret over the madness of his friend, Charles Fenno Hoffmann, but the words are more self-revealing:

> His present misfortune—rather blessing—is but the sequel to a long experience of unwhole habits of thought.—This going mad of a friend or acquaintance comes straight home to every man who feels his soul in him,—which but few men do. For in all of us lodges the same fuel to light the same fire. And he who has never felt, momentarily, what madness is has but a mouthful of brains. What sort of sensation permanent madness is may be very well imagined—just as we imagine how we felt when we were infants, tho' we can not recall it. In both conditions we are irresponsible & riot like gods without fear or fate.—It is the climax of a mad night of revelry when the blood has been transmuted into brandy.—But if we prate much of this thing we shall be illustrating our own propositions.[10]

In the Spring of 1853, Dr. George Adler, Melville's companion on his trip to England in 1849, was confined to Bloomingdale Asylum at about the same time Elizabeth Melville and Maria Gansevoort both noted Melville's own low spirits. This nervous condition left Melville with fears for himself, but also made him difficult to live with, particularly before the Levant trip. His granddaughter, Eleanor Melville Metcalf, tells of her mother's complaints over Melville's fits of temper, possibly brought on by a guilty conscience resulting from a failure to provide an adequate income.[11] Van Wyck Brooks overstates the case when he sees Pierre's attacks of vertigo as Melville's own through these four or five years. But he is correct when he says that Hawthorne's later judgment of Melville as "overshadowed" was a right diagnosis of a man in poor mental health.[12]

Because of the bad health, an inability to settle financial problems, and a constant irascibility, the family and Melville agreed that he should go on an extended vacation. Mr. Shaw's loan enabled him to leave on October 11, 1856. At the time of departure, he was uncertain how long he would be gone. He only knew that, like Ishmael, the damp, drizzly November in his soul would dry out when he could "quietly take to the ship."

The despairing element of the *Journal* Melville kept of his travels suggests his deepest motivation in leaving home again. What had appeared to friends and relatives as basic reasons for his morbidity and a health-seeking vacation were, in fact, not the primary reasons. Rather, he was prompted by the theme of his last book—a need to find some religious conviction. Just before leaving, he purchased a copy of *Don Quixote* and marked this passage:

> ". . . a knight errant without a mistress is like a tree without leaves, a building without cement, a shadow without a body that causes it." M's comment: or as Confucius said "a dog without a master," or to drop both Cervantes & Confucius parables—a god-like mind without a God.[13]

His contemptuous use of *Fidèle* as the name of the ship in *The Confidence-Man* was pointed in satire, for he could not live without faith, nor abide an existence without God. The Levant trip, with its conclusion of greater despair, can be understood only in these terms.[14]

Melville landed in Liverpool on November 8, 1856, and visited with his friend, Hawthorne, before he left for the Mediterranean. He had not seen Hawthorne since 1853. The long separation apparently did not bother either of them; for in their three meetings in Liverpool they were their old philosophical selves, rambling over the problems of the universe and man's mysterious destiny. Out of these talks came Hawthorne's famous observation of Melville's tortured religious state:

> . . . Melville, as he always does, began to reason of Providence and futurity, and of everything that lies beyond human ken, and informed me that he had "pretty much made up his mind to be annihilated"; but still he does not seem to rest in that anticipation; and, I think, will never rest until he gets hold of a definite belief. It is strange how he persists—and has persisted ever since I knew him, and probably long before—in wandering to and fro over these deserts, as dismal and monotonous as the sand hills amid which we were sitting. He can neither believe, nor be comfortable in unbelief; and he is too honest and courageous not to try to do one or the other. If he were a religious man, he would be one of the most truly religious and reverential; he has a very high and noble nature, and better worth immortality than most of us.[15]

Perhaps Melville informed Hawthorne directly or Hawthorne merely inferred that this trip to the Holy Land was explicitly to find the religion Melville sorely needed. Hawthorne hoped he would uncover such a measure of truth, for he saw Melville on the point of a dangerous mental break:

> I saw him again on Monday, however. He said that he already felt much better than in America; but observed that he did not anticipate much pleasure in his rambles, for that the spirit of adventure is gone out of him. He certainly is much overshadowed since I saw him last; but I hope he will brighten as he goes onward.[16]

These two observations, pieced together, have an ominous sound: Melville's despondency had become so pronounced that the coming journey had to bring about either peace or "annihilation."

Except for occasional glimpses of light, the long trip to the Levant, and the return through Italy, Germany, and England, were days free of adventure. They failed to live up to the grand hopes that Melville had anticipated for a similar trip in 1849:

> This afternoon Dr. Taylor and I sketched a plan for going down the Danube from Vienna to Constantinople; thence to Athens on the steamer; to Beyrouth & Jerusalem—Alexandria & the pyramids. . . . I am full (just now) of this glorious *Eastern* jaunt. Think of it! Jerusalem and the Pyramids—Constantinople, the Agean, and old Athens![17]

His first glimpse of Constantinople on the actual trip was through a heavy fog. His first walk through the streets ended in claustrophobic panic when he felt himself lost and strangled in the narrow, close alleys. He walked thereafter with his hands in his pockets to thwart the many thieves in hiding. His most striking impression came from the grim sight of an Armenian funeral with "Juggling & incantations of the priests—" and the miserable cries of the bereaved woman who called to the dead as though there were the possibility of resurrection.[18]

Descriptions of stones, dust, cemeteries, broken-down houses, mosquitoes and flies, unbelievable poverty, religious fanatics, and moods of total disillusionment fill the *Journal*. Melville's first sight of Greece, when viewed from the ship as a "colossal sugarloaf," turned out to be a warren of huts on streets cluttered with filthy goats and sharp stones. Salonica, the site of famed Olympus, was actually one large bazaar:

> Quite large, but filthy. Streets all narrow, like cow lanes. And smelling barn-yards. Very silent. Women muffled about the faces. All old. No young. (p. 71)

The romantic glamour cast over the Middle East in travelogues disappeared for Melville in the yellows and grays of a "used up—superannuated" Asia.

Alexandria offered him no pleasure either. It lived in its antiquity, a "Dust colored city," of high blank walls and mysterious passages. But it presented him with a terrifying visit to the pyramids. There he was overcome with awe and terror as he came face to face with the genesis of God:

> I shudder at the idea of ancient Egyptians. It was in these pyramids that was conceived the idea of Jehovah. Terrible mixture of the cunning and awful. Moses learned in all the lore of the Egyptians. The idea of Jehovah born here. (p. 118)

The "god-like mind without a God" shrank before the mystery of God that might be solved there, or it trembled for fear that there was, after all, no mystery to be solved. Melville's final note on this whole impressive incident strikes the mood of the entire Levant part of his pilgrimage:

> And one seems to see that as out of the crude forms of the natural earth they could evoke by art the transcendant (novelty) of the pyramid so out of the insignificant thoughts that are in all men, they could by an analagous art rear the transcendant conception of a God. But for no holy purpose was the pyramid founded. (p. 124)

Disillusioned by the Greek isles, which lacked the virgin freshness of Polynesia, choked by the dust and stench of Constantinople and Alexandria, and terrified by the mystery of the pyramids, Melville found in the Holy Land the dust grayer and more profuse, the stones in greater number, and his own loneliness weighing on him like a millstone:

> I am emphatically alone, & begin to feel like Jonah. . . . I have such a feeling in this lonely old Joppa, with the prospect of prolonged detention here, owing to the surf—that it is only by a stern self-control & grim defiance that I contrive to keep cool and patient. (pp. 129-32)

The stones and other sterile objects registered the absence of God:

> The mind cannot but be badly and suggestively affected with the indifference of Nature & Man to all that makes the spot sacred to the Christians. Weeds grow upon Mount Zion; side by side in impartially equality appear the shadows of church & mosque, and on Olivet every morning the sun indifferently ascends over the Chapel of the Ascension. (p. 142)

The misery intensified because Melville was on a religious pilgrimage. Others might be out there as part of the nineteenth-century Protestant evangelistic travel vogue. But he was in the Holy Land out of a need too deep to be sopped by tourist attractions:

> In pursuance of my object, the saturation of my mind with the atmosphere of Jerusalem, offering myself up as a passive subject, and no unwilling one, to its weird impression, I always rose at dawn & walked without the walls. (p. 145)

A willingness to believe exposed him to disillusioning traumatic experiences.

Before his trip he had wished for an end to the cynicism of *The Confidence-Man*. But when viewing the Holy Sepulchre, he could only comment:

> No country will more quickly dissipate romantic expectations than Palestine—particularly Jerusalem. To some the disappointment is heart sickening. Is the desolation of the land the result of the fatal embrace of the Deity? Hapless are the favorites of heaven. (p. 154)

Instead of writing "some," Melville could have inserted "Herman Melville," for this heart-sickening entry marks a low point of the trip. It followed upon his unmoving experience at Bethlehem and forced a decision to remain no longer in a God-forgotten land. The long journey only proved what he had tentatively concluded in "The Piazza": just as there is no land of enchantment at the rainbow's end, so there is no more to be found of God in His Holy Land than at home in Pittsfield.

Melville left Judea on January 27, 1857. He had been there since January 7, too long for a man who could say "How it affects one to be cheated in Jerusalem." (p. 142) The ambivalence of skepticism and hatred of his own disbelief continued after he left the site. He felt swindled by his experience in Cyprus: "Found it as hard to realize such a thing (Venus's rising from the foam) as to realize on Mt. Olivet that from there Christ rose." (p. 164) The isle of Patmos reminded him of another Christian myth he could not accept; but again he despised his own cynical state:

> Patmos is pretty high, & peculiarly barren looking. No inhabitants.—Was here again afflicted with the great curse of modern travel—skepticism. Could no more realize that St. John had ever had revelations here, than when off Juan Fernandez, could believe in Robinson Crusoe, according to De Foe. When my eye rested on arid height, spirit partook of the barreness.—Heartily wish Niebuhr & Strauss to the dogs.—The deuce take their penetration & acumen. They have robbed us of the bloom. If they have undeceived anyone—no thanks to them. Pity that ecclesiastical countries [are] so little attractive by nature. (pp. 166-67)[19]

Niebuhr and Strauss were only whipping boys for him off Patmos. He had come full circle from his original state of disbelief, to a need for certification of belief, to an actual religious pilgrimage, to a despairing condition of disbelief. Yet at this final stage of the Holy Land interlude he still wished his own Niebuhr-rationale to the dogs.

The rest of the journey was an epilogue. Melville placed in a forgotten corner the anguished religious loss of the Levant experiences and thereafter became a tourist. Overcrowded streets and heights still bothered him. But in the *Journal* entries during his stay in Italy and England, a comparative buoyancy emerges, as seen particularly in his visits to Milan and Oxford. Altogether, the entries toward the end of the trip, from Sicily on, show a Melville more concerned with what he experienced as an ordinary traveler than with endless examinations of a tortured mind.

Melville left from Liverpool on May 6, 1857 and arrived in New York on May 19. As a trip designed for spiritual rebirth or awakening, the pilgrimage had been a total failure. Melville's disillusionment with the barrenness of Jerusalem, his apathy at Nazareth, and his skepticism at Olivet, Cypris, and Patmos left him in a worsened condition. Like Taji, he had gone to discover a meaning for existence or a relief from his anxieties, only to find that "The pains lie among the pleasures like sand in rice, not only bad in themselves, but spoiling the good." (p. 268)

The years from 1857 to the end of his life saw Melville as a quiet, sedentary, occasional author consciously striving to control the titanic rebellion that now and then blazed up within him.[20] From the time of his arrival home in May, 1857, through 1860, he attempted in various ways to attain a balanced view of life or to occupy himself in some activity which would allow freedom for speculation without cutting him off from social connections. He cooperated with Elizabeth and the others in their request that he not resume writing and so began a new career as a lecturer. The three-year, boring, generally remunerative lecture series proved to him and the listeners that oratory was not his forte. The inspired storyteller who had charmed Hawthorne, the Duyckincks, and so many others in the Knickerbocker set, and the gallant who had captivated Sophia Hawthorne and Sarah Morewood appeared at the lectern as a subdued, low-voiced academican when he delivered the three lectures on "Roman Statuary," "The South Seas," and "Travel." Another sea voyage—this time on the *Meteor*, captained by his brother Tom—took him away from home between May 30 and November 11, 1860. This too failed either to revive the Polynesian mood which haunted him as a memory or to provide him with the clue to where happiness was to be found, if at all. But a turn of events occurred at this time which enabled him to sublimate the physical ills and spiritual restlessness.[21] A quietism set in, a comparative serenity, which allowed him to get outside himself through the turmoil of the Civil War.[22]

Compassion in Melville for his fellow man can be found throughout his works, an expression of humanitarianism which precluded a hatred for any man. He understood or tried to understand even the Claggarts, Brands, Jacksons, and Clarets; pity for them ran deeper than a hatred for what they did, or for what they represented. This sums up his feelings on the War. He regretted the split in the Union and deplored the fact of blood shed in futility, as he says at the end of the second "Jack Gentian Sketch." But his love for mankind, and the fact of war's destructive power inflicting yet another wound on the "poor, drifting sea-weed," drew Melville away from the bleak moods he suffered on and off since 1851 and returned him to an acceptance of the coordinate responsibilities of society he had previously minimized or rejected.

When Melville was refused a post in the Navy because of his age, he committed himself to the War in his own fashion through the writing of war poems. Poetry was a new medium for him, although some time soon after 1857 he had written nineteen poems, most of them impressions of his Levant trip.[23] Failure to find a publisher did not deter Melville from writing poetry. As early as 1859, with the writing of "Portent," a poem which envisioned the consequences of John Brown's actions, he evidenced an interest in verse patterns rivaling his earlier enthusiasm for the novel. Thereafter he wrote feelingly throughout the years of the War on the blight that had fallen "On the world's fairest hopes."[24] In the best of these poems—"The Conflict of Convictions," "Apathy and Enthusiasm," "Misgivings," and a few others—the War is an awful demonstration of the fall of man as an irreversible fact, with the loss of innocence dramatically enacted by a country ironically convinced of its unique perfection. The blackness he had depicted in "Benito Cereno" a few years back, he intimates, was always there beneath the fair surface of America whether Captain Delano knew it or not. The eruption of national violence in 1861 had always been an eventuality as a manifestation of the constant struggle of evil to overcome good. All of the poems take this as a basic fact and then portray the individuals caught up in the catastrophe. The poems, little known at the time, were collected by Melville after the war and published as *Battle-Pieces and Aspects of War* in August, 1866, just ten years after his last publication.

The book met with mixed reviews, mostly on the negative side, which classified the author as a "versifier." It also had virtually no sale. By this time Melville was indifferent to the critics and the reading public. The youthful emotional reaction to the savage reviews of *Mardi* was one he would not tolerate in himself in 1866.[25] Evidence of this appeared sometime in 1865 when he purchased John Ruskin's *Modern Painters* and scored and underscored lines from "Of Vulgarity":

> . . . to men not of his kind he cannot open himself, though he tried it through an eternity of clear grammatical speech. By the very acuteness of his sympathy, *he knows how much of himself* he can give to anybody. . . . *Whatever he said, a vulgar man would misinterpret*: no words that he *would use would bear the same sense to the vulgar man they do to them*. . . .[26]

Melville, however, did give "much of himself" in *Battle-Pieces*, regardless of the vulgar audience. Themes from his earlier works echo in the poems but are less important than the overall sense of sadness. Melville did arrive at a state of quietude, as noted, but reconciliation with the world on its terms robbed him of joy. It was precisely in this lost enthusiasm that Melville identified his fallen condition with the vanquished South. The pain caused by frustrated dreams was subsumed, however, in poetic exhortations to the victorious Union armies to practice charity in their reformation of the country:

> Patriotism is not baseness, neither is it inhumanity. The mourners who this summer bear flowers to the mounds of the Virginian and Georgian dead are, in their domestic bereavement and proud affection, as sacred in the eye of Heaven as are those who go with similar offerings of tender grief and love into the cemeteries of our Northern Martyrs. And yet, in one respect, how needless to point the contrast.[27]

The "Supplement" to *Battle-Pieces* rings with this compassion.

A more intimate and dramatic identification of the poet's crushed feelings and sense of failure can be seen in the portrait of the still heroic, but patiently resigned General Lee:

> No word he breathes of vain lament,
> Mute to reproach, nor hears applause—
> His doom accepts, perforce content,
> And acquiesces in asserted laws;
> Secluded now would pass his life,
> And leave to time the sequel of the strife.[28]

Battle-Pieces lauds Lee, Stonewall Jackson, and a host of others who fought and died meaninglessly, men who "were driven/by Fate to arms." Their valor lives after them, even though Fate forced them into the war, caused their deaths, and awarded the victory to the North. A man has no control of the events of his life. He merely summons his strength, fights, endures or dies, without ever understanding the inexorable tragic movement of events. This is the overall theme of *Battle-Pieces*.

It remained as Melville's conviction for the rest of his life.

The one last significant event thereafter, bearing on the writing of *Clarel*, was an appointment of the then-forgotten author to the Custom House as Inspector 75, on December 5, 1866. The duties there were tedious and unheroic; they must have appeared to him as comic relief after the imaginative adventures with Taji, Ahab, and Pierre. To a man who had sailed all over the world, the circumscribed area of a "District Officer in the Customhouse" would seem to have been unbearable. Nevertheless, his family noted how improved his health became as a result of his daily attendance at business.[29] Equally important, the position afforded Melville an adequate income to provide for his family and, at the same time, gave him ample time for reading. From 1866 on, Melville collected and read numerous books on criticism and poetry. It can be seen now that all of this was preparatory to the writing of *Clarel*, a work he did not begin in any systematic way until sometime after 1870. It seems appropriate that much of the poem was written in what Vernon Parrington called "his tomb in the Custom House where he was consuming his own heart."[30] Although he suffered there the daily pain of lost ideals and anonymity, he was hardly "consuming his own heart" in daily activities which kept him safely removed from the materialistic world he despised. Using the post as a kind of monastic retreat, he wrote other poems and prepared carefully for the one long poem which was to sum up a lifetime of thought, frustrated ambitions, defeats, and resignation. When it appeared, the poem emerged as a natural flow from all the earlier writings and anticipated the few remaining works Melville was to produce. As such it constitutes the high point in any understanding of Melville's life and art.

IV

A Century of Readers

> But I don't know but a book in a man's brain is better off than a book bound in calf—at any rate it is safer from criticism.
>
> Letter to Evert Duyckinck: December 13, 1850

On June 2, 1876, *Clarel* was published by G. P. Putnam's Sons. Peter Gansevoort paid for the costs of the two volumes with a check for twelve hundred dollars but never saw the manuscript nor the poem in print: he died on January 4. Melville was deeply touched by this unsolicited generosity and dedicated the book in loving memory to his uncle. The joy that an author should have with a monumental work completed, especially after a long hiatus, was missing because of the death of his friend and also, in April, of his sister, Augusta. In addition, he had reverted to a morbid state in the months immediately before publication. Elizabeth wrote of this confidentially to Catherine Lansing, who by then had become very close to Melville:

> The fact is, that Herman, poor fellow, is in such a frightfully nervous state, & particularly now with such an added strain on his mind, that I am actually *afraid* to have any one here for fear that he will be upset entirely, & not be able to go on with the printing—He was not willing to have even his own sisters here. . . . If ever this dreadful *incubus* of a *book* (I call it so because it has undermined

> all our happiness) gets off Herman's shoulders I do hope he may be in better mental health—but at present I have reason to feel the gravest concern & anxiety about it—to put it in mild phase—. . .[1]

The extraordinary length of the poem—over 18,000 lines—and its heavy philosophic and religious emphasis did not recommend it to the professional critics nor to the reading public. Followers of Longfellow and Lowell, and other popular poets, were unreceptive to the naked, sometimes wrenched lines of a poem that violated all the sounds, patterns, and thoughts of acceptable verse. But Melville never expected wide circulation or acclamation: he knew the areas explored in *Clarel* would be repugnant to the optimists of his age. This indifference to the public's reaction accounts for the restrained inscription on the first page:

> If during the period in which this work has remained not undivulged, any of its properties have by a natural process exhaled; it yet retains, I trust, enough of original life to redeem it at least from vapidity. Be that as it may, I here dismiss the book—content beforehand with whatever future awaits it.[2]

Ten years before, Melville had published his first volume of poetry, *Battle-Pieces and Aspects of War*. Though hardly a critical or financial success, the book at least managed to keep the once-famous author's name before the public. When *Clarel* was published, however, the name of Herman Melville was relatively obscure. Only this can account for the fact that two of the three most important weeklies—*Harper's Weekly* and the *Nation*—and the four leading monthlies of the day—*Harper's, Scribner's, Atlantic,* and *North American Review*—failed to review the poem at all.[3]

The first notice on record, in the *New York Daily Tribune*, reintroduced the "Typee" Melville, the then-forgotten "narrator of marvellous stories of tropical life and adventure." The reviewer remembered the poet of the stirring lines of "Sheridan's Ride," but he regretted that *Clarel*, "in design and execution," remained a puzzle and a hopeless failure:

> There is thus no plot in the work; but neither do the theological doubts, questions, and disputations indulged in by the characters, and those whom they meet, have any logical course or lead to any distinct conclusions. . . . The verse, frequently flowing for a few lines with a smooth, agreeable current, seems to foam and chafe against unmanageable words like a brook in a stony glen; there are fragments of fresh, musical lyrics, suggestive both of Hafiz and of William Blake; there are passages so rough, distorted, and commonplace withal, that the reader impatiently shuts the book. It is, in this respect, a medley such as we have rarely perused,—a mixture of skill and awkwardness, thought and aimless fancy, plan shattered by whim and melody broken by discords. . . .[4]

He concluded that Melville obviously intended a profound meaning in the poem but failed miserably in the execution.

The reviewer in *The World* also found little to praise. He thought Melville's facility for words led off into wild digressions, into rambles which obscured all meaning. He considered the philosophic content of the poem the least appealing. If the poem had any merit at all, it could be found only in the "bold, clear, and judicious descriptions."[5] *The Independent*, one of the leading religious weeklies, failed to review the poem, but it did condemn the work in pontifical fashion:

> Poetry is scarce lately—in bound volumes, at any rate. We have, however, a few books of verse on our table. *Clarel: A Poem and Pilgrimage to the Holy Land* (G. P. Putnam's Sons), by Herman Melville, is a vast work, extending through a couple of 16 mo. volumes. It is destitute of interest or metrical skill.[6]

The review in *The Library Table* was also a masterpiece of vague statement:

> . . . The verse is flowing and musical, the hero and his companions meet with the customary adventures, see the customary sights, and, during their journeyings, chance upon much that surprises and interests them and furnishes abundant food for thought. The poem is a long one, and it seems to us might judiciously be somewhat curtailed, but we doubt not it will meet with some readers who will not object to linger with the author by the way and who will think it none too long. . . .[7]

The irony here was the inclusion in the same issue of lengthy, highly detailed, glowing accounts of Annie Thomas's *A Narrow Escape* and Mary Mapes Dodge's *Theophilus and Others*, works known now only by antiquaries. The slick account in *The Galaxy* caviled at Melville's title and ignored the poem itself:

> We confess that we are puzzled by the title of Mr. Herman Melville's last volume—*Clarel*. . . . How a book can be a poem in the Holy Land, or a pilgrimage, we really cannot discover. The fact of the matter, set forth in simple English, is, that *Clarel* is a poem which narrates and comments upon a pilgrimage in the Holy Land. We are by no means in a captious, or a dissenting, or even a fastidious mood, but we cannot praise Mr. Melville's poem or pilgrimage, or poem-pilgrimage. It is not given even to the gods to be dull; and Mr. Melville is not one of the gods.[8]

The judgment in the *New York Times*, on the other hand, at least indicated a reading of the poem. It found merit in the descriptive passages, but suggested that a "writer of Mr. Herman Melville's undoubted talent" would do better to revert to prose, that his "genius is evidently not of the kind which must express itself in numbers."[9]

The notice in *The Academy* gave unqualified praise but without precise reference:

> . . . (it is) a book of very great interest, and poetry of no mean order. The form is subordinate to the matter, and

> a rugged inattention to the niceties of rhyme and meter here and there seems rather deliberate than careless. In this, in the musical verse where the writer chooses to be musical, in the subtle blending of old and new thought, in the unexpected turns of argument, and in the hidden connexion between things outwardly separate, Mr. Melville reminds us of A. H. Clough. He probably represents one phase of American thought as truly as Clough did on one side of the Oxford of his day. . . . We advise our readers to study this interesting poem, which deserves more attention than we fear it is likely to gain in an age which craves for smooth, short, lyric song, and is impatient for the most part of what is philosophic or didactic.[10]

The reader for *Lippincott's Magazine* was far more reserved. His delight on hearing that the author of *Typee* was writing again turned to disappointment on finding a long, dull poem. He considered Melville's intention honest, but his conclusions erroneous and his execution awkward and pedestrian. He wondered how Melville could think that all men are plagued with such doubts or why the poet should pose so many philosophic and religious problems without offering a single solution.[11]

In England the book fared little better. The snide account in *Westminster Review* dismissed Melville's work as completely unintelligible; such an ambitious undertaking with so little to show for it seemed an absurdity:

> Talleyrand used to say that he always found nonsense singularly refreshing. He would certainly have set a high value on *Clarel*.[12]

With one exception, then, the contemporary critical reception was even more indifferent and negative than Melville had anticipated.[13] Those who found any merit at all in the poem saw some slight aesthetic appeal in the local color and scenic description. Yet they failed to see any relationship between setting and subject matter. Nor did they grasp Melville's use of characters for the development of his thought.

Almost a half-century went by before *Clarel* was given any further attention, when Frank Mather rediscovered the poem and judged it to be the work of a very great mind. He pointed out that because of the inherent difficulties in the poem he was probably the only man alive who had read both volumes. Despite the obvious flaws, he thought the poem grew with each new reading, until it became for him the best poetic statement of the pervasive nineteenth-century theme of faith-doubt.[14]

Two years later, Raymond Weaver called himself the second reader of *Clarel* and doubted there would be a third. Nevertheless, he agreed with the general note struck by Mather: "*Clarel* is by all odds the most important record we have of what was the temper of Melville's deeper thoughts during his long metaphysical period." He saw the major theme or the recurrent note of the poem as the hero's "parched desire for companionship." As to its future success, Weaver agreed with Melville's wry comment in a letter to James Billson, that it was "a metrical affair, a pilgrimage, or what not, of several thousand lines, eminently adapted for unpopularity."[15] Significantly, Weaver gave to the poem only four and a half pages of a long biographical essay, with over three of these mere quotations.[16] If Mather began a twentieth-century approval of the poem, Weaver added nothing to that consent. Neither did the English biographer, Raymond Freeman, win over any readers to *Clarel*. He observed that the movies can do a better job than Melville did, and that Melville's concern for philosophy and his naked verse led only to utter boredom: ". . . this dull precision accounts in part for the 'boring' part of the poem."[17] He scorned Melville's ignorance of the subject matter proper to poetry:

> He never learned, neither in verse nor in prose [*sic*], that his philosophy and religion, his transcendentalism and piety, are of little *essential* value in poetry, and indeed of none if by their presence they exclude imagination.[18]

Lewis Mumford read *Clarel* with far more perception and yet arrived at the same sad conclusion:

> It is unfortunate that Melville diverted into the ingenuities of a foreign versification the energies that should have gone into the mastery of the theme itself. But matter and manner are always one; and because Melville did not find harmonious form for his intuitions, we are deprived of a good part of them, and those that remain we must pick, like precious shards, from the refuse heap of the poem. He was a true poet; but formal verse was not his medium; and the relentless probity of his mind, the keen reaching into the heart of a dilemma, lacked in these lengthy verses an appropriate vehicle. Melville was wrong when he said that some of the aroma might have exhaled during the years *Clarel* remained unpublished; the aroma had never been there.[19]

Although he found the poem awkward in expression and obscure in meaning, Mumford believed that the "precious shards" should be examined. For example, Melville anticipated an era of social skepticism in his assessment of the balance that must exist between the ideal and the real. He was fifty years ahead of his time in excoriating a society founded on science and in prophesying the destruction that faces a nation moulded into an industrial culture. He thus foresaw all the "disillusion of social revolutionists." On the other hand, Mumford observed, Melville was not pejorative. His awareness of the historic cycle—of Christ following Osiris, for example, of an era of doubt, in turn, followed by another of doubt and uncertainty—gave him little consolation. In a way, it constituted his own religious statement. Such faith hardly goes beyond animal endurance, Mumford concluded, but it at least makes life livable.[20] Mumford called attention to the autobiographical nature of the poem as well, viz., Melville's stoic affirmation of life and man's heroic capacity. His praise of the poet's social skepticism emphasized a theme that has been continued in much of the Melville scholarship today. Despite his failure to find aesthetic merit in the poem, Mumford's was the first genuine treatment in any comprehensive fashion.

Willard Thorp was impressed by the seal that Melville placed at the end of the poem: the affirmation of faith in the Epilogue gives meaning to Clarel's spiritual pilgrimage. In Thorp's judgment, the triumphant ending shifts the meaning from the anguish of Arnold and Tennyson closer to the consolatory messages of Meredith and Hardy. This can be understood, however, only as it bears on the whole Melville canon; for *Clarel* becomes a final statement or a resolution of the earlier works. Thorp's only regret was that in his determination to achieve clarity Melville sacrificed the "poetry" of the work.[21]

The first real enthusiast for the poem appeared in 1939, in the French critic Jean Simon. He considered the work as a great soul-study projected against an authentic historic background. He found in it sections of great poetry, perceptive analyses of a tortured era, and a correct assessment of the religious problems of the day. Simon's criticism included a shrewd but unfounded guess about the dates of composition of the volumes: volume I was written before *Battle-Pieces* (1866), at a time of spiritual crisis, when Melville desperately needed something to believe in; volume II came in the later years, when Melville abandoned the religious search, after he accepted an "isolated life of silent meditation."[22]

F. O. Matthiessen did not share Simon's enthusiasm for the poem. He considered *Clarel* "practically unreadable because of Melville's inexplicable choice of rhymed tetrameter as the medium for philosophic meditation,"[23] a poem altogether of very little merit. It "might have been formed into a whole, but again he let himself be swamped by too many indistinct characters; and their discussions of religion became as tediously abstract as the details in *White-Jacket* had been heavily concrete." Had Melville included women in the work to any extent, a greater variety would have resulted; but Melville's mistake was to judge their absence in any philosophic inquiry an absolute necessity.[24] Like Thorp, Matthiessen regarded the Epilogue as a distinct Christian expression and a reasonable statement of hope.[25]

Bernard Kimpel included *Clarel* in his study of Melville's later life. He believed that the poem affirmed an emotional faith rather than a rational conviction, but one held tenuously in the poem. For Kimpel, *Clarel* expressed the positive need for man to believe in God and the inability to find a way. This unavailing search impressed upon Melville the fruitlessness of battling against overwhelming odds; it accounted for the difference between the rebellion and pessimism of *Pierre* and *The Confidence-Man*, and the resignation and quiet hope of *Clarel* and *Billy Budd*.[26]

•

Henry Wells set a pattern in 1943 for the present-day general appreciation of *Clarel*. Echoing Hoadley and Mather, he said that each new reading of the poem threw new light on its greatness and emphasized its modern appeal:

> His verse is never elegant, unctuously soft but is toughly imaginative, like the best verse of Emily Dickinson, Emerson, and Thoreau. . . . in the restraining measures of a short-line verse the reticence and deep reserve of energy in the New England spirit find their best expression. Throughout *Moby-Dick* the allegory is vague and portentous: often lost, even to its author, in a romantic cloudland. In *Clarel* style is outwardly less glowing while actually a greater fire burns within. Economy and intellectual clarity replace lavishness and mental fog.[27]

Wells thus found merit in the clarity and profundity that Matthiessen and Freeman had scored. Even more, he regarded Melville's wedding of Palestine background and tortured inquiry a deliberate analogue of Dante's *Inferno* and *Purgatorio*, and the use of characters to develop ideas a parallel to the *Canterbury Tales*.[28] Wells's enthusiasm for the poem, which went beyond Simon's, was tempered by the thought that *Clarel* would never become popular except with readers of Dickinson, Emerson, and Dante.[29]

The first complete study of *Clarel* was made by Walter Bezanson, in 1943. Although there were references to the other Melville works, the author's concern was with *Clarel* as a work of poetry and as a reflection of Melville's thought late in life. Bezanson emphasized the strong parallels that exist between the poem and Melville's *Journal*; between the poem and Melville's sources, particularly Arthur Stanley's *Sinai and Palestine in Connection with their History*; between the poem and the poet's difficult years that led up to the writing of the book. This interpretation of *Clarel* concentrated on the characters as individual expressions of the spiritual problems Melville posed in the poem. His dissertation, complementing Wells's cogent observations in the same year, brought an entirely new reading of, and, in turn, a new audience to the poem. Anything written since necessarily has taken them both into account.[30]

In England, also in 1943, William Plomer brought out a selection of Melville's poetry and included excerpts from *Clarel*. He expressed the traditional complaint that it is a great labor to read the poem, for too much of it "trundles along in low gear." Plomer thought the difficulty could be overcome, however: ". . . the reader is left with an extraordinary expression of a man of the 19th century trying to free himself from the incubus of conscience, the weight of tradition and the lumber of a whole civilization, and to look backwards or forwards, inwards or outwards, for living realities."[31]

Sedgwick's study of the inner life of Melville, in 1945, stressed *Clarel* and *Billy Budd* as companion pieces. Sedgwick read them as Melville's calm acceptance of the universal tragedy of human existence and an indication of a move away from the "radical Protestantism" of youth to the warmth of the Catholic Church. Not that Melville ever seriously accepted the Roman Catholic dogma; rather, that he saw the Church as truthful, or devoted to the heart, and Protestantism as meaningless, or dedicated to the head.[32] No other scholar before or after Sedgwick weighed Melville's Catholic sympathies so heavily as this.[33]

The new acceptance of *Clarel*, begun by Wells and Bezanson in 1943, failed to persuade Van Wyck Brooks in 1947. In

The Times of Melville and Whitman, Brooks praised Melville for his ambitious approach to literature, but concluded that his floundering could have been avoided if he had received even a little philosophic training.[34] Brooks thought the defect remained less obvious in Melville's prose. But when this facility for writing prose disappeared he turned to verse, and this resulted in his sophomoric approach to philosophy: "As for the philosophical poems, these were too often inexpert, a marriage of wooden rhetoric and refractory thought that turned him into a still more awkward Clough, especially in the ambitious *Clarel* with its jogtrot metre and its characters vaguely drifting in and out."[35]

Nathalia Wright's expert analysis of Melville's use of the Bible pointed out how much and in what way *Clarel* was derived from Scripture. In particular, she saw Melville bringing his life-long use of the Ishmael symbol to a literary peak, with all of the major characters in the poem as Ishmael in one way or another.[36] Accordingly, *Clarel* fits in with all of the other works where loneliness is the theme; that is to say, where Melville studies man, he finds him in sad isolation at the beginning of the work and leaves him at the end in the same sorrowful condition. The Ishmael theme in *Clarel*, and in all the other works, Wright contended, argues against solutions to problems and, therefore, does not allow for a happy ending.

In the same year, Geoffrey Stone wrote his biography of Melville, admittedly from the Roman Catholic viewpoint. He judged *Clarel* as a second-rate poem but also as clear evidence of a first-rate mind at work. Stone concluded that Melville's praise of the Church in *Clarel* never involved doctrinal matters and that the arguments presented for it by certain characters were only on the natural level. Even the Epilogue denied man's supernatural goal after life: it implied that life is to be "found on the subrational level . . . mere animal persistence."[37] Stone's reading of the poem reinforced Mumford's conclusions regarding the overall stoical theme.

Richard Chase scored *Clarel* for aesthetic weaknesses. He believed, however, that the poem must be read for a fuller understanding of Melville's life-long search for a conducive culture. The search in this late work was "for an intelligent point of view,"[38] in an age of sterility where "life has withdrawn its richness and its ecstasy and is no longer tragic but simply progressive."[39] Chase saw little value in a reiteration of the search theme. But he was struck by the change which allowed Melville to find the "point of view," a fact that marked a high road in the poet's life.

When Newton Arvin published his biography of Melville in 1951, he expressed qualified enthusiasm for this novel in verse. He granted that there were major artistic blemishes. Yet he regarded the visual and emotional truthfulness of many passages as remarkable: ". . . in general the sense of place, the feeling for scene, is masterly in *Clarel*."[40] Although Arvin admired the poet's occasional success with symbols, he was less impressed by Melville's staggering in the dialectical play of the poem. Even with such unevenness, Arvin thought the theme emerges clearly, viz., the poet's awareness and acceptance of good and evil in a world created by an inscrutable God.[41] In the same year, Leon Howard lamented Melville's weak poetic form in *Clarel*. He recognized, however, that Melville did come to grips with the deepest conflicts of the age and with the "human problem of belief which had bothered him for so long." Even though the dominant mood was skepticism, Melville "could recommend an acceptance of the rude elements of belief found in the impulses of the 'heart'."[42] Howard saw the poem as a significant turn from philosophy to psychology, which then brought the poet to a fuller understanding of man.

As noted earlier, Melville's first English biographer, John Freeman, rejected *Clarel* as a dull poem and as a work that added nothing to the reputation of the American poet. His second English biographer, Ronald Mason in *The Spirit Above the Dust*, praised *Clarel* extensively, despite the poetic weaknesses: "*Clarel* is nothing less than the most substantial and significant attempt that Melville's considerable intellect was ever to make to rationalise and resolve the paradoxes which his intuition had bred in his imagination."[43] Mason, like Sedgwick before him, admired Melville's resolution of these paradoxes, citing the poem as an act of faith in a world where there are no panaceas for pain and sorrow.[44]

In a casual aside as part of his long study of Melville, Lawrance Thompson judged *Clarel* as merely another example of the poet's deep hatred for God. He found the poem full of characters who were "hate-shod" like Pierre and "fire-worshipping" like Ahab.[45] Although it had little value as poetry, *Clarel* demonstrated Melville's continuing quarrel over God's betrayal of man, including the forsaken Christ. Thompson maintained that theories which depend upon the mature poet's acceptance of life's ambiguities are destroyed in the light of the textual evidence of *Clarel*, and of *Billy Budd* after it.

Arvin's reading of *Clarel* as a statement of New Manicheanism[46] was repeated in Frank Griffith's thesis. Griffith examined all of Melville's works as expressions of a search for God, with a concentration on *Mardi*, *Moby-Dick*, and *Clarel*. In these three works, Melville's heroes refuse to give up their search for God even when they are faced with the awful possibility that He might be devil too. The tragic theme lies in their failure to find absolute answers on the nature of God, good and evil, and the universe. Griffith found the dilemma resolved in *Billy Budd*: only there can be found Melville's sincere belief in the coexistence of a just Deity and a temporary evil.[47]

Howard Horsford's edition of Melville's *Journal* appeared in 1955 and necessarily contained allusions to *Clarel*. Horsford complemented Bezanson's earlier findings of the parallels that exist between the work and the *Journal*, but he went further in judging how dependent Melville was on the diary: "*Clarel*, so far as narrative goes, is virtually an elaborated recapitulation of the Palestinian section of the *Journal*."[48] Like Bezanson, and implicitly supporting the early speculation of Simon, Horsford found volume I to be highly personal, written not too long after Melville's return home in 1857, and volume II clearly written after the War, in typical Melville fashion, i.e., he composed the second half out of prolific readings on the Holy Land.

James Baird's study of Melville as a primitivist presented nothing new in the critical estimates of *Clarel*. For Baird, the poem contained "some of the worst aberrations of versification in the English language—yet [Melville's] total range of poetic sensitivity triumphs over these faults."[49] Baird rejected the many primitive symbols, such as the cross, as evidence of Melville's Christianity, arguing that Melville in his spiritual voyage had traveled beyond Christ and the Christian God. As a consequence, Melville found the peace that comes with the stoical acceptance of the mysteries of the universe. In a judgment totally different from Sedgwick's and Mason's, Baird called this the logical conclusion of the true Protestant artist.[50]

In his study of Melville, Milton R. Stern included *Clarel* as further evidence of Melville's naturalism, one based on rationalism, empiricism, objectivity, and relativism. Each of Melville's heroes is like *Clarel*, "who tries to reconcile the disparities between his own history and the assumptions which a pilgrimage requires."[51] Each of the questers ends in futility because idealism is the philosophy of fools. Thus Stern sees *Clarel* as an extension of *The Confidence-Man*, where the main character is "searching for a causality that is more than something merely external to man's moral sphere."[52] *Clarel* is one of Melville's "tragedies," i.e., where the quester's pilgrimage never results in purgation of the world, no lessons are learned, no moment of communal wisdom is shared, and where the quester is defeated without any hope extended for the reader to plunge back into earth's conflicts.[53] Stern believes that such a view, expressed in *Clarel* and the other major works, properly constituted Melville as the spokesman for the breakdown of western society after two thousand years of idealism.[54]

The second complete study of *Clarel* as a poem was finished by Mother M. Denis Mahoney in 1958. She regarded the poetry as inferior: "aesthetic criticism must be justifiably hard on this, Melville's only sustained effort in verse."[55] She did not suggest that the poem should not be read. On the contrary, *Clarel* must be studied as the metaphorical sunrise after the despair of *Pierre* and *The Confidence-Man* and as a poem that makes the vision of *Billy Budd* understandable. Mother Denis's study examined the long struggle by Melville for faith in spiritual isolation, his tendency toward asceticism, and his insistence upon the need for suffering in the universe. All of this led her to conclude, with Howard before her, that Melville solved his problems as a psychologist, and that when he left metaphysics, as he did in the poem, he came to a better understanding of himself and of mankind in a universe created by a personal and benevolent God.[56]

In 1959, Michael Ziek also made a full study of the poem but from a historian's point of view. He gave particular attention to Melville's concept of democracy and attachment to the Catholic Church. Concerning this attachment, Ziek found the poet's Catholic sympathies centering on a deep belief in supernal love, insistence upon the efficacy of prayer, asceticism and Christian compassion, respect and admiration for Jesus as divine and for Mary as His mother, a firm belief in original sin and personal sin, and an utter distaste for Protestantism. Zeik's conclusions echoed Sedgwick's, although Zeik, like Stone, was reluctant to label Melville a Catholic.[57]

The most important single contribution to appreciation of *Clarel* occured in 1960 with a new edition of the text by Walter Bezanson. Unlike the original edition, and that of Weaver's, it appeared in a single volume, completely annotated. A lengthy introduction and a series of notes to the text included all of the material of his 1943 dissertation, and went deeper into detailed analysis of the poem's ideas. He insisted that the seeming weaknesses of Melville's craft—the cramped lines, archaic expressions, and stop and go movement—were carefully arranged to show constriction as the tragedy of modern man.[58] He saw the poem demonstrating Melville's religious dilemma, noted earlier by Hawthorne: "He can neither believe, nor be comfortable in his unbelief; and he is too honest and courageous not to try to do one or the other." As such, the theme of *Clarel* centers on the loss of faith and how one can "endure the overwhelming sense of a shattered vision."[59]

Merlin Bowen also brought out a study of Melville in 1960. In it he tacitly agreed with Thompson in regarding all of Melville's works as expressions of a long encounter of the isolated man with an indifferent nature, God, and the universe. Bowen agreed with Wright that the theme of the poem is, once again, Ishmael's search for a life-sustaining balance, "a vision adequate to the needs of both heart and head."[60] He pointed out that Melville cannot be understood in terms of *Mardi, Moby-Dick*, and *Pierre* alone. One must go to the later Melville for a clarification of all the earlier doubts and rebellions. Thus *Clarel* is

> a complex, deeply considered, and carefully elaborated work of art, the fount of its author's ripest maturity, enriched by reading and meditation, chastened by the experience of national and domestic tragedy. . . . Art has no final answers, but if it is Melville's last fully considered judgment that we want, we must turn to *Clarel*. And quiet though it is, that answer, in its emphasis upon endurance and affirmation, is closer to defiance than surrender.[61]

In the same year, Richard Fogle also insisted upon *Clarel* as required reading for any proper judgment of Melville. He saw in it, however, two major structural flaws: one, the fact of distinct and unrelated plot lines of the love affair and the pilgrimage; and two, the lack of connection between the conflict of ideas and the actions of the personalities involved. Both impair the aesthetic effects and thereby impose difficulties for the reader as he tries to understand the unfolding arguments. Fogle identified Melville with the character of Mortmain because he is the only one to experience both despair and faith, the alternatives for humanity offered in the Epilogue. He saw evidence of this in the mystical event when the eagle snatches Mortmain's black cap and carries it heavenward, a sign that he was "visited by the mercy of heaven."[62]

John Bernstein singled out two lines as a leitmotif in his reading of Clarel:[63]

If Luther's day expand to Darwin's year
Shall that exclude the hope—foreclose the year?

He considered Melville a continuing rebel in these late years, for the poet takes sides with the three revolutionaries, Celio, Mortmain, and Ungar, who argue against the existence of a benevolent God and the natural goodness of man. Like Bernstein, John Seelye discovered in Melville's emphasis on the quality of endurance a modern expression of existentialism: heroic virtue can be achieved by any man who accepts the limited possibilities he is offered in life. In this, the poem is not unique for it echoes an earlier statement in *Moby-Dick*: ". . . our souls are like those orphans whose unwedded mothers die in bearing them: the secret of our paternity lies in their grave, and we must there to learn it."[64]

Bernstein and Seelye offered a reading of *Clarel* in line with modern proposals concerning the human predicament, but inclusion of the poem as a part of a larger study of Melville necessarily limited their evidence and overall arguments. In 1971, two studies appeared at the same time, as though their authors had discussed at length these existential problems and solutions posed by Melville in the poem. Father Joseph Knapp began and ended his book[65] in praise of Melville's artistic control of the voluminous material. He saw *Clarel* as America itself at a dead end of belief, yet continuing a search for anything of spiritual value; with spokesmen for her nineteenth-century reliance upon Protestant fundamentalism, evolutionary progress, and the autonomy of science, and with spokesmen against these three positive positions. Unlike so many other readers of the poem, he found the Epilogue as no appendage or afterthought, but as a logical conclusion to key cantos and to the overall poem. This conclusion, he maintained, was Melville's surest conviction at the end of his life: the man who can confront with equanimity the reality of alienation and continuing conflict with God's will wins a victory over himself precisely as he takes on the natural virtue of endurance in the fact of that reality. Stanley Brodwin, at the same time, complemented this judgment with an examination of *Clarel* as a prime example of modern man's search for the authenticity interpreted by Kierkegaard and Heidegger. He interpreted *Clarel*, therefore, as the victorious "inner man" when he becomes aware of what he must be and do as he crosses over the "frontiers of eternity."[66] Ray B. Browne, in the same year, included *Clarel* as part of a larger study of Melville's life-long concern over the human plight and his repeated affirmation of humanism. Like Knapp and Brodwin, he identified Clarel with the alienated universal man who believes in little more than life's dominance over death but rests or continues thereby in quiet hope.[67]

The surge of interest in *Clarel* since 1960, with particular notice taken of the poet's prophetic expression of alienation and endurance, demonstrates how far the circle of criticism has run since *The Independent* reviewer observed that the poem "is destitute of interest or metrical skill." The overall reactions to the poem since its publication in 1876 include a majority of readers who complained of Melville's failure to couch ideas in an attractive form, although they believed the profundity of ideas would always command attention. After the contemporary reviewers voted the book down, a few readers like Matthiessen and Brooks concluded that, if anything, *Clarel* could only damage Melville's reputation. But they, at least, read the poem before they condemned it; too many Melville admirers ignored the book completely and then went ahead with evaluations of the poet's life and work.[68] *Clarel*, it is safe to say, will never become a popular poem with the public, notwithstanding the interest since Bezanson's edition. Its awesome size, constricted verse, and occasionally obscure subject matter discourage even some Melville enthusiasts. Nevertheless, this sketch of a century's reading discloses an obvious increasing respect for the poem by those who are willing to meet the poet on his terms. And it will continue upwards, to a limited level, because of the subject matter, not in spite of it, and because the poem is one of the most moving experiences in American literature.

V

The Pilgrimage Revisited

> . . . that the more spiritual, wide-seeing, conscientious and sympathetic the nature, so much the more is spiritually it isolationed, and isolation is the mother of illusion.
>
> "Rammon"

The first canto of *Clarel*[1] introduces the main character, states his problem, and elliptically presents possible solutions. The major theme and liturgical motif of the poem emerge, too, for the canto opens appropriately on the Vigil of Epiphany. A young, nonbelieving theologian, Clarel, arrives in Palestine as a modern Magus seeking the place of Jesus's birth, hoping for the revelation of a new faith or a reaffirmation of the one he has discarded. His background is unknown. He is one who has been "long confined/Apart like Vesta in a grove/Collegiate," responding to the demands of his intellect but disillusioned with all the findings of "blind theology." He has come to Jerusalem to find the Rose of Sharon, to drink at the waters of Siloa. He finds instead, from the very beginning, that the ideal of the quest fades to nothing in the real experience:

> Romance of Mountains! But in end
> What change the near approach could lend.
>
> [I, i, p. 4][2]

The romance of the Rose disappears with the first sight of "Thy blank, blank towers, Jerusalem!" (I, i, p. 4). The blind arches and sealed windows, the "portals masoned fast," portray for him his own closeted condition. But they are not depressant enough to keep him from going aloft to view Mt. Olivet or from plumbing the depths of the "underformings in the mind."

The first canto is actually an Epilogue of another journey, summing up the plight of modern man in an age when faith is dead. More specifically, it presents a need by Clarel for belief in something outside himself, and the courage required if he is to discover some truth or peace. His journey through the Holy Land is to be his initiation into the awful mystery of tragic existence, in contrast to the youthful intellectual frustration which caused his trip to Judea. The journey will be an examination of the basic conflict between the head and the heart.

Throughout the poem Clarel looks for meaning in the "underformings" through the many people he meets. He approaches each new one as a teacher, assuming that in the resolution of their problems he might discover why he has arrived at a "dead pool" of existence. The poem thus becomes a series of meetings, with moral and philosophic conversations held on good and evil, tragedy and happiness, democracy and independence, death and immortality, faith and science, progress, art, love, sex, and God.

Clarel's first meeting in Jerusalem is with Abdon, one of the "Lost children in the wood of time" (I, ii, p. 8). Abdon is a Black Jew, one of the remnants of the Ten Tribes of Cochin. His journey to Palestine, by way of commercial Amsterdam, was a holy pilgrimage. But after a short while in the Holy Land he found in himself and in the land a spiritual aridity. He was able to endure thereafter only by the dream of return to his native India. His bitter renunciation of Judea complements the blank towers of Jerusalem and anticipates Clarel's own final disillusionment. Abdon's function ends with this; except for an occasional glimpse of him thereafter, Clarel forgets him.

On his first morning in Jerusalem, Clarel roams through the sacred places of Scripture where Christ taught as a boy in the Temple, where He was crucified and buried, and where He appeared to Mary after His resurrection. Imaginatively, Clarel casts himself back into the time and place of Christ, then back and forward through the ages of other religions and pseudo-gods—Allah, Brahma, and Buddha—through the "Tribes and Sects" (I, vi, p. 24) of Christianity, until his anguish over the "gulf of dizzying fable lost" (I, vi, p. 24) has him crying for the lost Word:

> I too, I too; could *I* but meet
> Some stranger of a lore replete,
> Who, marking how my looks betray
> The dumb thoughts clogging here my feet,
> Would question me, expound and prove,
> And make my heart to burn with love—
> Emmaus were no dream today!
>
> [I, vii, p. 27]

His need for a risen Christ is met at once, ironically, in a half-mad evangelist, Nehemiah. Nehemiah conducts him through Palestine with little care for the geography of the land: Judea has meaning for him only as a reminder of favorite passages in Scripture. Along the way he distributes tracts telling of Christ's Second Coming, of the need for penance, and of the coming holocaust. Clarel sees at once that he can learn nothing from Nehemiah, just as he could gain nothing from Abdon. But the old man's sincerity and warmth endear him to Clarel, and he humorously accepts him as his Virgil.

In the following days, the two wander through the historic land, with little to mark the passing time. One day Clarel sees a humpbacked young man whose appearance betrays utter despair. Instinctively, Clarel would speak some words of fellowship, but the shyness that plagues him prevents it. He overhears the man's lament as though the words were his own:

> "Equivocal!
> Woo'st thou the weary to thee—tell,
> Thou tomb, so winsome in thy grace?
> To me no reassuring place."
>
> [I, xi, p. 35]

Clarel learns that his name is Celio, that he comes from a distinguished Roman family intimately connected with the hierarchy, and that he has renounced Catholicism. He is now in Judea, like Clarel and Abdon, in a last attempt to give meaning to his life. But Celio's mission ends in quick failure. He dies outside the walls of the city, cut off from God and society. His death seems to be an act of his will, as though he refuses to live in a world from which God has removed Himself:

"But died he twice?
He comes not back from Paradise
Or Hades now. A vacant tomb
By Golgotha they show—a cell,
A void cell here. And is it well?
Raiser and raised divide one doom;
Both vanished now."

[I, xv, p. 48]

Clarel sensed in Celio an alter ego, but his inability to speak prevented the friendship they might have had. Clarel suspects that their relationship would have served no purpose, however; both of them were islands of despair set in disparate seas:

Can these a climax share?
Mutual in approach may glide
Minds which from poles adverse have come,
Belief and unbelief? may doom
Of doubt make such to coincide—
Upon one frontier brought to dwell
Arrested by the Ezan high
In summons as from out the sky
To matins of the infidel?

[I, xvi, p. 50]

No word was exchanged between them, yet the encounter with Celio disturbed him, for he saw in the excommunicate all of his own doubts and rebellion. Celio's failure, like Abdon's, seemed to presage his own. The weight of the spiritual meeting would have become unbearable for Clarel except that at this time he receives his first gift from Palestine.

Walking with Clarel one morning on the outskirts of the city, Nehemiah offers his tracts to a group of Jews who are singing a dirge at a Wailing Wall. They ignore him. But afterwards, one of them, a beautiful young girl named Ruth, smiles at them and almost at once Clarel falls in love. He visits Ruth later, and the original impulse develops into what Clarel thinks is an ecstatic love. He learns of her background through these visits but more through Nehemiah's accounts. Ruth's father, Nathan, was a farmer in Illinois, a God-fearing man. Tragedy, in the form of his parents' death in an avalanche that swept away the whole village, suggested to him that there was no providential god. Reading Thomas Paine thereafter convinced him, and he became a militant atheist. But in a short time he met a Hebrew lady, named Agar, married her and was converted to the Jewish faith. In time, he became more of a Jew than his wife and, against her wishes, moved the family—two children by then—to Palestine. He farmed the arid Judea soil but spent more time defending his land against marauding Arabs. At this point, Clarel meets Nathan and his wife and daughter.

The strictures cast on Jewish maidens make any courtship difficult so that much of Clarel's time is spent with Nehemiah. In their many walks, Clarel meets two other individuals who are to have a major influence on him. The first is Vine, an obvious recluse, who immediately senses that he and Clarel have much in common as skeptics. He joins Clarel and Nehemiah in their subsequent walks and through his cynical remarks emphasizes Clarel's own religious doubts. The second is Rolfe. His forceful personality captures Clarel at once. His readiness to lecture on any and all subjects and to argue both sides of any question, delights and awes the student. A defense of Roman Catholic priests by Rolfe puzzles Clarel until he realizes that Rolfe's open mind on all things is really camouflage of a skepticism, only a shade different from his and Vine's. Rolfe knows that if a man is to live he must believe in something. At the present time, Rolfe sees in the Catholic Church the only creed to offer anything of worth. At this point of his life, Clarel needs stronger arguments than those of Rolfe regarding the Church, namely, her historic endurance and emotional appeal. Like Nehemiah, Rolfe provides for the time only a kind of serious amusement for Clarel.

Along with Vine, Rolfe, and Nehemiah, Clarel is invited on a pilgrimage to visit Siddim, the Dead Sea, the ancient Copt monastery of Mar Saba, and Bethlehem, as part of a routine tour of the holy places. Clarel's new love for Ruth dissuades him, although a deeper reason lies in his dread of these dead sites.

> Loath was he here to disentwine
> Himself from Ruth. Nor less Lot's land,
> And sea, and Judah's utmost drought
> Fain would he view, and mark their tone:
> And prove if, unredeemed by John,
> John's wilderness augmented doubt.
>
> [I, xlii, p. 133]

He chooses, instead, to visit Ruth. In place of the usual hospitality, he finds strangers in mourning who tell him that Nathan has been killed by a band of Arabs. In keeping with Jewish custom, Clarel is refused admittance until the period of mourning is over. His failure to see Ruth or Agar compounds his sorrow, and he decides to join the pilgrimage to gain "Relief from dull inaction's pain" (I, xlii, p. 134). The pilgrims leave the Inn at dawn, with Clarel full of dread over the coming events.

This marks the end of Part I of *Clarel*. This first section presents the distraught theologian in a strange land where the truths he came to find are seemingly nonexistent. Chance offers him a substitute romantic solution in the person of Ruth and then takes it away temporarily through the death of her father. The death and the separation of the lovers anticipate the future tragedy, but, more specifically, set the scene for Part II—the Wilderness.

New characters introduced in the pilgrimage are Djalea the guide, an Anglican priest named Derwent, a rich fat banker and his future son-in-law, and a man clothed in black named Mortmain.

Djalea leads them out the Via Dolorosa, past the Ecce Homo Arch, through St. Stephen's Gate, and outside Jerusalem. Their first stop is at the Garden of Gethsemane, where the first of many quarrels takes place between the meliorist Derwent and the misanthropic Mortmain. Afterwards, in the role that becomes him, Rolfe informs the group of Mortmain. The bastard son of a noble Swedish lady, he left a loveless home for Paris, where he became a utopian evangelist, preaching, fighting to make the world a better place:

That uncreated Good
He sought, whose absence is the cause
Of creeds, and Atheists, mobs and laws.
[II, iv, p. 155]

The insurrection of 1848 that promised to cure all the social ills only substituted new versions of the old abuses and left Mortmain despairing of any good in a world where man can shape events. He became a solitary person, hating man for what he made of God's world, hating particularly those optimists who see prosperity everywhere in a world of progress. Unlike Clarel, he has not come to the Holy Land to discover for himself some penultimate truth: he is beyond such a quest.

But this man
No cloister sought. He, under ban
Of strange repentance and last dearth,
Roved the gray places of the earth.
And what seemed most his heart to wring
Was some unrenderable thing:
'Twas not his bastardy, nor bale
Medean in his mother pale,
Nor thwarted aims of high design;
But deeper—deep as nature's mine.
[II, iv, p. 158]

On the first day of the pilgrimage, the group passes along Bethany, in the shadow of Mt. Olivet, and out into the desert wilderness of Bahurim and Adommin. This road to Jericho inspires Nehemiah to paraphrase the tale of the Good Samaritan and its message of Christian compassion. Djalea's amused but courteous reaction to the "romance" told by a demented man is underscored by the pilgrims' sight of the murderous spears just now thrown by Djalea's guards at marauders. The incident presses home for Clarel the dichotomy between the ideal and the real, between the tale of Scripture and the fact of the unholy land. Nor do the miles and miles of stones and sand and endless waste remind him of the love Christ brought out of this barren earth. He knows that Scripture records that John found wild honey here. If so, he wonders, why is it "a land/Direful yet holy-blest though banned?" (II, xii, p. 179). In the wilderness he sees the emblem of man's fallen condition, but nowhere can he find the symbol of redemption.

The depressing scenery of the desert overcomes the banker and Glaucon; they obviously had been ill-advised in the choice of an entertaining tour. They join a passing caravan and return in higher spirits to Jerusalem. As hedonists they avoid the crags and bitter roots of life and advise in song that all others should do the same:

"Tarry never there
Where the air
Lends a lone Hadean spell—
Where the ruin and the wreck
Vine and ivy never deck,
And wizard wan and sibyl dwell:
There, oh, beware!

"Rather seek the grove—
Thither rove,
Where the leaf that falls to ground
In a violet upsprings,
And the oracle that sings
Is the bird above the mound:
There, tarry there!"

[II, xiii, p. 185]

The song has no echo for the pilgrims as they ride on the rim of the black gorge of Achor, in the shadow of the Quarantanian mountain. Provoked by Mortmain's anguished cries, they imaginatively recall the forty days of fast in the desert and the Devil's assault on Christ's virtue. They remember, too, out of a growing fear, the lamentation of Moses over Jericho and his natural desire to be back again in fertile Egypt. In contrast to them, Achor and the mountain become Mortmain: he decides to remain alone there for a couple of days and then meet the group at the river Jordan. They leave him, in awe over such a decision; all but Djalea, who regards Mortmain's action as normal and sees in the melancholy man a strength of courage and purpose hidden to the rest. The journey continues to the Crusader's Tower in Jericho, where camp is struck for the first night in the wilderness.

The second day of the pilgrimage is given over to exploration around Jericho. In the morning, Clarel and Rolfe meet a Syrian monk. He tells how he spent forty days and nights in the mountains to atone for his sins of doubt and how, while there, was visited by the Devil. Whether it was autosuggestion or an actual contest between God and Satan for his soul, he does not know. But now he lives out his life in expiation, knowing that the ambiguities will never be solved in life, that only in death will this double vision become one.

> 'Content thee: in conclusion caught
> Thou'lt find how thought's extremes agree—
> The forethought clinched by afterthought,
> The firstling by finality.'—
>
> [II, xviii, p. 201]

Clarel refuses the Monk's advice; he is not ready to pray with the Syrian, "His will be done." First he must discover for himself what God's will is and, even more, who God is before he can make any act of faith.

At the foot of the mountain, they meet a geologist named Margoth. After the stunning effect of the ascetic Monk, Rolfe and Clarel are immediately repelled by this "Hegelized/Convert to science" (II, xix, p. 203), with his measurement of the world by slide rule and his reshaping of the earth with a hammer. Although none of the pilgrims accepts Nehemiah's Scriptural account of the Holy Land, they reject at once the materialism of this German Jew. In conversation with them he attempts to prove the Bible a tissue of lies in the light of scientific evidence. He abuses Nehemiah and scorns any belief that cannot be tested by instrument. He insists that this ancient "holy" land must make way for progress:

> "Stale is she!
> Lay flat the walls, let in the air,
> That folk no more may sicken there!
> Wake up the dead; and let there be
> Rails, wires, from Olivet to the sea,
> With station in Gethsemane."
>
> [II, xx, p. 207]

On the third day the group arrives at the river Jordan, where memories of the peaceful St. John are lost in a tribute demanded by Arab bandits. In another example of command presence, Djalea talks the Arabs out of the ransom, and the pilgrims are safe to wander about. Although no Catholic, Rolfe sings from a Catholic prayer book to celebrate their arrival at the Jordan. Derwent and Vine join in the hymn, although it is apparent to the orthodox Nehemiah that

> While they at best do but fulfill
> A transient, an esthetic glow;
>
> [II, xxiv, p. 223]

Nehemiah cannot sing with them, but he performs a more meaningful act in tasting the waters of the Jordan. Despite the bitter quality of the brakish waters, it tastes like sugar to him.

The hymn persuades a wandering Dominican priest that the group is Catholic. When he learns otherwise, he is even more pleased, for it enables him to discourse on the contributions and benefits of the Catholic Church. He argues that her endurance for over a thousand years in a state of genuine Christian democracy, with an appreciation for man and his needs that Science can never know, attests to the fact of her divinity; at worst, the longevity proves man's basic need for faith. He argues that in the final analysis, despite schisms and heresies, the only authentic creed is that of the Catholic Church. Were she to disappear chaos would be the result.

> If Rome could fall
> 'Twould not be Rome alone, but all
> Religion. All with Rome have tie,
> Even the railers which deny,
> All but the downright Anarchist,
> Christ-hater, Red, and Vitriolist.
>
> [II, xxv, p. 229]

Derwent's comment after the Dominican leaves is more gentle than Margoth's snarling words, but it is equally negative as a Protestant rejection of dogma: "The world is now too civilized/For Rome" (II, xxvi, p. 233). Rolfe, although hardly a believer in Catholic theology, argues for the Church's principle of order and obligation in a world that demands liberty and freedom and receives license and shame. He predicts a future when Protestantism will be only a tool in the great battle fought between Rome and Atheism:

> Protestantism being retained
> For base of operations sly
> By Atheism.
>
> [II, xxvi, pp. 233-34]

Clarel tires of the arguments and seeks out the quiet Vine. In a rare, eloquent mood, Vine laments man's tragic wandering in a lost world. Clarel barely hears him in the sudden emotion which sweeps over him: he feels in Vine the presence of a soul mate.

Ah! call me *brother*!—
So feminine his passionate mood
Which, long as hungering unfed,
All else rejected or withstood.

[II, xxvii, p. 238]

Vine immediately senses Clarel's unconscious "thrill of personal longing" and recovers the reserve he momentarily dropped:

Lives none can help ye; that believe.
Art thou the first soul tried by doubt?
. . . .
But for thy fonder dream of love
In man toward man—the soul's caress—
The negatives of flesh should prove
Analogies of non-cordialness
In spirit.

[II, xxvii, p. 238]

The earlier identification with Celio was as nothing compared to the feeling of spiritual relationship that Clarel has for Vine. Except for promises to Ruth, his wordless but obvious approach to Vine is the first self-exposure since he came to the Holy Land, and it ends in a scornful rebuke.

The pilgrimage continues into the heart of the wilderness as the group arrives at the shore of the Dead Sea, on the third day. The fog, dust, and stench of the Dead Sea awaken images of Sodom and Gommorah, of Aaron's hermitage and death cell on Mount Hor. The "dead boughs stranded" remind them of the suicidal Maccabees. The feel of Hell sweeps over all of them, except for Margoth. Inexplicably, presentiments of death shake Clarel as he thinks of Ruth and her dead father. It is only by an exertion of his will that he forces from his mind the Dead Sea mood:

"Go, goblins; go, each funeral thought—
Bewitchment from this Dead Sea caught!"

[II, xxx, p. 246]

The infernal trance is lifted from him slightly when Derwent spies on an overhanging crag of Petra Rock a chalked drawing of the Southern Cross, signed

By one who wails the loss,
This altar to the Southern Cross.
[II, xxxi, p. 250]

The drawing has its "mystical" meaning explained in the twenty-one lines of verse scrawled below it. It suggests that the Cross of Christ has lost all significance for modern man, and that Christianity, like the Egypt, Greek, and Roman religions before it, is merely another dead cycle of belief. An answer is inscribed on the stone by Margoth, who cares neither who wrote it nor what despair caused the writing:

I, Science, I whose gain's thy loss,
I slanted thee, thou Slanting Cross.
[II, xxxi, p. 252]

The lateness of the day and the promise to wait for Mortmain force the pilgrims to pitch camp on the shore of the Sea. Their depression deepens with the ghastly appearance of Mortmain upon his return. Unlike the Monk who came back from a longer vigil on the same Quarantanian mountain filled with awe for God and content with his pain, Mortmain rejoins his fellows and cries out jeremiads like a man possessed.

"Repent! repent in every land
Or hell's hot kingdom is at hand!
In pause of the artillery's boom,
Yea, yea,
While now the armed world holds its own,
The comet peers, the star dips down;
Flicker the lamps in Syria's tomb,
While Anti-Christ and Atheist set
An Anarch the red coronet!"
[II, xxxiv, p. 259]

He sees sin and evil everywhere, with man's only escape through renunciation of the world. To show the way, he acts against Djalea's practical advice and drinks the bitter waters of the Dead Sea, exhorting the others to follow suit. Later, in a quieter mood as the group gazes at the stars, the fixation sends him into a further diatribe against man and his sinning ways. He shocks the others when he traces the source of all sin back to woman:

> ". . . O fair Medea—
> O soft man-eater, furry-fine:
> Oh, be thou Jael, be though Leah—
> Unfathomably shallow!
> . . . .
> In thee the filmy cell is spun—
> The mould thou art of what men be:
> Events are all in thee begun—
> By thee, through thee! Undo, undo,
> Prithee, undo, and still renew
> The fall forever!"
>
> [II, xxxvi, p. 264]

During the night while all the others sleep, Nehemiah dreams a vision of eternity with God calling for him to come to the New Jerusalem. He rises in his sleep and walks into the Black Sea. Vine discovers the floating body on the next morning and, before calling out an alarm, murmurs his envy of the peace given to the dead "saint." The pilgrims mourn Nehemiah's passing, except for Margoth who sees it as merely the working out of the laws of chemistry. The Arabs bury Nehemiah while Derwent reads an appropriate service from the evangelist's book. As the body is interred an avalanche of stone and sand pours down the mountainside, and out on the sea a kind of "aqueous light" appears for a moment, like a dim sign from heaven.

Part Two ends with Nehemiah's death on the fourth day of the pilgrimage. No new truth has come to Clarel in the wilderness. Just as the Jerusalem episode ended in Nathan's death and Clarel's separation from Ruth, so the search in the desert yields only another tragedy. Nehemiah's death forces on Clarel thoughts of sin, evil, man's inhumanity, and the overall waste of existence. Vine's earlier advice that no means are available for the avoidance of suffering takes on meaning in the wilderness experience.

Part III of the poem—Mar Saba—fills out a three-day interlude at the Copt monastery, high in the Judah Mountains. During the fourth day of the pilgrimage, the group rides up the mountain, passing the many niches in the rock where ancient hermits lived out their penitent days. On one of the cliffs they meet a young minstrel from Cyprus, singing a gay song. He is on his way to the Jordan River to dip his mother's shroud in the bitter waters, as part of an old Greek custom which fuses "The funeral urn with fair caress/Of vintage holiday divine" (III, iv, p. 289). His gaiety and general optimism contrast sharply with the wasteland mood that grips the travelers and remind them of the paradox that death is but a part of life.

Late into the night they climb, all the while discussing theological and philosophical problems. As they had done before at Gethsemane, Derwent and Mortmain rage at each other over the world's condition and hope for the future. Clarel detects for the first time an insecurity in the minister, and he wonders if even he has been touched by the death and evil experienced in the wilderness. The sound of a bell ends the altercation and the pilgrims enter the monastery grounds. Once again, however, an ironic contrast of peace and violence is struck, just below the monastery gate, when Djalea thwarts a band of Arab thieves who demand tribute for entrance into the holy place.

Mar Saba is an oasis in the desert, including sleeping quarters, food and wine, and ample grounds for visitors to roam in pleasure. The weary group, unaccustomed to travel so late at night, prepares for sleep, when they are interrupted by a boisterous Greek purveyor from the isle of Lesbos, who sings out that night is not for sleeping but for drinking and dancing. Derwent's immediate lusty response sets the example for the rest. Throughout the night they drink, dance, and sing, in sharp contrast to the devotional atmosphere of the convent. The Lesbian's joy sours for a moment with the sight of Mortmain lumped in a corner, his black cap a sign of death threatening the "good fellowship in feast." Like Derwent in a similar situation at Achor, this "juicy man" dismisses Mortmain as mad and resumes his drink and song.

Later in the night, an old weatherbeaten sailor joins the group. Like the Ancient Mariner, except here persuaded by others, he tells his story. His name is Agath. Years ago, when a pestilence broke out in Egypt he smuggled a Moor aboard his ship, *The Peace of God*. When it foundered on rocks in the teeth of a gale, and all were lost except himself, he concluded that the Moor was the Devil's aid and actually caused the sinking. Afterwards, with ten other sailors, he journeyed on foot from Joppa to Mar Saba to offer his prayers to God. Wandering outside the walls one day, he was beaten, stripped, and left for dead by Ammonite robbers. Monks found him, brought him back to the monastery, and nursed him until the present time. Meanwhile, his mates left for other shores, leaving him again a solitary.

The Lesbian responds to the tragic tale with another riotous song. Just as the banker and his son-in-law had no time for sorrow, neither does the Greek merchant allow sad spirits to weigh him down. Derwent, too, urges Agath to be of good cheer. The Bacchic songs ring wilder until all, except Mortmain and Clarel, forget their troubled past. But as the Lesbian is about to start another song, a dirge echoes through the room:

> Lord, have mercy.
> Christ, have mercy.
> Intercede for me,
> Angel of the Agony.
> Spare me, spare me!
>
> [III, xiv, p. 334]

It comes from the monks in their early morning litany, chanting the first ritual celebration of the feast of Mar Saba. It is the fifth day of the pilgrimage. The feast day is highlighted by the performance of a masque on the theme of Cartaphilus, the Jew who wanders in loneliness looking for the New Jerusalem. The monk's acting as the cast-off Jew impresses Clarel but puzzles him as well: are persons like Cartaphilus and himself designed by fate or God to suffer loneliness?

Perplexed and saddened by the little drama, Clarel voices his concern to Derwent on the next morning. The minister's response shocks Clarel. Derwent confesses that he does not really believe in all of the things he advises. Like Rolfe, he acknowledges the need for some belief, even if it is only a faint outline of some long-forgotten truth:

> Less light
> Than warmth needs earthly wight.
> Christ built a hearth: the flame is dead
> We'll say, extinct; but lingers yet,
> Enlodged in stone, the hoarded heat.
> Why not nurse that?
>
> [III, xxi, p. 362]

He tells of his own youthful pursuit of unalterable truths, no different from Clarel's one-dimensional demands of God and man. Years of unfullfillment chastened his ardor, however, and he is content now to take a middle course in all matters, knowing that tomorrow will probably come and as a beautiful day. Clarel leaves the minister, deflated by the crass confession of meliorism, and wanders aimlessly into a monk's cave. Before gaining admission, a skeletal inmate there demands from him the countersign, "Death." The word itself, as a sepulchral echo from the living-dead monk in the wake of Derwent's shallow revelation, and an overall feeling of waste in the journey, fills Clarel with dread. He leaves the cell at once, and in panic reaches out for memories of Ruth, as he did in a similar condition at the Dead Sea. This time she comes alive in his mind but only as a speaker of the ambiguous words, "Dost tarry, tarry yet?" (III, xxiv, p. 374).

Observing the rules of polite behavior, Derwent visits the

Abbot after his talk with Clarel. The old man's pride in jeweled possessions and rich relics of ancient saints amuses Derwent, who finds in the interview only confirmation of his beliefs concerning Catholic ornamentation and mummery. Derwent leaves the Abbot and joins the Lesbian in a climb down onto the lower levels, where the River Kedron forms a cool fountain. The Lesbian points out a Palm Tree on the side of the mountain that was planted there over a thousand years ago by St. Saba himself. The minister's innocuous comment implies the modern unconcern for time and symbols. They pass by a cell where the demented monk who frightened Clarel warns them against their drinking joys, but the two dismiss him as "a crazy friar." The monk's jeremiad echoes Mortmain's warnings of the past, as the two look aloft and see a great bird soaring away with Mortmain's black skull cap in his claws. The grim omen unsettles Derwent and his companion, enough for the Lesbian to let down his guard in fear: "The devil's in these eagle-gier" (III, xxv, p. 378).

They find no relief as they enter a cell, called "Habbibi's home," where the walls are covered with crazy scribbling. The writing tells how the inmate there was commanded by heaven to write as penance for his sins, but that all who read must be wary of what they interpret: for there is no real heaven, only another hell over hell which man mistakes for heaven. Although Derwent feels a "touch of gliding care" from his exploration, he quickly dispatches the mood with a little jig, demonstrating how a man can be happy in any circumstances.

Vine, too, wanders about on the sixth day, and comes in sight of the palm tree. He sees it as an emblem of a lost Paradise and a sign of wish-fulfillment; it serves as reminder that all things pass, just as the palm itself one day will be gone. On a ledge below him, Mortmain sees the tree and it becomes for him yet another death symbol. But, paradoxically, it suddenly inspires him with hope for an everlasting life in which the "uncreated Good" can be found, in which outcasts like himself can know the meaning of love:

"Envoy, whose looks the pang assauge,
Disclose thy heavenly embassage!
That lily-rod which Gabriel bore
To Mary, kneeling her before,
Announcing a God, the mother she;
That budded stalk from Paradise—
Like that thou shin'st in thy device:
And sway'st thou over here toward me—
Toward *me* can such a symbol sway!"
[III, xxviii, p. 388]

Further down on another ledge, Rolfe sights the tree, and it swells in him idyllic memories of an Eden existence he knew in earlier days. Instead of the memories warming him, the tree symbol informs him that all joy is in the past and that a return is impossible.

"Renouncer! is it Adam's flight
Without compulsion or the sin?
And shall the vale avenge the slight
By haunting thee in hours thou yet shalt win?"
[III, xxix, p. 391]

Clarel actually comes to a ledge that fronts the palm, but his troubled thoughts on death, Ruth, and marriage leave him blind to the phenomenon. Instead, he wonders if a blue-robed brother he sees there caring for doves in "gracious calm," like a modern St. Francis, can know a happiness in celibacy such as married men know. Late into the night he muses over the virgin peace experienced by Blessed Mary, St. John, and St. Francis. He wonders if sex is really an integral part of love, or if it brings with it an impurity that destroys. Clarel's thoughts are not those of a lover anticipating joyful reunion with his love. They are the qualms of a celibate who fears he is about to make a tragic mistake.

The pilgrimage resumes at dawn of the seventh day, but Mortmain is absent. Clarel finds him dead, his filmed eyes fixed on the palm tree, an eagle's feather set upon his lips.

The hushed group—diminished now by two in death—watch the friars bury the body outside the walls of Mar Saba: the monks refuse Christian burial to pagan blasphemers. Like Celio, Mortmain is cast out even in death.

As a refuge for the tired pilgrims, Mar Saba provided Clarel with the comforts of a physical haven. But his search for a meaning for life provided no clue at this ancient religious site. Instead, Mortmain's invectives and sudden death, the memories of Nehemiah's wasted goodness, and an inability to recall the image of Ruth impress upon him the awful fact of nothingness.

The fourth and last part of *Clarel* is ironically called "Bethlehem"; these modern Magi[3] crossing the desert from Mar Saba have participated too deeply in life's tragedy to admit the romance of a Messiah. They are joined by a new pilgrim, Ungar, a military man in mufti, visibly marked by a livid scar on his neck and powder burns on his temple. He is a native of the Southwestern United States, a soldier of fortune since his defeat as a Confederate officer.

Toward evening the group arrives at a monastery outside Bethlehem. As at Mar Saba, they are warmed by the monks' hospitality, this time by the Capuchins at the monastery of the Church of the Nativity. On the following morning—the eighth day of the pilgrimage—Ungar takes Mortmain's place as he rails against the pious platitudes of Derwent. He resents Derwent's Anglo-Saxon tolerance of the Orient and asks all the others to imitate Christ, particularly in their dealings with other ethnic groups. He condemns the present age for its lack of Christian virtue and exhorts them all to emulate the Christians of the Middle Ages.

During the day, they visit the Church of the Star erected over the site of the Manger. A youthful Tuscan Franciscan conducts them around the holy place, and his religious zeal animates the group, Derwent excepted. The priest senses Ungar's deep passion and tells him that his sword is appropriately the sign of the cross, as it was for St. Ignatius and St. Martin of Tours. Ungar is so struck by the observation that he is subdued for the rest of the day. His companions are similarly awed by the monk's firm convictions and gentle manner, so that the remainder of the visit at the Church is conducted in awe and respect.

On the ninth night of the pilgrimage Clarel shares his room with a young Frenchman from Lyons. The young man came to Jaffa for a business firm, and, having a day's holiday, thought he would have a look at Jerusalem. What he has in mind is enjoying himself with the beautiful Jewish women. He tells Clarel that of all the women he has had, the Jewish ones are by far the most voluptuous and the easiest of virtue. He suggests that Clarel should imitate him, that the hedonist's way leads to joy, if only "you'll put up your monkish thong!" Clarel finds it difficult to sleep after the Lyonese's provocative suggestions to ". . . look at straight things more in line/Blue eyes or black, which like you best?/Your Bella Donna, how's she dressed?" (IV, xxvi, p. 497). But in the morning when he finds the salesman gone as mysteriously as he arrived, Clarel forgets the Frenchman and his licentious temptations.

That night the company leaves for Jerusalem. They arrive on the outskirts of the city shortly before dawn of Ash Wednesday. They pass by a cemetery where laborers are working at a grave. After a few questions, Clarel discovers Ruth and Agar are the ones being buried; he learns that a combination of fever and grief over Nathan's death brought on the sudden end. Clarel defies Hebrew custom and gazes on Ruth's face, kisses her hand, and then cries out, while the bodies are interred. After five days, Rolfe, Vine, and the others reluctantly leave Clarel, although he is unaware of their presence or their departure. Throughout Lent he wanders dazedly over the sites of Christ's Passion and Death, attempting in vain to identify with the tragedy of Christ. He follows other pilgrims through the rites of Holy Week, sharing with them the solemn mood of Good Friday but seeing the day as a melancholy termination of Christ's mission. Promises by the Saviour of a resurrection in three days as a conquest of death are for Clarel as illusionary as his own hopes for Ruth to return from the tomb. The Passion, Death, and Resurrection are constructs of a mythical past; the death of Ruth is real, and now, and irreversible.

The cheer, so human, might not call
The maiden up: *Christ is arisen*:
But Ruth, may Ruth so burst the prison?
[IV, xxxiii, p. 520]

Weeks pass by. Despite his acceptance of Ruth's death and the awful possibility of life's nothingness, Clarel joins another group of pilgrims on the feast of Pentecost, as they wind their way along the Via Crucis.

Thus the poem comes full circle, with Clarel resuming his endless quest for an unattainable faith.[4]

VI

Clarel — "One Dripping Trophy"

> *Clarel*—published by George P. Putnam's Sons, New York—a metrical affair, a pilgrimage or what not, of several thousand lines, eminently adapted for unpopularity.—The notification to you here is ambidexter, as it were: it may intimidate or allure.
>
> Letter to James Billson, October 10, 1850

Toward the end of his life, Melville wrote a short poem called "Art." In eleven lines it tells of the anguish suffered in the creative process when the poet must impose form upon the wild urges that inspire him.

> In placid hours well-pleased we dream
> Of many a brave, unbodied scheme.
> But form to lend, pulsed life to create,
> What unlike things must meet and mate:
> A flame to melt—a wind to freeze;
> Sad patience—joyous energies;
> Humility—yet pride and scorn;
> Instinct and study; love and hate;
> Audacity—reverence. These must mate,
> And fuse with Jacob's mystic heart,
> To wrestle with the angel—Art.[1]

In the earlier years of writing, with *Mardi* and *Moby-Dick* as best examples, Melville attained a unity of emotion and idea that sprang out of spontaneity, out of an inspiration that allowed him to bypass or ignore the strictures on form that most authors follow in their attempts to reconcile life's antimonies. The prophetic element constituted the stuff of his art, or enabled him to narrate, interrupt, editorialize, reminisce, rhapsodize, shift from third to first person and back again, and, generally, to invent expression and structure according to the needs of the story. His creative imagination functioned freely in this early period of prolific writing, reinforced intellectually by an aesthetic belief that art should be formless because life itself is without meaningful shape, or without recognizable features by which it can be finally understood. Unfortunately, this rationale for prophetic expression was never verbalized at length and defended: Melville was too busy in the original creating.

After 1856, when poetry became a central interest for him, Melville consciously studied the problems of form. The overpowering profusion of words that constituted the strength and weakness of the earlier works gave way to what he described as the desideratum of art:

> Not magnitude, not lavishness,
> But Form—the Site;
> Not innovating wilfulness,
> But reverence for the archetype.[2]

Probably during or slightly after the Palestine trip, he learned, as Lawrence Barrett expresses it, that "poetry, which is a human thing, is poetry only so long as it partakes of ordering form."[3] This is the meaning of the two poems just now quoted. It is the dominant theme of *Billy Budd*: order and form in the universe exemplify for man the need to impose order and form in his own creative life. Leon Howard would regard this, however, as retrospective distortion. He contends that the radical shift from spontaneity should not be construed as evidence of a conscious improvement in aesthetics but as proof of Melville's loss of the earlier poetic inspiration that had triumphed over amateur craftsmanship.[4] Another critic insists that even the earlier "successes" came from a writer who had little comprehension of what he wrote, and that his accomplishment with "one book" augured the failures that were inevitably to come to an author who had never mastered his craft.[5]

Such pejorative judgments rule out the Melville after *Moby-Dick* and *Pierre* who struggled with his imagination to perfect a new art form; they mark the works written in the last half of his literary life as necessarily inferior. There is no question that he turned to poetry in the middle of emotional depression and, unfortunately, in the worst slump in American poetry.[6] There are poems in *Battle-Pieces* that stand as scarred evidence. Because of them and because the poetry operated on a different level than *Moby-Dick*, there are some critics who echo Robert Penn Warren's hasty conclusion that Melville on the whole was "a poet of shreds and patches."[7] But this kind of critical dismissal does not account for the many lovely lyrics of "Fruit of Travel Long Ago," for the deep feeling and sustained imagery of *Battle-Pieces* and the *John Marr* poems, for the poignancy and challenge of *Billy Budd*, or for the consistent philosophic inquiry of *Clarel*.

In this shift from the early "inspirational" writing, Melville deliberately avoided the radical protestantism that produced *Pierre*; he practiced in its place an extroversion that did not admit of the moral autonomy of the individual.[8] The concentration on form actually became a prop for what Warren calls his "new state of consciousness, in which his spontaneous ego or self-consciousness no longer played an all-commanding role."[9] Thus the reader who easily identified Melville with Wellingborough Redburn, White-Jacket, Ahab, and Pierre stumbles when he looks for the same clear reflection in *Clarel* and *Billy Budd*. A different kind of author is at work in the later pieces, one who demands a different kind of attention.

Clarel does make a particular demand, for its enormous length and jogging meter advertise a task to be accomplished rather than a pleasure to be enjoyed. The reader who was overwhelmed by *Moby-Dick* and *Pierre*, even when he could not grasp all the loose ends, has to work hard and long at *Clarel* before he can arrive with the protagonist on the lonely Via Crucis at the end. In addition, the four-beat line, in interminable couplets and intertwining quatrains, appears to undercut the weightiness of the philosophic, religious, and social questions. The blank verse Melville handled so well in "The House Top,"[10] might have provided a better medium to sustain the reader's interest and to complete the panoramic vision of the poem. But his concern after the 1860s was not so much with Gothic and Elizabethan expression as it was with poetic discovery of the naked thing itself:

> Gems and jewels let them heap—
>   Wax sumptious as the Sophi:
> For me, to grapple from Art's deep
>   One dripping trophy.[11]

During this time, "wrestle," "struggle," "grapple," "order," "form," "measure," "reverence," "dignity," and similar limiting words suggest the lexicon Melville used in a continuing examination of man's troubled existence in the universe. The prospectus for art he set through such language was not determined by a bankruptcy of imagination, as some critics insisted; it was rather a proper complement for philosophic conclusions on the circumscription of human activity. Like Matthew Arnold slightly before him, and Housman and Hardy later on, he longed for the glandular wisdom of youth at the very moment he knew of its ephemeral existence:

>   How lovely was the light of heaven,
> What angels leaned from the sky
> In years when youth was more than wine
> And man and nature seemed divine
> Ere yet I felt that youth must die
> . . . .
>   But will youth never come again?
> Even to his grave-bed has he gone?
> And left me lone to wake by night
> With heavy heart that erst was light?
> O, lay it at his head—a stone.[12]

But even this expressed wish for a pastoral life of ease rings hollow, for the poet knows that encouraged nostalgia and melancholy are artificial moods. Closer to the truth of man's possibilities and the proper area for creative art, Melville came to believe, are those human efforts which make life tolerable in a disordered universe, which produce a psychical harmony out of contradictory impulses and allow a man in the middle of pain to assert his identity.

> Wandering late by morning seas
> When my heart with pain was low—
> Hate the censor pelted me—
> Deject I saw my shadow go.
> In elf-caprice of bitter tone
> I too would pelt the pelted one:
> At my shadow I cast a stone.
>
> When lo, upon the sun-lit ground
> I saw the quivering phantom take
> The likeness of St. Stephen crowned
> Then did self-reverence awake.[13]

Clarel is the "One dripping trophy" Melville hoped to gain, a poem which sums up these studied conclusions on life and art. It is an uneven work: vivid figures of speech, soaring Elizabethan soliloquies and dialogues, and rich musical effects are singularly missing; syntax and meter are occasionally wrenched; ellipses of thought occur because of the deliberate understatement; and shadows or "eclipses" pervade the Holy Land pilgrimage. But the poem triumphs over these minor flaws. It records a sustained objective inquiry into the condition and causes of modern skepticism. It displays the keen, observant eye of a poet who sees the great and the picayune expressions of human behavior; it exposes the heart of a man in love with humanity. It prophesies events and attitudes of times to come, and calls out warnings as though there is a chance for aversion. As such, *Clarel* is one of the most moving experiences available to the reader who will meet Melville's challenge; it stands among the best poems ever written in the United States.

Melville wrote *Clarel* over a period of almost twenty years, beginning the poem, however sketchily and only in his mind, sometime in 1857, and concluding with its publication in 1876. Except for some singularly overpowering passages in Part II, the tone, expression, and subject matter of the poem are handled with a consistency that defies the shifts and vagaries of twenty years. In this connection, at least, Melville fulfilled his own Greek architectural principles of art. In his earlier work such consistency of structure and expression was at best intuited. *Moby-Dick* and *Pierre*, as examples, depended for their esthetic success upon a heroic concept and the subsequent disillusion that each hero suffers rather than on the form they took on. In them the gap between the vision and the reality made for tremendous shifts of mood and expression, resulting in an effect of polyphony and of logical inconsistency. *Clarel*, on the other hand, is written deliberately in a lower but sustained key.

The protagonist is introduced in the first canto as a disturbed young theologian who has lost his faith:

> "Other cheer
> Than that anticipated here,
> By me the learner, now I find.
> Theology, art thou so blind?"
>
> [I, i, p. 3]

When he is last seen, the same despairing theologian walks wearily on the Way of the Cross, his few illusionary hopes dashed. He has come through an experience of the wasteland, has learned the meaning of death, but has no more faith or knowledge than he had seven months before:

> "They wire the world—far under sea
> They talk; but never comes to me
> A message from beneath the stone."
>
> [IV, xxiv, p. 522]

Throughout the hundreds of pages in between, this sad sense of emptiness and loss is maintained. Occasionally, hopes are raised when Clarel believes his despair can be lifted. But all too quickly reality returns, and he knows there can be no change. The tone is thus one of Hebraic lamentation. Without direct borrowing of lines or incidents, the sorrows of Job and Jeremiah are paralleled in Clarel's sad journey. The tragic human condition, in which reclamation can come only from a source outside oneself, echoes the sad cries of Ecclesiastes. The Wailing Wall that Clarel finds so outdated in his first meeting with Ruth, and the persistent theme of the Wandering Jew are major motifs so that Biblical and traditional lore of Palestine pervade the poem.[14] The tight verse form and the structured Greek outline emphasize this Hebraic tone ironically, for at no point in the poem is there any glorification of man beyond his remarkable endurance and resiliency. Humanism is raised time and again by Melville, as it was by Job, but only as something to question. In *Clarel* Melville wrote a Hebrew poem in a Greek mold.

Melville's strictures on form, despite adherence to Grecian principles, are not realized fully in *Clarel*. The poem resembles an epic in its size and grandeur of subject. But the verse pattern and the language choice work intentionally against the epical effect because Melville's purpose was to show the modern tragedy of constriction in verse which fits the theme. The four-beat iambic lines, in irregularly end-stop couplets, blend with occasional quatrains of shifting rhyme. This results frequently in a jogging effect where the terse statement unexpectedly cuts off the thought or the emotion. While no poet should be held to an elaborate exposition of his characters and actions, the steady beat of a tetrameter line in a poem of such enormous size produces ellipses that result in obscurity. This can be seen at the end of Part I, after Nehemiah has drowned. Melville describes an avalanche that occurs precisely when a faint sign from heaven peeps through the Dead Sea's fog. The intended irony staggers in the descriptive lines, leaving the reader perplexed on whether the phenomenon is literally a physical fact to be explained or a transcendent sign to be accepted as proof of Nehemiah's redemption. Nor can the previous events connected with the foolish evangelist provide an answer because Melville refused to mock him in his most childish performances:

Up in thin mist above the sea
Humid is formed, and noiselessly,
The fog-bow: segment of an oval
Set in a colorless removal
Against a vertical shaft, or slight
Slim pencil of an aqueous light.
Suspended there, the segment hung
Like to the May-wreath that is swung
Against the pole. It showed half-spent—
Hovered and trembled, paled away, and—went.
[XX, xxix, p. 274]

A few of the philosophic disquisitions are marked by the same incompleteness. Such serious matter suffers especially where the meaning might have been clarified by a few additional lines of simple statement. These were not mere oversights, however, for Melville believed that success in these areas would come from a pyramid of thought compressed by the density of form. But the result now and then is a collapse of the pyramid, such as the one that occurs at Mar Saba. There, Derwent attempts to convince Clarel that burrowing too deeply into the mysteries of the universe leaves one only sadder:

But go back—well,
Reach to the years of first decay
Or totter: prithee, lad, but tell
How with the flamens of that day?
When brake the sun from morning's tents
And walked the hills, and gilded thence
The fane in porch; the priest in view
Bowed—hailed Apollo, as before,
Ere change set in; what else to do?
Or whither turn, or what adore?

What but to temporize for him,
Stranded upon an interim
Between the ebb and flood? He knew.—
You see? Transfer—apply it, you.
[III, xxi, pp. 361-62]

It is obvious that Derwent's clichés inform us further of his shallow nature. But the dialogue with Clarel unfortunately never arrives at the point of intellectual conflict the scene seems to anticipate. The sharp dichotomy of thought that engaged Ahab and Starbuck, or Pierre and Mr. Falsgrave, fades away in hints, presumptions, and promises. Indeed, so incomplete are these philosophic arguments that Derwent's actual meliorism is in the poem an accusation only and not a demonstration.

The versification in *Clarel* does not allow for shifts of meter to give vibrancy or richness of tone. The variations Melville used in *Battle-Pieces*, particularly in one of the best, "The March into Virginia," rarely appear in this poem. The one substantial change that Melville did effect in *Clarel* was the song he interspersed, but too infrequently for any real relief. For example, he included only one sorrowful lyric of fifteen lines in Part I, which includes over four thousand lines. The other three sections of the poem are only slightly relieved by metrical shifts, such as the hedonistic song of Glaucon (II, xiv, p. 185), the hymn sung by the Dominican (II, xxv, p. 229), the ironic echo of the Dominican's hymn muttered by Margoth (II, xxvi, p. 230), the Cypriot's gay words (III, iv, pp. 286-90), the drinking scene at Mar Saba (III, xi-xiv, pp. 331-32), the liturgical chant of the Saba monks (III, xvii, p. 346-47), the Lesbian's advice (III, xx, pp. 354-55), and a few other five or six-line lyrics. Otherwise, except for an occasional hexameter line closing out a canto, the thousands of lines follow in repetitive beat the simple measure Melville chose for the poem.

The language of *Clarel* complements the versification. Melville deliberately suppressed his natural facility for rich metaphorical expression.

> But wherefore this? such theme why start?
> Because if here in many a place
> The rhyme—much like the knight indeed—
> Abjure brave ornament, 'twill plead
> Just reason, and appeal for grace.
>
> [I, iv, p. 18]

The combination of a "powerfully prosaic vocabularly"[15] which resulted and a sublimation of emotion produced an anti-poetic, tough-minded poetry which anticipated the modern idiom. The nouns are particularly plain: "petition," "cleft," "laic," "gravitation," "clink," "chat," "conjecture," "ornament," "fiddle-strings," "similitude," "symposiarch," "worldlings," and many other equally flat words. One of them—"thrill"—appears repeatedly until its meaning is lost. Nor do the adjectives generally extend beyond their dictionary meanings: "mistimed," "befogged," "dubious," "serene," "placid," "commemorative," "homely," "obsolete," and countless similar prosaic expressions. As he did in all of the poetry, Melville included in *Clarel* the conversion of nouns through suffixes: "thoughtful," "wishful," "mindless," "briny," "weedy," "showery," "flinty," "clownish," "touchy," "napkined," "oceanic," "glenned." The verbs of *Clarel* convey the same dullness: "misapply," "heathenized," "cheerfulize," "construe," "cried," "fidgeted," "quaffed," "mitigate." The verbs, in fact, are so innocuous they have to be looked for by the reader. This produces a great number of ellipses, where the verb in the construction must be discovered in some previous sentence. The adverbs, similarly, are not emphasized: "inwalled," "religiously," "away," "anew," "jauntily," "here"; nor are they instrumental in achieving shades of meaning not carried by the verbs. Melville's earlier Shakespearean usage of puns is missing in the poem. The few he does use stand out because of their rarity: Nathan's boyhood is marked by the tragedy which is to cling to him throughout his life, particularly in the birth of his daughter, Ruth—"But time instead contributes ruth"; Glaucon puns on the hated word "death" when he exclaims, "For heaven's sake"; the adjective "grave" describes the Judea pilgrims, but it is intended more as a noun to stress the theme of death; Derwent calls himself Dante and the Lesbian his Virgil, which prompts the Lesbian to a play on words: "what daunts ye, friend" (III, xxv, p. 376); Derwent is "reverent" as he tries to "screen" his feelings, with the word functioning literally as a filter for sand; an "anchorite" is actually fettered at Mar Saba; the one-legged Don Hannibal "stumped" around Fleet Street as a socialist agitator.

This "powerfully prosaic vocabulary" fits perfectly the mood and tone of the poem, however. Had Melville written of an idyllic Polynesia in this kind of language, the effect would have been ludicrous. But the examination of an age of disbelief set against the aridity of a desert demanded that the poet be as ingenious in the other direction; that is, he had to present one large objective correlative of sterility and hang on it multiple prosaic and barren figures. He went even further in this direction. Instead of presenting only the flattest language of the nineteenth century, Melville filled the poem with archaic language as well.[16] The result is a curious blending of the contemporary with an age long dead, a fusion of the modern idiom with a pseudo-Scriptural language. Thus in a kind of Spenserean echo, men are "wights," "carles," and "kerns." A sense of the past is invoked through expressions like "unglad," "days fleet," "ills that gride," "thither," "amort," "gyve," "shoon," "bethinking," "weened," "keepeth," "showeth," "fane," "thrall," "flamen." Such words are freely mixed with modern, common words out of industry, business, modern history, law, newspapers, and street idiom: "Title-deed," "fly page," "tile," "balloon," "coffee," "cigar," "luggage," "messmate," "connivers," "hee-haw." The archaic expressions, the deletion of relative pronouns and conjunctions, the simple language, and the naked lines all combine to cut away artificiality and convention so that man and the age alone remain fixed for examination.

These self-imposed, severe restrictions and the occasional syntactical flaws are minor in the overall effect, like the blemishes easily found in Shakespeare's plays and Chaucer's poems. The poem contains an abundance of perceptive insights on the nature of man in the universe, provocative political, social, and religious questions with tentative solutions, revealing personal disclosures, all woven into the single-purposed mission of the young theologian; that is, the integrity of the plot and the consistent tone of the poem are not dissipated through careless digressions, contradictory moods, or intrusions of language foreign to the needs and movement of the poem. *Clarel* does not incorporate the ecstatic passages which enriched earlier novels and short stories: Babbalanja's vision and conversion; White-Jacket's plunge into the sea; Ishmael's rejection of hell-fire and Ahab's boasted assault on the sun; Pierre's correction of inherited reality; and Delano's final comprehension of Benito's plight. Such epiphanies are in the past for the author of *Clarel.* They are discoveries in a romantic period when dilemmas seemed to have explanations available, and when a quest appeared to have a reachable goal. Clarel and the other sincere pilgrims exist in a situation where transcendent values and certitude are not convenient, and where identity of self emerges painfully only after heroic acceptance of the circumscribed universe which hems in man. It is precisely in this conclusion and procedure that Melville makes a final statement of his life-long puzzlement over life's ambiguities; it is in this assertion that he appeals directly to an audience in the twentieth century.

The poem contains rich and fruitful images which are sustained and emphasized as significant symbols.[17] One of them is dust, a source of great annoyance to Melville on his trip to Palestine.[18] When Clarel appears in the opening canto he is covered with dust:

> Beside him in his narrow cell
> His luggage lies unpacked; thereon
> The dust lies, and on him as well—
> The dust of travel.
>
> [I, i, p. 3]

His attempts to shake it away are fruitless. He learns this symbolically through the little poem he finds in the lining of his trunk:

Only Judea my feet did roam;
And mainly there the pilgrim clings
About the precincts of Christ's tomb.
These palms I bring—from dust not free,
Since dust and ashes both were trod by me.
[I, ii, p. 11]

He finds dust on the Tomb of the Holy Sepulchre (I, iii, p. 12), dust covering the wasted cities that once knew the greatness of Hebrew kings and the Christ Messiah (I, x, p. 32). Dust covers the rubbish heaped at the Wailing Wall where Clarel first sees Ruth (I, xvi, p. 52); it is a desert that creeps into the cracks of homes and pores of men (I, xxiv, p. 82). Dust presses on the pilgrim the awfulness of the Rim of Achor (II, xiv, p. 189), and the incongruity of an oasis palm at Mar Saba (III, xxv-xxx).

Dust pervades the poem as a constant irritant to the senses and as grating evidence of Asia as a "used-up superannuated" land. It also provides a major symbol of man's substance in the pejorative sense and of man's paradoxical potential for the creation of his own significant nature out of such common matter. Melville's uncanny associative powers might not have linked this dust imagery to the Catholic Church's ritual assertion on Ash Wednesday of man's ignominious composition: "Memento, homo, quia pulvis es, et in pulverem revertis," that is, "Remember, man, that you are dust, and into dust you shall return."[19] The coincidental movement of Clarel through the Holy Land from Epiphany Sunday to Ash Wednesday and the emphasis on dust as the genesis of man suggests, however, that Melville was aware of the Church's ceremonial act of belief in an immortal spiritual existence and so began the poem with such imagery because he had the culminating Ash Wednesday defeat of his hero in mind. Whether or not there was a deliberate parallel to the Church belief for ironic underscoring, echoes like this are to be found throughout the poem, becoming, in fact, rhythms rather than resonance.

The dust imagery is reinforced by a constant usage of stones. Clarel's initial impression of the blank towers, of the sealed windows and blind arches of Jerusalem, becomes for him a nightmare of stones:

> In divers ways which vary it
> Stones mention find in hallowed Writ:
> Stones rolled from well-mouths, altar stones,
> Idols of stones, memorial ones,
> Sling-stones, stone tables; Bethel high
> Saw Jacob, under starry sky,
> On stones his head lay—desert bones;
> Stones sealed the sepulchres—huge cones
> Heaved there in bulk; death too by stones
> The law decreed for crime;
> . . . .
> stoned to death
> Was Stephen meek; and Scripture saith
> Against even Christ they took up stones.
> . . . .
> Behold the stones! And never one
> A lichen greens; and, turn them o'er—
> No worm—no life; but, all the more,
> Good witnesses.
>
> [II, x, pp. 170-71]

For Nehemiah, however, stones present only another task that God imposes upon man. Thus he tells the other pilgrims that he does God's work as he attempts to clear the road of millions of stones (II, x, p. 175). For Vine, stones have no meaning beyond themselves: they are porous bits used to pelt his own shadow (III, v, p. 295), or to build a "monument to barrenness" (III, vii, p. 303). Petra is a vast crag of stone, appalling to the pilgrims in the hellish desert as a "scene/Of Nature's terror" (II, xxx, pp. 247-49).[20] Jerusalem is a "Stony metropolis of stones" (IV, ii, p. 408). As such, it evokes Agath's memory of the island of tortoises and stones, "In waters where no charts avail" (IV, iii, p. 415). Stones in motion sound out the meaninglessness of life for Clarel in the burial of Ruth and Agar at the Gate of St. Stephen, the martyr who was stoned to death.

They laid them in the under-glooms—
Each pale one in her portioned place.
The gravel, from the bank raked down,
Dull sounded on those slabs of stone,
Grave answering grave—dull and more dull,
Each mass growing more, till either pit was full.
[IV, xxx, p. 514]

Together, the stones and dust control the wasteland imagery of the poem and reinforce a pervading atmosphere of sterility and death.

This wilderness motif cuts deeper into the reader's consciousness through a strong contrast of sea imagery which runs throughout the poem. The images are so multiple that "There is no alternative except to grant that the narrator is an ex-sailor," as Bezanson points out.[21] For example, when Clarel tells Rolfe of Nehemiah's strange tale, Rolfe's reaction is described in terms of one who has been to sea.

As when upon a misty shore
The watchful seaman marks a light
Blurred by the fog uncertain quite;
And thereto instant turns the glass
And studies it, and thinks it o'er
By compass: is't the cape we pass?
[III, ii, p. 283]

The nautical sensibility appears throughout the poem. Mortmain's drawing of the Southern Cross and his inscription concerning Christ's wasted death have precise meaning for the sailor who takes a bearing from that constellation. Clarel's loneliness can be shared only by the rebel sailor cast away on a forgotten island.

Days passed; and passed a second one,
A third—fourth—fifth; and bound he sate
In film of sorrow without moan—

Abandoned, in the stony strait
Of mutineer thrust on wild shore,
Hearing, beyond the roller's froth,
The last dip of the parting oar.
[IV, xxxii, p. 515]

With the keen eye of a mariner, Agath is the one who sights Jerusalem in the distance. Used to disaster, he calls out, "Wreck, ho—the wreck!" (IV, i, p. 408), and echoes one of the central images of the poem. The Rim of Achor is beyond Rolfe's comprehension of terror so that he views it in stark contrast to the glorious visions Balboa must have seen on his voyages; to Vine, used to nature in depression, it is a Crag of Agonies "Bare as an iceberg seamed by rain/Toppling awash in foggy main/Off Labrador" (II, xiv, p. 188). The sea is a constant referent as though its familiarity will clear away any obscurity or heighten the sentient immediacy Melville expects in his reader. Rolfe's waning influence on Clarel is like a ship diminishing to a white speck on the horizon for the "one estranged" on the shore. An Arab riding a camel through a distant valley, lance pointing to the sky, is seen as a "wreck with one gaunt mast" (II, xiii, p. 182). Rolfe is viewed far below Mar Saba as a petrel diving in the "sweep of overcurling tide" (III, xxix, p. 389). This fleeting glimpse of the bird is only part of a larger picture of the sea in turmoil, a descriptive passage by Melville at his best as an imagist. The same sharp perception appears also, but with auditory more than visual effects, when the poet tells of the great rollers onto Borneo's shores (III, xv, p. 334); and when he likens the symphonic sounds of an organ to those of the sea's storms and tides (IV, xv, p. 457).

The sea imagery follows no pattern. The omniscient narrator concentrates on the story of the pilgrimage and adds other dimensions through these random similies and simple or extended metaphors. Thus the movement of flying sand in the desert reminds the poet of the ocean:

Sands immense
Impart the oceanic sense:

The flying grit like scud is made:
Pillars of sand which whirl about
Or arc along in colonnade,
True kin be to the water spout.

[II, xii, p. 178]

The desert itself once ran with water, a legend tells, until it was congealed because of ". . . crime and earthquake, throes and war" (III, i, p. 280). Although the desert terrifies all those who look to nature for consolation, the sea is not the good alternative of Ishmael's soliloquies in *Moby-Dick*; it provides no termination of misery for the landlocked narrator and pilgrims. The sea is filled with rocks and wrecks of ships (II, xiii, p. 182). The crags of Judah's mountains are smooth and inviting compared with the icebergs off Tamura (I, xiv, p. 46). The dorsal fins of sharks at every turn dispel the landlubber's romantic dreams of the sea as the great, inviting haven (II, ix, pp. 169-70). The sea lies outside the congealed land where pilgrims can only dream of escape. But it is a watery wasteland; like the desert, it is nature in its most pitiless form. There are four tales told in this connection, all of them told by the two ex-sailors of the group, Rolfe and Agath. Rolfe tells the first, of a captain victimized by inevitable disaster: his first ship was pierced on waiting rocks, his second crushed by an infuriated whale (I, xxxvii, pp. 120-22). Agath tells the other three tales, and they also portray the viciousness of the sea. The stories reinforce the multiple sea images and further pronounce on the "wrecked" condition of the landed pilgrims. They do more, for they demonstrate that while there is no haven on the ocean, like fool's gold the water stirs in the pilgrims memories of gardens, sweet streams, marigolds, lavender, and acres of golden wheat, all images lost in the sea. These land alternatives to the sharks and wrecks of the sea are illusions quickly lost in the modern, dust-covered, stone civilization. The sea only emphasizes the loss.

The controlling images of dust, stone, and the sea produce the sterile atmosphere proper to Melville's portrayal of man's tragic existence. The image of the Cross similarly runs throughout the poem, like an iron rod binding the pilgrims to the bleak facts of reality. The Cross symbolizes pain and sorrow. It must be carried or endured, not as a redemptive act guaranteeing immortality but simply because there is little else in life except suffering. Thus Mortmain's Slanted Cross readily imprints itself on the consciousness of the travelers (II, xxxi). In the same way, despite his rebellion and blasphemy, Celio returns to the fact of Christ's Cross and mourns only that the death-act failed to achieve the promised freedom.

> How long?—'Tis eighteen cycles now—
> Enigma and evasion grow;
> And shall we never find thee out?
> What isolation lones thy state
> That all we else know cannot mate
> With what thou teachest? Nearing thee
> All footing fails us; history
> Shows there a gulf where bridge is none.
> . . . .
> By what art
> Of conjuration might the heart
> Of heavenly love, so sweet, so good,
> Corrupt into the creeds malign,
> Begetting strife's pernicious brood,
> Which claimed for patron thee divine?
> [I, xiii, pp. 43-44]

A white cross gleams on the back of the patient ass appropriately ridden by Nehemiah (II, I, p. 146). And although he is shocked by Brother Salvaterra's simple analogy of his sword as a cross, Ungar is quick to see how his professional use of the sword actually is a devotion to the Cross (IV, xiv, p. 453). Even Vine hints at the Cross as he weaves a crown of thorns (IV, xv, pp. 456-57). Derwent's aesthetic praise of the more romantic Greek cross evokes scorn in Rolfe: he argues that it is only the Latin cross that "realistically" depicts the fact of suffering (III, xviii, p. 349). His argument has precedent, for the Latin cross was the driving force of his idol, King Louis IX, who died in a desert like Siddim (II, xiii, pp. 181-82). Most important for Clarel, the ten-day journey leads to his return and the death of Ruth, both events analogous to those of Good Friday and the death of Christ on the cross and His looked-for resurrection.

> But when Good Friday dirged her gloom
> Ere brake the morning, and each light
> Round Calvary faded and the TOMB,
> What exhalations met his sight:—
> Illusion of grief's wakeful doom:
> The dead walked.
> . . . .
> But Ruth—ah, how estranged in face!
> He knew her by no earthly grace:
> Nor might he reach to her in place.
> And languid vapors from them go
> Like thaw-fogs curled from dankish snow.
>
> Where, where now He who helpeth us,
> The Comforter?—tell, Erebus.
>
> [IV xxxii, pp. 517-18]

Other sustained images also tighten the poem.[22] The death image, for example, carries from beginning to the end. It is begun in Jerusalem when Abdon points out to Clarel a marble slab over the grave of his wife. It assumes personal import for Clarel shortly after in the death of Nathan, for the taboo at his wake separates the young lovers forever. Death becomes a good, or less a terror, when Nehemiah completes a sleepwalking existence in his innocent suicide "Upon that Pentateuchal shore" (II, xxviii, pp. 268-69). It becomes again a grim symbol at Mar Saba in the armored figure of a Count who abjured his name for "Lazarus" (III, xxiii, p. 367). Death and the echo of "Lazarus" are a ritual there as a mad monk, Cyril, demands of Clarel the password "Death" before passing by his "sloping theater of skulls" (III, xxiv, p. 373). The image is raised to a higher and more personal significance in the death of Mortmain and in his burial outside the friars' walls:

> Where vulture unto vulture calls,
> And only ill things find a friend:
>
> [III, xxxii, p. 400]

The image, mood, and fact of death culminate in the poem and for Clarel in the death of Ruth in "dead" Jersualem, where Celio, a spiritual brother, had also died. The tragic event leads into one of the best lyrics Melville ever wrote, an obvious digression to console himself and the reader, cantos before the Epilogue.

Dirge

> Stay, Death. Not mine the Christus-wand
> Wherewith to charge thee and command:
> I plead. Most gently hold the hand
> Of her thou leadest far away;
> Fear thou to let her naked feet
> Tread ashes—but let mosses sweet
> Her footing tempt, where'er ye stray.
> Shun Orcus; win the moonlit land
> Belulled—the silent meadows lone,
> Where never any leaf is blown
> From lily-stem in Azrael's hand.
> There, till her love rejoin her lowly
> (Pensive, a shade, but all her own)
> On honey feed her, wild and holy;
> Or trance her with thy choicest charm.
> And if, ere yet the lover's free,
> Some added dusk thy rule decree—
> That shadow only let it be
> Thrown in the moon-glade by the palm.
>
> [IV, xxxi, pp. 514-15]

Bird imagery also pervades *Clarel* but, like the sea imagery, only in random fashion. The figures are too numerous for listing, but their function generally is to add the bird's capacity for augury to the grim tragic imagery and events. The osprey, in particular, gazes in "hollow stare" on a hollow world; and even the kites and hawks fear to approach the Dead Sea. Ruth is a "sparrow," too vulnerable in a world preyed upon by eagles.

> Seven furious horsemen fling their flight
> Like eagles when they launching rush
> To snatch the prey that hies to bush.
>
> [II, xxiii, p. 218]

An eagle steals the sailor's cap, pecks his brain, fights him in the air and in the sea, and finally flies away, victorious in another diabolic victory of nature.

> "A curious story, who e'er heard
> Of such a fray 'twixt man and bird!"—
> "Bird? but he deemed it was the devil,
> And that he carried off his soul
> In the old cap, nor was made whole
> 'Till some good vicar did unravel
> The snarled illusion in the skein,
> And he got back his soul again."
>
> [III, xxvii, p. 382]

An eagle also steals Mortmain's skull cap (III, xxv, p. 377); and another, perhaps the same one, leaves a feather as a token of glory on the dead man's lips (III, xxxii, p. 399).

The image of light is one that seems to have a pattern. It has particular significance toward the end of the poem when it is used to point up how the light or illumination from heaven is extinguished in the modern world. Thus Part IV begins ironically with the pilgrims approaching Christ's birthplace as modern Magi. But the star that shone over the manger for Amerrian, Apelius, and Damazon can no longer be seen.

They failed not, for a light was given—
The light and pilotage of heaven:
A light, a lead, no longer won
By any, now, who seekers are:
Or fable is it? but if none,
Let man lament the foundered Star.

[IV, i, p. 403]

Shortly before, Derwent's comment over Agath's tattoo sums up a cynical age that mocks the lost light:

"Why, why so blue?"
Derwent again: and rallying ran:
"While now for Bethlehem we aim,
Our stellar friend the post should claim
Of guide. We'll put him in the van—
Follow the star on the tattooed man,
We wise men here."

[IV, ii, p. 412]

Derwent scoffs also at Ungar's devotion to medieval times and calls it "Dark Middle Ages, time's midnight!" (IV, xi, p. 439). Ungar answers that man's strength in that era constituted its own light as a reflection of a starlit heaven. His answer is couched deliberately in ironic terms, as the narrator substitutes the modern symbol of electricity for God's stars:

A something in the voice or man
Or in assumption of the turn
Which prior theme did so adjourn,
Pricked Ungar, and a look he ran
Toward Derwent—an electric light
Chastising in its fierce revolt!
Then settled into that still night
Of cloud which has discharged the bolt.

[IV, x, p. 441]

Clarel cannot mock the dead light, despite Derwent's cynical words of caution. He would give his life for "one beckoning star." During the night ride from Bethlehem to Jerusalem, he sees above the Cistern of Kings just such a one, probably the star the Magi saw. But when he passes Shaveh and arrives at Siloam, the only light that gleams for him comes from the torches of diggers as they prepare graves for Ruth and Agar. The city itself is one vast grave, ". . . fix'd in blight/No hum set forth, revealed no light" (IV, xxix, p. 510). In the days that follow, the November hills reflect only "brown light," and Mt. Olivet looms in "dusked" outline. The "eclipse" of faith and happiness raised throughout the pilgrimage by the narrator is complete for Clarel, who is now "overshadowed." Clarel's grief over the lost light is shared by Melville in the Epilogue:

> Degrees we know, unknown in days before;
> The light is greater, hence the shadow more.
> [IV, xxxv, p. 523]

The lost light is the given of Clarel's future life, and of the world, but is hardly the end for Clarel, or for the world, as the rest of the Epilogue concludes.

In a world where the light of heaven is extinguished, all objects are colorless, gray, or black. The absence of light actually signified death for Melville.[23] This is Pani's meaning in *Mardi*: "Blindness seems a consciousness of death."[24] Even in black, white, and gray Palestine, however, Melville uncovers a few contrasting colors, though they always lead back to gray and black. Ruth, for example, provides Clarel with a polarity of choice in her white and Rose of Sharon coloring. The whiteness of infinity that Melville described in his earlier works envelops Ruth for Clarel so that the morbid fears her love raises in him throughout the pilgrimage make her death only a painful abstraction. Thus her white unknowingness sinks him in a despairing meditation on sex and marriage, as he gazes over the Siddim Plain from Mount Saba (III, xxx-xxxi, pp. 391-98). Similarly, the rose provides only an illusion of peace, for it is the "Rose of Sharon" land, defended by Ruth's father, that causes his death and the separation of the lovers. The same perplexity haunts Celio, earlier in the poem, as he sees in Christ the dichotomous white and red:

> Whatever ribald Future be,
> Thee shall these heed, amaze their hearts with thee—
> Thy white, thy red, thy fairness and thy tragedy.
>
> [I, xiii, p. 44]

The false promise of red is like the green in the dream that Agar has of gardenlike America. As a gardener, she cultivates "her cherished pots of herbs and flowers," with the same care she gives to rearing her fragile Ruth. But her hopes for vernal blossoming through Clarel as Adam and Eve in a modern Garden of Eden (I, xxviii, p. 90) end in the stones heaped on a rude grave. Like Agar, Derwent persists in coloring the world he refuses to see as gray or black. He raves over the blue or rosy skies (III, xxi, p. 357), and he counsels the troubled student:

> This shaft you sink shall strike no bloom:
> The surface, ah, heaven keeps *that* green;
> Green, sunny . . . .
>
> [III, xxi, p. 364]

His song lauds the violet grape and extols the rose (III, xiii, p. 328). The Prodigal also covers the world in pleasant colors. His flying trip from Jaffa is a day's outing in "green" Jerusalem. It is a land of purple grape that Cape Horn never knows, and of voluptuous Hebrew maidens of "rosy feet." His feminine colors mirror those of the other young hedonist, Glaucon, who ridicules Mortmain's black cap and urges all of the group to wear pink.

> "Pink, pink," cried Glaucon, "pink's the hue:—"
>
> 'Pink cap and ribbons of the pearl,
>   A Paradise of bodice,
> The Queen of Sheba's laundry girl!"—
>
> [II, ii, p. 148]

Melville did not intend any rigid color pattern in the poem. Vine is beyond the spectrum, and Rolfe's bronze features cast him as a neutral. But the pinks and the greens, whites and purples emphasize by contrast the pearl-gray of the Ass and Nehemiah. They set apart for stress the black of Abdon's skin, of Agath's Moor on the *Peace of God*, of Ungar's powder burns, and of Mortmain's skull cap. They dramatize the colorless Clarel who absorbs or reflects all of the colors.

Melville used the palm tree as another organizing image, in the same way that he used the doubloon in *Moby-Dick*. Accordingly, in some of the most brilliant passages of the poem, the tree becomes for Derwent, Vine, Mortmain, and Rolfe the reflection of their hopes and memories (III, xxv-xxx, pp. 376-91). The tower figure similarly enables the pilgrims to rise for the moment above the awful reality of flat existence. So Clarel goes aloft after his first disappointed sight of blank Jerusalem (I, xviii, pp. 67-68). After the vigil over the waters of the Dead Sea, the pilgrims' journey ascends to the twin towers of Mar Saba, where escape from the perilous desert is possible (III, vii, p. 303). In the same way, the depression over Mortmain's death lifts for the group only when they sight Bethlehem from their position in the nearby hills (IV, i, p. 408). Even after Ruth's death and burial Clarel attempts an ascent, but his view from Mt. Olivet ends in fog (IV, xxxiv, p. 522). Like lush colors, the tower changes the vision of reality, but only as a distortion. In the same way that gray and black remain constant, regardless of the beholder's preference, the man who goes aloft must inevitably return to the flat earth.[25]

All these clustered images of dust, stones, sea, the Cross, death, birds, light, colors, trees, and towers constitute the one fractured image of Jerusalem, the central image of the poem. The city for Melville's contemporaries held a different meaning, a sacred one nurtured by Christian evangelists and fostered by tourist agents. Provincial usage of "New Jerusalem" for America and acceptance of the Holy Land as the handwork of God were facts of life in the nineteenth century.

Arise, shine out, for your light has come,
The glory of Yahweh is rising upon you,
the night still covers the earth
and darkness the people.

Above you Yahweh now rises
and above you his glory appears.
The nations shall come to your light
And kings to your dawning brightness.[26]

Out of the memory of his own dismal visit there in 1857 and a rejection of the myth of any city as God-touched, Melville disclaimed this vision of a resurrected Jerusalem and agreed with the same prophet's account of what was actually there.

What a harlot she has become,
The faithful city,
Zion, that was all justice!
Once integrity lived there,
But now all assassins.[27]

Just as he used cetology in *Moby-Dick* and additional nautical effects in other works for documentary atmosphere, so he used stone and dust, blank walls and blackness, bitter waters and pockmarked land, and countless different images of aridity picked up from the other stops on the pilgrimage, to limn Jerusalem, the image of nineteenth-century sterility. The city is full of blind alleys and sealed gates, guarded ironically by Turkish troops. Its greatness lies only in its shrouded past.

Under such scenes abysses be—
Dark quarries where few care to pry,
Whence came those many cities high—
Great capitals successive reared,
And which successive disappeared
On this same site. To powder ground,
Dispersed their dust blows round and round.
[I, xvi, p. 52]

The promise of peace that lured Nathan and his family to the Holy City led to barrenness and death. When examined, the glorious Gate of David only divides the waste of desert into two separate drought holes (I, xxiv, pp. 79-80). "Zion's old magnificence" was and is a colony of leper-huts (I, xxvi, p. 85). The romantic hope Clarel had placed in the Holy City dies in the discovery that nothing

> More lonesome looks than this dead pool
> In town where living creatures rule.
>
> [I, i, p. 7]

Each new site discovered drives from him the imagined glory of Christendom.

> But much as distant shows the town
> Erst glorious under Solomon,
> Appears now, in these latter days,
> To languid eyes, through dwelling haze,
> The city St. John saw so bright
> With sardonyx and ruby? Gleam
> No more, like Monte Rosa's height,
> Thy towers, O New Jerusalem?
> To Patmos now may visions steal?
> Lone crag where the lone ospreys wheel!
>
> [IV, ii, pp. 408-09]

The reality of Jerusalem is not light, glory, and rising, as Isaiah proclaimed: it is death. It is a "Ruined City," one vast coffin, an appropriate burial place for Ruth.

> Here the city old,
> Fast locked in torpor, fixed in blight,
> No hum sent forth, revealed no light:
> Though, facing it, cliff-hung Siloam—
> Sepulchral hamlet—showed in tomb
> A twinkling lamp. The valley slept—

Obscure, in monitory dream
Oppressive, roofed with awful skies
Whose stars like silver nail-heads gleam
Which stud some lid over lifeless eyes.
[IV, xxix, p. 510]

Jerusalem the Wreck,[28] the dead gray city, holds all the parts of *Clarel* in one fragmented image.

The pattern of imagery and the constricted verse of *Clarel* fit perfectly the severe structure of the poem. Melville carefully constructed the work in four somewhat equal parts, with Part I longer because of the required exposition.

The structure suggests comparison with *The Divine Comedy*. The hero is discovered at a point of despair in Jerusalem, a gray city of walking dead. He meets a guide who alerts him to the need for grace from heaven and for the penance required for salvation. The two leave Jerusalem as Part I ends and wend their way downward to Jericho and the Hell of the Dead Sea. This Wilderness in Part II plumbs man's nature and potential for destruction. Such a land holds no promise for the pilgrim and brings death to the guide. The Purgatory of Part III is climbed by Clarel, and its mountain of Saba offers a measure of peace after the black hole of Achor. The Bethlehem of Part IV appears as a Paradise from the distant Judah mountains, but, in reality, is another point in the circle of despair for the pilgrim. It leads back to Jerusalem and the original lost condition. The final movement of the poem suggests Melville's sad comment on Dante's vision of the quest achieved.

The form of the poem includes also a pervasive motif of escape. Melville used the technique many times before. In *Typee, Omoo,* and *Mardi* the hero frees himself from an intolerable situation, even though "freedom" is won in chaos. Pierre escapes a "Saddlemeadow" innocence and wins the disorder of civilization and death at the end of his flight. Ishmael, like Redburn, escapes from the city into the enigmatic sea where he comes to a fuller understanding of life, or at least of himself. Total escape from society and responsibility is managed only by Bartleby, when he fulfills his preference for death over life.

The same escape technique is used in *Clarel*. As an innocent at the beginning of the poem, Clarel distrusts his intellect, has no feeling for the universe, and has come to the Holy Land as a last chance for survival. He escapes unwittingly from Jerusalem into the wilderness, examines there the values offered by the world through his fellow pilgrims, meets tragedy face to face upon his return, and reverts to his original depressive state but now aware that he alone can bring some order of peace into his life. His escape, like Ishmael's, is significant because he knows he must get out of his spiritually stagnant condition; it is, therefore, a voluntary pursuit of a goal rather than a simple flight away from an intolerable condition. Accordingly, there is next to no suspense in the poem. Whereas the reader wonders how White-Jacket will stand up to a flogging, or whether Starbuck can win Ahab away from Fedallah, or if Delano will ever see through Babo's camouflage, in *Clarel* the inexorable movement toward tragedy precludes any suspense. It is true that at the end of Part I Melville anticipates future events and change.

> They part, Farewell to Zion's seat.
> Ere yet anew her place they greet,
> In heart what hap may Clarel prove?
> Brief term of days, but a profound remove.
>
> [I, xliv, p. 138]

Similarly, Clarel's sudden fearful recall of a forgotten Ruth, on the night before the departure from Mar Saba, looks forward to the catastrophe. But neither the wonder over the unfolding of future events nor the attempt to understand the mysterious symbols seriously enters into the poem.

Melville is the omniscient narrator who controls the telling of the story. He balances straight narration with dialogue; indeed, most of the philosophical problems are presented in the form of a Platonic dialogue. Melville allows the characters to speak their own minds and, in some cases, to narrate long tales. He also enters their minds so that their ruminations come directly from them. The combination of narrative, dialogue, soliloquy, and introspection gives an effect of drama, with depth perception of the characters a major concern for Melville. He does intrude now and then: to account for a canto which follows (III, xxv, p. 374); for a mood change in the succeeding lines (III, xi, p. 313; IV, xxv, p. 491); for a personal reaction to one of the characters (IV, v, p. 422). But rarely in these infrequent cases does Melville intrude with enthusiasm, except for the open declaration of the Epilogue. Instead, he maintains a distance from the events and characters so that the reader is left, as he is with Shakespeare, unable to identify the author's personal voice.

Within the limits for dramatic turns imposed by the narrative scheme, Melville achieved remarkable effects through timing, with some instances like cues for stage entrances. Mortmain, for example, returns as a prophet of hell and destruction from his mountain retreat at a time when the other pilgrims are engulfed in the mood of Sodom's waste (II, xxxiv, pp. 258 ff). After the ascent to Mar Saba has begun with the terror of the Dead Sea still upon them, the group hears in the distance the cheery song of a Cypriot, which suggests to them that comfort and ease await at the monastery (III, iv, p. 286). When Ungar completes one of his bitter tirades against humanity, Clarel wonders why one should be scrupulous over behavior if all that he says is true: why not live a life of sensual enjoyment? At this point, the Prodigal enters and offers him just such a way of life (IV, xxvi, pp. 491ff). Contrast like this is rhythmic in the poem: the bitter experience in the Siddim desert gives way to an all-night revelry which, in turn, is interrupted by solemn penitential psalms sung by the monks. More important to the overall meaning of the poem in this connection, is the contrast of movement and fortune for Clarel. His despair at Jaffa is converted to hope through love for Ruth; the joy is dashed at once by separation and the horror of the wilderness, where he literally cannot remember her features; hope revives at Bethlehem in anticipation of reunion with Ruth but is crushed again in the graveyard discovery. The pastoral mood of Bethlehem itself, notwithstanding Ungar's sour presence, also affords a contrast: it intimates a classical, false resolution of the impending tragedy, with an aura of comparative peace that lulls Clarel until he is completely unprepared for the shattering events that follow at Siloam. These neat devices of contrast and timing afford change of pace and shadings of meaning which are vital in the poem. But they do not divert attention nor deliberately relieve the reader's comprehension of the awesome facts through a series of rhetorical tricks; the mood of the poem remains constant as though the poet cannot compromise the truth of Clarel's tragedy. Thus he ends many of the cantos with stark symbols[29] and runs the arid imagery like coarse lace through the entire narration.

In such a heavily didactic poem Melville used very few epigrams, despite the opportunity offered by the octosyllabic line. And the allusiveness that marked his early work appears less in *Clarel* than its enormous length would suggest. Melville's grasp of history and science, his prolific reading and speculation in philosophy and religion appear, of course. But the rambling style of *Mardi*, and the protruding essays of *Moby-Dick* and *Pierre*, which only incidentally bear on the plot, are rarely found in *Clarel*. The poet curbed his imagination and guided it on a well-charted course. Even the episodes harmonize with the epical structure and contribute to the grim spirit of the poem. In no other work did Melville so restrict himself to his immediate task. His subject required the tautest of forms, and the form could not allow any deviation.

This singular work of Melville is even more remarkable in that it is almost completely free of the opposing spirits of comedy and terror. The terror emerges from every page, but the comic spirit which informed Melville's early work is either dead or thoroughly chastened.[30] The earlier Rabelaisian humor cannot be found in the poem. But the tone of *Clarel* does not allow for exaggeration or the tall tale, inflated language, biting satire, burlesque, or risqué scenes. In their place is the faint smile over things remembered or incongruities observed. It was Brother Benignus Muscatel in the past who provided Rolfe with the hymn book he uses while he sings over the brackish waters of the Dead Sea (II, xxiv, p. 222). The man who builds the coffins at Mar Saba is Brother Placido. In this passage Melville allowed himself the only real comic scene of the poem. Don Hannibal rests in one of the coffins, half a corpse himself, with an arm and a leg missing. He invites his friend Derwent to join him.

"Take a chair,
Don Derwent; no, I mean—yes, take
A—coffin; come, be sociable."
[IV, xxv, p. 490]

Derwent's stuttered preference for a bench awakens in the reader Ishmael's similar early acquaintance with coffins.

The coffin scene persuaded Melville that he was in the comic mood, for he ends the canto with the intimation that the following section is to be humorous:

And now—not wantonly designed
Like lays in grove of Daphne sung,
But helping to fulfill the piece
Which in these cantos finds release,
Appealing to the museful mind—
A chord, the satyr's chord is strung.
[IV, xxvi, p. 491]

The discourse that follows between the two young men involves the virtue of Clarel's restraint and the Lyonese's sensual abandonment and twitting of such puritanism. The tone is light, although the heavy overtone of sensuality bewilders and frightens Clarel. The Prodigal's hedonism takes on a grimmer tone when Clarel learns afterwards from a displaced Russian that the young man is, in fact, a wandering Jew bitterly concealing his Hebrew identity. There are thus no laughs in this satyr's passage of comic reversal, despite Melville's warning beforehand. There is only another awakening for Clarel.

The frolic at Mar Saba, already mentioned, similarly achieves a chilling effect. The pilgrims dance and drink in an effort to drive out the low spirits haunting them. Just when they have forgotten their experience in the wilderness the piercing cry of lamentation calls them back to the fact of their bleak existence. All of the joy Melville imparted to his dedicated drinkers on the *Neversink*, men who were "suckled at a puncheon," or to Dr. Long Ghost, who comes alive when he imbibes strong liquor, is missing in the *danse macabre* at Mar Saba. Neither Melville nor the pilgrims have a genuine humor for the revel. The effect is one of comic incongruity, which heightens the encompassing tragedy.

Throughout his literary career, Melville never faltered in the mastery of dramatic technique. *Billy Budd* contains as much compelling action and clear motivation as anything written in the early years. Dramatic moments can be found in *John Marr* and *Timoleon*. *Clarel*, too, contains deep conflict between the head and the heart, but not in the sense of a drama that concerns flesh-and-blood figures. The minor characters of the poem are clearly limned and recognizable. But the major ones are the embodiment of ideas, important only so long as they function as vehicles for the ideas. Because of this, Clarel's frustration at the end of the quest produces no catharsis for the reader: the hero's failure is little more than a large question mark at the end of a philosophic debate.

Melville carefully introduces his characters in proper setting. As noted above, the confused Clarel appears literally from nowhere, the dust on his clothes symbolizing his gray, orphaned condition. Nehemiah seems to come out of the sun, like a modern Elijah or a Virgil dispatched from heaven. Celio appears in a group of demoniacs, and Ruth enters at a wall of sorrow. Vine is first seen lying on the ground in the Sepulchre of Kings. Agath, a man of sorrows, comes on the scene immediately after Derwent says he wishes to hear some adventures and after Rolfe sees the scimiter which split so many skulls. The Cypriot meets the pilgrims after they have heard his gay song ringing across the mountain. Margoth, a mechanical man, is seen off in the distance, with his hammer in hand as though he were a physical part of the mountain.

In addition to the proper setting, Melville gives most of his characters names of allegorical or allusive significance. The name of Clarel fits the hero ironically: he is more opaque than he is clear or "clair," with his condition at the beginning of the poem one of complete bewilderment. Clarel's similarity to Clare and Clara also suggests the feminine side that requires development; that is, Clarel's whole purpose in Palestine is to uncover the meaning of the heart.

The name of Nehemiah is also significant. It comes directly from the *Second Book of Ezra and Nehemia*,[31] the "cup bearer" of the Persian King Artaxerxes and appointed by the King as Governor of Jerusalem: his specific mission was the rebuilding of Jerusalem. As "God's Comforter" this Biblical figure has his counterpart in Melville's millenarian who makes ready the Lord's Second Coming through distribution of tracts. As the builder of Jerusalem's walls despite his enemies' scorn, the ancient Nehemiah is imitated by the evangelist's feeble attempts to remove the stones from Judea. Just as the Biblical Nehemiah called himself the worst sinner before God, so Melville's character identifies himself as "The Sinner Nehemiah" (I, vii, p. 28) and "the chief of sinners" (II, xxvii, p. 240). The prophet requested the best of timber to rebuild the tower over the temple, whereas the beams of the evangelist's house "Were wreck-stuff from the Joppa strand" (I, xxii, p. 74). In creating this lovable and foolish character, Melville adhered closely to the Bible to produce ironic effects.

Melville also used a Scriptural model for Ruth, with certain variations. In the book by Samuel, Ruth was a Moabite woman who left her people to marry a Jew, Boaz of Bethlehem. Melville has Ruth pledged to marry a Gentile, Clarel, thereby renouncing her parents' faith. Just as Ruth followed the reapers in the field and brought corn for Naomi, so Melville's Ruth each day brings old Nehemiah a loaf of bread. Ruth's loyalty to Naomi extends to death and parallels in spirit the coincidental deaths of Ruth and Agar.

> Wherever you go, I will go,
> Wherever you live, I will live.
> Your people shall be my people,
> and your God, my God.
> Wherever you die, I will die

> and there I will be buried.
> May Yahweh do this thing to me
> and more also,
> If even death should come between us![32]

The advice by Naomi to her daughter-in-law concerning proper behavior with Boaz parallels Agar's words to Ruth. The parallel ends in the filial devotion, for Melville differed with Samuel in that he did not intend marital happiness for his Ruth. She symbolizes virtue but cannot know the meaning of happiness. She merely fulfills the role of pawn in Clarel's tragedy.

Other than those of Ruth and Nehemiah, the names and actions of the characters in the poem do not come from the Bible. Ruth's father, Nathan, has no connection with David's prophet, except for his similar refusal to compromise with the truth. Abdon's would seem to be a random name, one perhaps remembered by Melville from maps he had studied in 1857 or later on when he set to work on the poem. Abdon was a little town that existed before Christ, south of Tyre, about five miles off the Mediterranean. The only remote connection between Melville's minor character and the town is the allusion to the remnant of the original Twelve Tribes living in Abdon's native Cochin, in India (I, ii, pp. 8-9). The town of Abdon was in the northwest section of Judea, inhabited by the First Tribe of Asher.

The real name of Mortmain is unknown to the author; his only identification is the "dead hand" nickname. It complements his vision of a world dead through sin and injustice and anticipates his death in solitude. Equally severe is the harsh sound of Ungar, the Anglo-American Indian. It echoes Cooper's famous Uncas; it also rhymes with the livid scar on Ungar's neck. Melville punned with the name; first, with the "gar" as a spear, or Ungar's prominent sword; and second as a jibe on the enemy he fought, the G.A.R. reduced by the negative prefix. Agar's name, so close to the soldier's, has an entirely different meaning. Agar means "green," coming from the gelatinous substance made from seaweed, a word Melville possibly picked up in his South Sea travels. The green quality dominates, expressing Agar's love for flowers and her functional innocence. Melville probably saw another meaning in her name, as a variant on Hagar. As Hagar, she affords Ishmael-Clarel a love he never received from a natural mother. The characteristic Ishmael name, in turn, extends to Djalea, the Lebanese Druze. Melville hints that he was "an Emır's son," but one who is "Exiled, cut off, in friendless state" (II, vii, p. 163). As an exile, he can be traced more directly to his lineage as a "Duruz" to the Arabic Ismail al-Darazzi, founder of a religious sect in Syria, or Lebanon. Even if this tracing to the Arabic tailor is without significance, the archetypal Ismail figure is repeated in Djalea. Also his respect for Christianity connects him with that ancient Arab Muslim group that adopted many Christian beliefs and devotions without becoming Christians.

Other names in the poem have certain immediate interest. Where Agar's name emphasizes the good qualities of green, Glaucon's name also signifies green, but as a lush, surface color that brushes off at once. The coloring suits the hedonic approach to life. It also complements his adoption of the color pink as a symbol of vitality. The Cypriot is another sensualist, his name bearing the traditional meaning of a licentious person, a prostitute, a worshipper of Aphrodite. His scarlet cap fits his name. His name and cap suggest a complex personality, for they contrast sharply with his mission, viz., going to the River Jordan to bathe his mother's shroud. The name also comments paradoxically on the "cypress" mood Clarel wishes to dispel in his later talk with the Prodigal. The name of the Prodigal fits this wandering Jew, too. His two names sum up the polarities of his nature: his tormented, wandering, wasted side in the harsh sound and Biblical echo of "The Prodigal" who has returned home; and his lush, sensual side in the voluptuous "The Lyonese's." The licentious suggestion carries over to the Lesbian, a "Mytilene, a juicy man" (III, xi, p. 320). It goes even further, for a homosexual hint is offered: he arrives with the Arnaut—a handsome giant among men—urges conviviality among men, and, in a short time, is holding hands with Derwent (III, xi, p. 319). The connection of Lesbos with female homosexuals was sufficient for Melville to invert the meaning by calling this man "The Lesbian."

The soft sound of Derwent's name blends with the memory of the Lake country and the River Derwent and sums up his liquid personality. The romanticizing of reality fits his name perfectly: at one point, he tells Clarel how often he cantered on the English downs. Agath's name is well-chosen, too. It comes from "agathos" and sums up the basic goodness of this man of sorrows. His tragic experiences and courage in the face of them are consistent with Melville's memory of the unworked tragic theme of Agatha, whose name also summed up her life.[33] Don Hannibal Rohon Del Aquaviva has a similar tragic background, although his new face for life belies a suffering life. His name, which combines the military echo of the Carthaginian general and the buoyance of the waters of life, mocks the fact of his amputated arm and leg. Brandy, or wine in this case, also has an ironic twist in the name of Vine. Melville deliberately set Vine in a pastoral background, with explicit reference to Theocritus and Virgil. The pastoral carries over to the image of Christ and the Tree and the Branch. Vine is seen in an arbor; like a vine he leans on the ground, or leans against a wall. When Vine joins in the drinking revel at Mar Saba, he thereby completes the wine meaning of his name. Melville plays with the name throughout the poem, but more suggesting the thorn of the vine than the blossom.[34]

Melville jested with Habbibi, the name of the scribe who wrote nonsense on the Mar Saba walls. It is a wry word, particularly with the scribbling an obviously grim comment by Melville on his own writings. The name probably has some derivation from the prophecies of Habbacuc, better known to the Hebrews as Hab. The self-deprecation of the prophet who answered a call from heaven to write, and his thundering warnings to society, come close to Melville's own belief and experience.[35] The poet uses irony, too, in the name of Celio. The hump on his back and defiance of God argue against his ever becoming "a being of heaven." The name of Brother Salvaterra, on the other hand, has no double nor inverted meaning, unless it is the obvious "Salvation." His decision to leave the charm of the Arno Valley for the "dull calm of desert" might confound Derwent; but he is clear in purpose and realization, for, as his name indicates, the "holy land" of Bethlehem has brought him a peace he could never find in Italy. In the same way, the name of Margoth is a perfect tag. He has come to the Holy Land, unlike Brother Salvaterra, to rip it open for investigation. His name fits the hun image which he evokes: his symbolic hammer which "mars" everything complements his snarling comments on all tradition and belief. As he did with Abdon, Melville added a slight additional meaning to the name through his memory of the city of Gath, a Philistine stronghold, northeast of Gaza.

Alone among the major figures of the poem, Rolfe is a neutral character in name as well as in color symbols. His is a common name, perhaps signifying a masculine quality (wolf) but yet not identifying him in any particular way. However, Melville chose the names deliberately, even Rolfe's. In some cases, they constitute little allegories, as in the cases of Ruth and Nehemiah and, perhaps, in that of Vine. In others, the names merely allude to a quality of the character observed by the narrator, as with Mortmain and Ungar. However used, they add a dimension to the personality and actions of the characters.

The pilgrims are also generally recognizable by their speech patterns. Such identification in verse can be made successfully only where the poet varies his meter and patterns or choice of language so that the wide range allows for perceptible differences. The hudibrastic medium restricted Melville, of course, so that all the lines are more or less the same in emotional effects. But even within this limiting frame, the characters take on a few identifying characteristics. Nehemiah's words constantly echo Scripture and urge a mystical relationship with God, so that each man can become "Young friend in Christ" (I, vii, p. 27). Rolfe's language is marked by clarity but withheld judgment, because his open mind demands that he take both sides of any given argument. He sounds always like a lecturer who rehearses his ideas in public. Vine communicates to the others in terse expressions, leading them either into nonunderstanding or into the belief that the terror he experiences is too painful for words. Derwent's words are the clichés of the dilettante: "queer," for the inexplicable, or "terrifying, my dear boy," when Clarel poses unanswerable theological questions, or "mad, mad enough," as an easy explanation for Mortmain's monomania. Both the Dominican and Brother Salvaterra speak feelingly out of a deep love for Christ and His creatures, with the latter's words a deliberate paraphrase of liturgical prayers. Don Hannibal explodes his words, with exclamation points pronouncing revolutionary ideas. The Prodigal lures Clarel with open-voweled, voluptuous language, particularly emphasizing his sibilants:

> "Let your Paradise exhale
>   Odors; and enlink the dance;
>   And, ye rosy feet, advance
> Till ye meet morn's ruddy Hours
>   Unabashed in Shushan's bowers!"
>
> [IV, xxvi, p. 499]

Mortmain and Ungar speak the same kind of language: words of fury bitten off in exhortation. Djalea compounds the mystery he carries about him, with enigmatic answers: "No God there is but God," or "Allah preserve ye, Allah great!" Agar's simple words come out of a simple love for hearth and home, for gardens and growing things.

This pattern of introducing characters and giving them appropriate names, setting, and speech never becomes rigid in the poem. Like Chaucer's technique in *The Canterbury Tales*, Melville ensured variety through omission of certain facts —Clarel's and Rolfe's backgrounds—and through repetition of characteristics to form a composite picture: Celio, Mortmain, and Ungar actually emerge as a single character in the final meaning of the poem. Melville's effects were not designed to delineate a cross-section of humanity so much as they were intended as a frame for ideas. Even so, this loose pattern, coupled with the poet's tight control of sustained imagery, restricted verse, and overall structure produced a poem which is almost unique in the nineteenth century. Although in *Clarel* the outward style is less glowing than in Melville's early work, the greater fire burns within. In it, economy and intellectual clarity replace lavishness and mental fog.[36] In this respect, and in many others as well, *Clarel's* appeal is directly to the twentieth century.

VII

Ideality and Reality in the Church

What motive was the master-builder's here?
Why these synodic hierarchies given?
Sublimely ranked in marble sessions clear,
Except to signify the host of heaven.
"Milan Cathedral"

The most startling discovery for the reader of *Clarel* is Melville's high regard for the Roman Catholic Church. This attitude pervades the poem as clearly as Clarel's pilgrimage follows the Catholic liturgical calendar: it opens on Epiphany Sunday and ends on Ash Wednesday; the hero's lamentation over Ruth's death covers the Lenten period of mourning and rises to a climax of expectation on Good Friday and Easter Sunday; Clarel's submersion in the city ends with his final appearance at the Via Crucis on the Feast of Pentecost. The sympathetic handling of Roman Catholic ritual, belief, and tradition contrasts sharply with Melville's previous observations on the Church. *Typee* and *Omoo,* for example, contain blasts at the French Catholic missionaries who brought the moral squalor of Christianity to the South Seas.[1] Only Father Murphy receives the author's praise, an accolade given to the tippling priest for "doing good works" for the natives, rather than for praying and hymning.[2] *Mardi* cuts deeper into the structure and teaching of the Church. The allegorical Maramma is the Roman Church, where men are forced into a sterile, unhealthy asceticism that does not admit of true love. There, Pani is blind—like Christodolus, the Abbot of Mar Saba in *Clarel*—and is symbolically fanned by dead leaves. The Church's claim as the one true institution descended from Christ is mocked by Babbalanja's story of the banyan tree.[3] Maramma deceives believers and mocks the sincerity of devoted pilgrims. Serenia, on the other hand, fulfills the Christian message. It has no churches or priests, but everywhere Alma is adored, joyously. There the heart rules in love and ensures peace in a land uncorrupted by precept or cant.[4] But the Catholic Church, for Melville, ignores Alma, or love, and sets up a structured institution in its place that resembles the foolish strutting and meaningless actions of the bird kingdom.[5] "Benito Cereno" similarly explores this wasted Catholic mission, but with less vindictiveness. Its theme, secondary to the overpowering one of innocence and evil in conflict, implies allegorically the failure of the Church to supply the spiritual needs of its members. "Follow your leader" as a motto for dogmatic infallibility holds meaning only in a dreamy romantic way, but when examined in the shadow of evil's reality it becomes another meaningless shibboleth.

These constitute some of the early representative Protestant or non-Catholic beliefs that Melville expressed. The idea of yielding one's will to institutional authority as an act of faith repelled him. Priests could not be unique interpreters of God's will. They are like other men, with no gift of Apostolic succession, no closer to the mystery that lies at the nut of the universe. Nor do they heed Christ's admonition to love one's neighbor. Melville cites their typical lack of Christianity in *White-Jacket,* viz., the Catholic priests in Callao refuse burial in consecrated ground to Protestants and cast them onto Volcano Island.[6]

Despite these earlier deep convictions, Melville singles out the Catholic Church in *Clarel* as worthy and devotes many pages to extolling her virtues. Where he catalogued her abuses in *Mardi*, he lists reasons for her continued existence in the poem. The scorn for all churches that Melville poured into the short story "The Two Temples" changes in *Clarel* to awe for an institution that sustained itself despite the corruption of man and the effacement of time. In no way does this attitude indicate a spiritual conversion to the Catholic Church. Instead, it denotes one more Romantic or Victorian poet who moved emotionally toward the Roman Church—each one unconsciously—but never arrived there.

Essential in Roman Catholic dogma is the Incarnation, which is the doctrine of supernal love concretized in the God-man, Jesus Christ. Through Him, charity becomes a realizable virtue as an expression of God's glory and, in turn, brings eternal reward. Love immerses man in this relationship with the God of love and impresses him with a capacity for joy and sadness: joy that love is obtainable through grace and good works, and sadness that it is not with him always. Through Christ man transcends his human condition in spiritual growth by means of the three theological virtues of faith, hope, and charity, with charity an absolute necessity. This constitutes a positive conviction based solely on love as the core of creation: the creation of the universe by God was the first and the greatest act of love. A fundamental premise of this doctrine, however, considers the sad aspect of man in his lack of perfection. This flaw traces back to the Garden of Eden and the subsequent loss of Paradise, or is explained doctrinally as the stain of Original Sin. The loss brought on another act of supernal love, in God the Father's gift of His Son as a Redemptor. But the Incarnation presumes, in turn, the Crucifixion and Redemption. It constitutes for man the noblest act he can perform, that of "substitutional sacrifice." The divine sacrifice has meaning, however, only insofar as man is capable of committing personal sin. It does not apply to the salvation of mankind in one great miraculous opening of heaven through Christ's act. Through the Redemption each man can earn his personal reclamation from sin and win his own eternal reward. There are other dogmas of the Catholic Church. But they have significance only in relationship with the Incarnation, Crucifixion, and Redemption as acts of love. In this doctrine the natural and supernatural are fused in the two natures of Christ and find identical expression in the natural and supernatural mission of the Church.

Melville never believed in this dual nature and purpose and rejected totally the supernatural aspect of the Church. The sympathy that he registers in *Clarel* comes essentially from admiration for her endurance as a natural institution. Rolfe voices this concern over the transience of all things and asks the Dominican if the Church is not merely another changing thing. The priest responds with simple faith.

> "Change? yes, but not with us. In rout
> Sword-hilts rap at the Vatican,
> And lo, an old, old man comes out:
> 'What would ye?' 'Change!' 'I never change.' "
>
> [II, xxv, p. 225]

He insists that whereas all human things change the superhuman quality of the Church does not admit of this flaw.

> "But Rome has lived a thousand years:
> Shall not a thousand years know more
> Than nonage may?"
>
> [II, xxv, p. 226]

Toward the end of the journey, when the pilgrims reach Bethlehem, Rolfe raises the subject again and echoes the priest's remarks on change in the world and permanence in the Church.[7]

> All shows and forms in Kedron had—
> Nor hymn nor banner made them glad
> To me. And yet—why, who may know!
> These things come down from long ago.
> While so much else partakes decay,
> While states, tongues, manners pass away,
> How wonderful the Latin rite
> Surviving still like oak austere
> Over crops rotated year by year,
> Or Caesar's tower on London's site.
>
> [IV, xvi, p. 462]

The Dominican's awe of the Church's endurance makes sense dramatically in the context of the poem. But these last lines are Rolfe's answer to Derwent as a Protestant spokesman and reflect more accurately Melville's view, particularly in the word "wonderful" expressing praise and mystery. The narrator observes, too, how the extraordinary continuity of Christ's Church becomes even more meaningful in its lineage rooted in Abraham:

> From Ur of the Chaldees roved the man—
> Priest, shepherd, prince, and pioneer—
> Swart Bedouin in time's dusky van;
> Even he which first, with mind austere,
> Arrived in solitary tone
> To think of God as One—alone;
> The first which brake with hearth and home
> For conscience' sake, whom piety ruled,
> Prosperity blest, longevity schooled,
> And time in fullness brought to Mamre's tomb
> Arch founder of the solid base of Christendom.
> [II, xx, pp. 204-05]

Its jealous preservation in the hands of the Ionian monks impresses him in the same way (I, xxxv, pp. 114-17), Admirable, too, is the patient loving care of the Calvary site by the Franciscans, where traditions rule. The Franciscans as a group "May claim more of similitude/To Christ, than any man we know" (IV, xiv, p. 455). Brother Salvaterra, the young guide in Bethlehem, is just such a man in Rolfe's eyes, his gentleness and patience marking him as a genuine follower of St. Francis (IV, xiii, p. 450).

Melville's deepest impression of the Church, then, is in her seeming triumph over time and her own incipient corruption. Throughout his life and particularly in his late years, Melville looked everywhere for such emblems of immortality. This accounts for the reveries in *Clarel* on the way to Mar Saba.

Translated where the anthem's sung
Beyond the thunder, in a strain
Whose harmony unwinds and solves
Each mystery that life involves;
There shall the Tree whereon He hung,
The olive wood, leaf out again—
Again leaf out, and endless reign
Type of the peace that buds from sinless pain?
[III, i, p. 277]

The palm tree at the monastery hints of this eternal leafing and signifies the possibility of permanance for transient pilgrims, including Melville himself. The wreck image that haunted him was one he would gladly give up if stone objects, like the Sphinx and twin-towered Mar Saba, could convince him in the same way of eternity. Similarly, the roses that occupied his late years actually disappointed him in their death and filled him with a longing for a metaphysical rose. It is no wonder that in his own attempt to find some anchor in the endlessly flowing seas of life the Church offered something secure and enduring.

Melville's basic inclination, after the 1860s at least, was to find a discipline of life as a way out of chaos. Although this approach was negative, it had him subscribe in spirit to the Catholic Church as the one port in the chartless sea of the nineteenth century; as a psychological solution for the emotional problems of the millions who believe in her.[8] And believe they must, for because of his castaway condition a man must find something to nourish his faith.

Ah, exile is exile, tho' spiced be the sod,
  In Shushan we languish—
Languish with the secret desire for the garden of God.[9]

The Syrian Monk's account of a harrowing experience on the Quarantanian mountain does not tell of any peace won through mystical communion with God. But the startling image of Christ's thorn that Vine holds in his hand after the narration emphasizes by contrast this need that he and the Monk and all men have to root themselves in some belief. The Monk comes to it in the Church, even though the mountain vigil supplied no final intimate knowledge, while Vine wanders lost, an outsider, a hopeless "drifting sea-weed of the universe." Rolfe's arguments, rather than those of the Dominican and Franciscan, present a fuller treatment of this psychological aspect of belief and are Melville's for the most part. Rolfe almost wills a belief in the Church simply because she represents the only land-element in an oceanic universe. He is impressed by her, for despite the multiple "sects that peak and pine," and the discovery of "new" principles of meliorism, science, pragmatism, and hedonism, the Church serenely adapts her creed without a single change of principle. The Dominican pointed this out earlier, when he said that the adjustment could be met easily because "Her art/Is simple, quarried from the heart" (II, xxv, p. 225).

Melville treats the Syrian Monk, the Dominican, and the Franciscan with respect, even more, with envy of their secure belief. He suggests that their Christian course is the proper one for exiles who languish in Shushan or who scream defiance at the Arch of Ecce Homo. Their lives typify "the old Christian style toward men" (IV, xx, p. 478). They portray the kind of life a man could live in the Middle Ages before the belief in progress supplanted the one of service to God and man. In the Middle Ages, a man like St. Louis could fuse the temporal and the spiritual in a rich and fruitful life; only then could a Charlemagne wear in humility the power of his crown (IV, x, p. 439). Jesus's admonition to care for the halt and the lame was then practiced in the way Churchmen ministered to the lepers. Men and women sanctified their lives by caring for these outcasts, oftentimes becoming cripples from the disease themselves(I, xxv, pp. 83-4).

Ungar particularly praises the Medieval spirit to Derwent, in whom he sees all of the abuses of modern latitudinarianism, because he would disabuse the minister of all rosy views of the New World's progress. He appears as a man born in the wrong time, one whose loyalties to a medieval Church and Crown could have completed his personality or, at least, reduced his black passion. Rolfe, too, urges on the other pilgrims a truer understanding of the Middle Ages. But his "manysidedness" embraces all ages, all climes, and all views. At one point Clarel sees Rolfe as though he were projected out of an ancient age, but the vision attests only to Rolfe's capacity for ambivalence:

> The student shrank. Again he knew
> Return for Rolfe of quick distaste;
> But mastered it; for still the hue
> Rolfe kept of candor undefaced,
> Quoting pure nature at his need,
> As 'twere the Venerable Bede:
> An Adam in his natural ways.
>
> [III, xvi, p. 342]

The medieval spirit, which brings an awareness of the Patristic Fathers venerated by the Catholic Church, is not in Melville's poem. The main concern, instead, is the modern predicament of man in a society cut away from such veneration, citing the previous eras merely as a touchstone to measure modern sterility. Accordingly, *Clarel* contains virtually no Catholic theology and tradition. Not that Melville was ignorant of them, as Nathalia Wright points out:

> And all the while he perused an amazing variety of related literatures: the Bible; Biblical commentaries; the writings of major Christian dogmatists from Augustine to Calvin and of the more famous saints; Jewish history; Rabbinical and medieval religious lore; seventeenth-century sermons and metaphysical essays; the great Christian poets, Dante and Milton; comparative accounts of religions and mythologies; and on the side of the opposition, the works of the Stoics, the deists, and the sceptics.[10]

Nevertheless, Wright concludes, Melville had no appreciation of the Church, nor of the great theological systems, nor even of a personal approach to the Deity; he was completely independent of dogma in his narrow religious concepts.[11]

This limited appreciation applies to *Clarel.* There are a few references to St. Paul and St. Augustine. St. Bernard of Clairvaux is mentioned once, and the blue-robed monk's similarity to St. Francis of Assisi impresses Clarel, just as the history of the Franciscans appeals to Rolfe. The Blessed Mother as a symbol of purity and motherhood comes into the poem three times. Melville evidences a reading of the history of monasteries and has Rolfe murmur a vague communal prayer:

> "So fade men from each other!—Jew,
> We do forgive thee now thy scoff,
> Now that thou dim recedest off
> Forever. Fair hap to thee, Jew:
> Consolator whom thou disownest
> Attend thee in last hour lonest!"
>
> [III, i, p. 278]

Melville admires the asceticism practiced by Nehemiah, Mortmain, and Ungar; and the poem rings with the Christian compassion of *Redburn* and *White-Jacket.* It lauds the Pope's charity in a protest against Russia's rape of Poland in 1831, while England and France stood by (IV, xii, p. 444). Melville's fondness for the Catholic display of icons, which he showed in *Redburn* and throughout the *Levant Journal,* accounts for Agath's tattoo of the crucifixion and for the poet's favorable treatment of the shrines at Bethlehem (IV, xiii).

Admiration for the medieval spirit, respect for the monks and friars, saints and icons of the Church, awe for the longevity of the Church, and awareness of Rome as a haven for wandering exiles sum up Melville's attitude concerning the Roman Catholic Church. All of this comes to an assessment of her virtues as a natural organization and to praise of her as better than anything else around.[12] This is not enough to satisfy Rolfe or Vine or Clarel, or any other spokesman for Melville in the poem. The Church could not provide the solution for Melville's life-long problem of "chronometrical" and "horological" excellence. Christ for Melville was *the* chronometer,[13] with the Sermon on the Mount the greatest of all miracles.[14] But Christ was a chronometer who could tell time only in heaven, and the Sermon on the Mount has no real application in this world:

> And where is the earnest and righteous philosopher, gentlemen, who looking right and left, and up and down, through all the ages of the world, the present included; where is there such an one who has not a thousand times been struck with a sort of infidel idea, that whatever other worlds God may be Lord of, he is not the Lord of this; for else this world would seem to give the lie to Him; so utterly repugnant seem its way to the instinctively known ways of Heaven. But it is not, and cannot be so; nor will he who regards the chronometrical conceit aright, ever more be conscious of that horrible idea. For he will then see, or seem to see, that this world's seeming incompatibility with God, absolutely results from its meridional correspondence with Him.[15]

The entire life of Christ defined charity, and it worked for Him. But Melville insisted in *The Confidence-Man* that not only do men not practice charity but that it simply cannot work in the modern world.[16] Were a man to follow in Christ's footsteps he would end up like Pierre. The mystical benefits of the Cross of Christ are, despite the teachings of the Church, man's heinous sins of malice.

> To us, disciples of the Order
>   Whose rose-vine twines the Cross,
> Who have drained the rose's chalice
>   Never heeding gain or loss;
> For all the preacher's din
> There is no mortal sin—
>   No, none to us but Malice![17]

Such sins are natural to man as a way of life. Knowing this, God should not have implanted in man's heart hopes for eternal salvation. Thus in *Clarel*, Celio's grievance centers on the heavenly promises by Christ and His admonition for men to lead the good life, when their accomplishment is impossible even for Him.

> *Behold the Man!*
> Yon Man it is this burden lays:
> Even he who in the pastoral hours,
> Abroad in fields, and cheered by flowers,
> Announced a heaven's unclouded days;
> And, ah, with such persuasive lips—
> Those lips now sealed while doom delays—
> Won men to look for solace there;
> But, crying out in death's eclipse,
> When rainbow none his eyes might see,
> Enlarged the margin for despair—
> My God, my God, forsakest me?
>
> [I, xiii, p. 42]

Great humanitarian that he was, Christ misinterpreted the nature of man and underestimated his tendency for perversion. Accordingly, Christ's mission stressed the ideal, when, in fact, men took these "golden grains" and changed them into "dubious dregs":

> Whither hast fled, thou deity
> So genial?
> . . . .
> Oh, men
> Made earth inhuman; yes, a den
> Worse for Christ's coming, since his love
> (Perverted) did but venom prove.[18]
>
> [II, xxi, pp. 209-10]

Acceptance of the Sermon on the Mount by the Catholic Church pleased Melville, but he considered her myopic in thinking it would work. *Clarel* stresses the ethics of Jesus but on a practical level where men's ferocity must be predicted and guarded against, a kind of contradiction of terms. The difference between *Clarel* and *Mardi* lies in this contradiction, or in the development of Melville's thought away from Taji's drive to gain the ultimate, to Clarel's final realization that all man can do is live moderately in a four-square world. The man-of-war condition of society gives the lie to Christ's command to turn the other cheek or to seek consolation in other sacrificial gestures. Thus Melville applauds Mortmain's youthful chronometrical vision, but he gives him the black death cap as a final symbol. Similarly, the romantic zeal displayed by Ungar in his earlier years failed because it overlooked man's bestiality; the scar on his neck and the burn on his forehead remain as evidence of unattainable sophomoric ideals.

Notwithstanding these distinctions that Melville made between chronometrical and horological measures of human expectancy and behavior, he agonized over the fact that such distinctions existed. Melville at times considered Christianity as approximating man's highest ideals, and he saw admirable human elements in the Catholic Church. He shared with her particularly the virtue of charity as the essential one in man's survival in society. The Epilogue to *Clarel* emphasizes an evolutionary process of nature, but its consolation or promise for the reader suggests the Church's equally vague definition of hope.[19] But he was completely unable to discover the meaning of faith. For him, God becoming man as Christ in the doctrine of the Incarnation proved false in the evidence of men's un-Christian actions. All of his experience verified the validity of Spencer's survival of the fittest principle, rather than the one advocated by Christ. Faith for him had to flow from charity, or charity from faith. Nor could the Church's argument on the supernatural "fact" of miracles as a basis for faith change his mind. The universe follows only natural laws. This is what the foolish Nehemiah fails to know in his imitation of Christ, when he is "miraculously" removing the stones from the road. Or the tragedy of Clarel might have been averted, or blunted, if he had not looked to Easter Sunday as the time for Ruth's "miraculous" resurrection. Miracles are like the pencil of light at Nehemiah's death compared to the awful fact of the avalanche: they defy reason. Melville could not accept them, or any other tenet, on blind faith.

This constitutes Melville's widest disagreement with the Catholic Church. He stressed this separation—a personal realization of truth—as early as *Redburn*, in the need for each man to write his own guide book, and *Mardi*, in Taji's painful renunciation of Babbalanja's compromise in a simple act of faith. The serenity that the Dominican and the Franciscan know in *Clarel* is wished for by Clarel and Melville, but its acquisition through faith is impossible.[20] Stone suggests that the argument that rages in *Clarel* between faith and science actually covers up Melville's own agonizing over an inability to throw over reason for faith.[21] Father Mapple's words in the Whaleman's Chapel plagued Melville and account for the same problem which he posed for Clarel:

> As with all sinners among men, the sin of this son of Amittai was in his wilful disobedience of the command of God—never mind now what that command was, or how conveyed—which he found a hard command. But all things that God would have us to—remember that—and hence, he oftener commands us than endeavors to persuade. And if we obey God, we must disobey ourselves; and it is this disobeying ourselves, wherein the hardness of obeying God consists.[22]

The titanism that Mapple and Melville inveigh against remained with Melville for the rest of his life, even though the expression was subdued after the 1860s. Clarel does not openly disobey, as did Taji, Ahab, and Pierre. But he cannot accept what he cannot know, and his knowledge at the end of his pilgrimage is as incomplete as it was when he left the ship at Jaffa. Clarel disappears after the celebration of Pentecost, but without wisdom, and without any consolation from the Redemption of Easter Sunday. Clarel, like Melville, is constitutionally unable to make the necessary act of faith. And because he cannot, he is kindred to Celio, both in defiance and in sorrow.

The sympathetic treatment of the Catholic Church in *Clarel,* then, includes the ethical and psychological. The essential matter of the Incarnation and a God of love, and the demand for faith where reason fails left Melville unbelieving. He accepted the Church's assertion of the need for discipline in action, but he repudiated all dogma. This acceptance of a discipline, or at least of its need in man, took Melville beyond the renunciating, rebelling, and despairing titans of the earlier works. The overall recommendation in *Clarel* is for man to make some declaration of purpose as a way out of chaos, even when his problems remain unsolved. This principle of self-imposed discipline to bring about order supports the simplistic argument that Captain Vere uses in *Billy Budd* to overcome the drumhead court and the inclinations of his own heart. It leaves to those in this world who live in faith and emotions the "Last Assizes," and enables leaders and other realists to deal with "the people" in an earthly, horological manner. It provides a practical solution for the individual in society and grants him a limited but ordered freedom. If such a discipline cannot provide the joy that Pan and Christ promised, it can at least lead one out of madness. It is, in fact, Plinlimmon's advice that could have saved Pierre.

VIII

Three Alternatives Rejected

> Ah, wherefore not at once name Job,
> In whom these Hamlets all conglobe,
> Own, own with me, and spare to feign,
> Doubt bleeds, nor Faith is free from pain!
>
> *Clarel* [III, xxii, p. 364]

The Catholic Church afforded Melville the closest approximation of the ideal to be realized in his life. Its basic beliefs in theory enable a man to transcend individual desires and national consciousness so that he can live in a state of harmony roughly equivalent to Serenia. But this is only an ideal. War, greed, sexual perversion, and malice control men, as Melville observed throughout his life. Christ would be crucified again were He to reappear.

> "O abyss!
> Here, upon what was erst the sod,
> A man betrayed the yearning god;
> A man, yet with a woman's kiss.
> 'Twas *human,* that unanimous cry,
> 'We're fixed to hate him—crucify!' "
>
> [II, iii, p. 153]

A God of love has no place in human hearts. The fallen nature of man precludes any possibility of Serenia. It sets him adrift in the universe, cut off from his fellowman, a wanderer afflicted with a vague memory of a better existence but with a keener sense of loss. Nor is there any hope that this Ishmael can be redeemed by a Prometheus or a Christ. The vague memory of a paradise to be reclaimed comes out of fairy tales heard by children, a memory and wish which cover over the nothingness of the universe and the absurdity of existence. A mature view puts away these fairy tales as it observes what man does in his inhumanity. Experience informs the truthful man that Christianity is all promise and no fulfillment, that the Sermon on the Mount—"the greatest of all miracles"—fails in application. This is the basic contradiction of the Catholic Church.

At the conclusion of *Pierre,* the "fool of virtue" dies in solitude, his sacrificial act and death final proof of naiveté. Early in his mission he discovers the inadequacy of the Protestant Church, specifically in the failure of Reverend Falsgrave to do Christ's work. Pierre assumes Christ's role himself, and accepts "crucifixion" as though it has eternal significance. But the sacrifice fails to redeem Isabel, Lucy, or himself. It is a futile act, signifying nothing. Melville brings the hero full circle: from innocence to the discovery of evil, round into the final silence of oblivion, with the clear message that such a quest for truth and goodness is impossible of attainment. In this sense, the beginning of *Clarel* is a sequel to *Pierre.*[1] The journey begins in silence with the young theologian unable to pray; the world he has fled holds no meaning. But the twenty-odd years between *Pierre* and *Clarel* brought a substantial change in Melville's thinking; for despite this similarity of Clarel to Pierre when first he appears on Epiphany Sunday, the fact of his presence in the Holy Land attests to an unwillingness to admit or to accept what Pierre finally came to know. Like Pierre, he is a solitary, one of Melville's "lonely outposts of the world." His landing at Jaffa, however, connects him with the magnetic chain of humanity in a series of relationships that differ only in kind from that of Ishmael and Queequeeg. Except during occasional periods of depression, Melville could not be satisfied with the awful fact of Pierre's discovery and death as the limitations of human existence.

But lo, arrested in event—
Hurried down Hades' steep descent;
Cut off while in progressive stage
Perchance, ere years might more unfold:
Who young dies, leaves life's tale half told.
How then? Is death the book's fly-page?
Is no hereafter? If there be,
Death foots what record? how forestalls
Acquittance in eternity?
Advance too, and through age on age?
Here the tree lies not as it falls;
For howso'er in words of man
The word and will of God be feigned,
No incompletion's heaven ordained.
Clarel, through him these reveries ran.

[I, xix, p. 70]

Like Pierre, Clarel sees his fabricated world destroyed by death with no acceptable explanation available; but unlike Pierre, he attempts again to impose meaning and value on his life thereafter. This is the essential difference in Melville's life between the composition of both works. The reality of tragic existence was the same for Melville when he created *Pierre* as it was when he came to sum up all such adversity in *Clarel.* The despair he gave to Pierre, however, was a passing observation of the world and human reaction to it, one that did not appear again after he had Israel Potter face up to the same calamities and demonstrate in his courage and tenacity what it is to be a man. Israel and Clarel are, accordingly, closer in spirit than Pierre and Clarel, with Potter's Judaic name anticipating Clarel's final appearance and lost-but-found condition.

Shortly after *Clarel* appeared, Melville wrote a letter to his brother-in-law, John Hoadley, commenting on his own violent metaphysical pursuits in the past:

> You are young; but I am verging upon three-score, and at times a certain lassitude steals over one—in fact, a disinclination for doing anything except the indispensable. At

> such moments the problem of the universe seems a humbug, and epistolary obligations mere moonshine, and the—well, nepenthe seems all-in-all.
>
> . . . .
>
> P.S. You are going (as I said before) but I ain't; and at my years, and with my disposition, or rather constitution, one gets to care less and less for everything except downright good feeling. Life is so short, and so ridiculous and irrational (from a certain point of view) that one knows not what to make of it, unless—well, finish the sentence for yourself.
>
> Thine.
>
> In these inexplicable fleshly bonds.
>
> H.M.
>
> N.B. I ain't crazy.[2]

The letter closely parallels Clarel's condition at the beginning of the poem. Clarel considers the world a humbug, has little inclination to attack it or reform it, and finds himself constitutionally unable to attach importance to anything. Yet just as Melville wrote *Billy Budd* after this despondent letter,[3] Clarel goes on to awaken a curiosity, to discover new truths, and to attempt a recovery in a new situation. Melville misunderstood his own nature, despite the long years of introspection and mourning over lost ideals. Contrary to the tone of the letter, he was constitutionally unable to accept these periodic bleak assessments of man and the universe as final. Although he could not assent to the positive teleology of the Catholic Church, neither was he able to live for long with the fact of nothingness or the fruitlessness of Pierre's mission to do good. If a quest proves time and again that a goal cannot be found, he believed a man instinctively and mysteriously resumes his exploration because there is no contentment in stasis, no peace in dreams and denial. Whether he is Ishmael, cast out into exile and forever seeking his father and a way home, or Prometheus, an altruist born to suffer without relief, the heroic man by his nature continues to a discovery of the truth of self and the universe, no matter how dark and endless the spiral staircase.[4]

Consistent with this view, Melville's "lassitude," manifest in Clarel at Jaffa, disappears at once in resumption of the endless search. Refusal by the hero to sink into self-pity and inaction constitutes the greatness of his character and the paradoxical beginning of his tragedy.[5]

Clarel begins his search like Redburn in the rejection of his father's guidebook. Scripture, tradition, mores, anything men think and say, none of these has any relevance for him. His journey has to be an absolute, personal experiment.[6] Clarel turns inward from Jaffa, and away from the West, and begins a spiritual journey as he searches outwardly for faith. Jerusalem becomes the testing ground or the beginning and end of his quest, with the supreme trial faced in the descent to Jericho and the Dead Sea; a literal descent to truth, or an awful discovery of evil. It is the plunge or vortex experience that marked White-Jacket's fall from the yard-arm, the geologist's wish in Pierre to bore through the earth to find its hidden meaning, Pip's unwanted leap into the sea, and Ahab's appeal to the whale's head to unfold its lodged secret.

Clarel assaults life in its most primitive aspect, viz., in a geographical area where vestiges of a past age of faith might be discovered, and where the low values of the present are cast into sharp focus. Throughout the search, Clarel uses the past to measure the present so that he can arrive at a truth which binds both eras and, at the same time, is operable for him in the future. The assault is made through the "friendships" he makes and loses, for the inexplicable "underforming of his mind" can possibly be completed by other tortured souls who also seek a solution in Judea. Life is tried for him in these meetings. The other characters become teachers, each presenting a different aspect of life and a possible way out of the maze that paralyzes him.

> But I, shall *I* my feet impel
> Through road like thine and naught redeem?
> Rather through brakes, lone brakes, I wind:
> As I advance they close behind.—
>
> [I, ii, p. 11]

Ultimately, they cannot really teach him. A man's personal experiences alone have substance for such learning; pain and sorrow are mere abstractions when they are used as words and tell nothing of the fact of inevitable tragedy. Thus he ends his journey alone, on the Via Crucis, the natural path for man.[7] Jerusalem provides no hint of a transcendent peace the past was supposed to offer. Even so, Clarel remains there knowing that life in all its bleakness must be faced and endured. All else is illusion and escape.

The whole direction of the poem, then, is toward a way of life for Clarel after faith has died for him. The different ways are expressed through the many characters he meets, "as if by a thousand examples from the lives of other men one might find an answer to one's own."[8] A veritable *tabula rasa,* he is "wishful from everyone to learn" (II, v, p. 159).

Clarel's experience in the Holy Land involves a series of eight possibilities, each one posed by a character, or a set of characters, each one representing a solution to the religious and psychological problem of faith:

1. Can he accept the orthodox western religion expressed in the words and lives of Nehemiah, the Dominican, the Copt monks, and the Franciscan?

2. If orthodox religion is unworkable for him, why not accept the modern substitutions of business, progress, science, and humanitarianism, as practiced by the Banker, the Presbyterian Elder, Margoth, and Derwent, the spokesmen for the new world?

3. Why not bolt from reason and gratify his sensual desires, as Glaucon and the Prodigal do?

4. Romantic love and maternal nourishment in Ruth and Agar can provide immediate surcease, but can they sustain the "traveler" for a lifetime?

5. If all three—religion, the new world, and romance—are without meaning, why not cast himself outside their influence and join the misanthropes, Celio, Mortmain, and Ungar?

6. Since such antisocial attacks avail no happiness, perhaps it is better to avoid society and its sorrow and imitate Vine and Agath?

7. Perhaps no one answer can be found, no one way of life is best. Therefore, is not Rolfe correct in an eclectic approach to life, his endless questions complementing continuous participation?

8. No answer can be found. It rests only with Allah, as the Druze says on the pilgrimage. One survives. Nothing else matters—questions, harangues, cajoling—for man cannot change the inexorable movement of fate.

Phrased in such a series of alternatives, the poem appears as a sentimental saga of a boy growing up. But Melville weaves the alternatives in and out of the hero's life so that the didactic effect which might otherwise have emerged remains somewhat concealed, even to Clarel. He does not take up the first question, resolve it, approach the second, resolve it, and so on through the end of his meetings with the different characters. The impressions are more blurred for him; he puzzles over them until the very end, when he plunges into the fact of tragedy in the death of Ruth, and attempts his own spiritual resurrection. The rest of his life will shape itself around this fact and out of the influences which prepared him for it. Although these eight life styles, or psychological, philosophical, and religious postures, constitute for Clarel a series of dramatic choices, they readily fall into two distinct categories; that is, if Clarel represents Melville in any one-to-one relationship, then the first three at no point in the narrative can offer any lasting attraction. Perhaps a case can be made for the sensual lure of the third because of Melville's primitivism in *Typee* and his ambiguity in the "Mysterious Night in London" scene in *Redburn.* But Fayaway and Kory-Kory never really win Tommo over to a life of ease as much as they present a temptation that the hero finally puts away in an escape to the *Julia.* And Wellingborough is not even an onlooker at the debauch he was fearful would take place. All of Melville's life and writings attest to a distaste for the licentious or casual handling of the senses. His antagonism for orthodox religion, commerce, and science is equally well documented. Melville faces Clarel with these three alternatives, however, because his options are open when he arrives in Palestine, as Melville's were at Jaffa in 1857. The first three alternatives will be discussed in the following pages, and the following chapter will take up the other five, more important possibilities.

1. Can he accept the orthodox western religion expressed in the words and lives of Nehemiah, the Dominican, the Copt monks, and the Franciscan?

Of the many outside persons of influence, Nehemiah is the first in the order of the poem to act on Clarel. But he is not first in importance, for his blind faith is unacceptable, even farcicial, from the outset. He is a protagonist of the heart, however, one whose open compassion for a man shunned by all others, a veritable "trunk of woe," wins him as a person to Clarel at once (I, xxvi, pp. 86-7). His scorn for material comforts impresses Clarel, as does his zeal in preparing the way for the Lord. But his unquestioning total acceptance of life is sophomoric. The Scriptures stir his heart and constitute a way of life, but his unthinking daily recreation of them is in a world which has lost God as a center. The sacred words of prophets, evangelists, and saints ignore the contradictory realities of life, and are as effective for humanity as are his attempts to remove stones from the ruins of Jerusalem. The tracts he distributes are munched by camels, speared by Arabs, and scorned by bandits, just as they would be were they distributed by Christ Himself. Such innocence unliberated by experience becomes degenerate.[9] Melville would have all the Nehemiahs, Pierres, and Billys live in a world with Adam where innocence could survive. But there is no such place. This is why Nehemiah is a "somnambulist" in the poem. He is literally asleep through many of the days he shares with Clarel; intellectually, he is perpetually asleep. On the last night of his life, like St. John, he dreams of heaven and appropriately walks in his sleep to that "New Jerusalem" which is, in reality, drowning in the Dead Sea. Earlier in the journey, when the crag of Petra stood out in grim representation of the wasteland and death, he slept there in peace. It is ironic, therefore, and yet fitting in Melville's consistent handling of such "sophomores," that he die in the wilderness. And yet he is not like Delano and Billy in their artlessness, for earlier in life he experienced terror and calamity to rival Job. He captained a ship with an obsessive will like Ahab's that ended in death for his crew and ignominious rescue for him. His second ship sank to the bottom of the sea thereafter, a victim of a whale's frontal attack.[10] Rolfe suggests that the two incidents account for Nehemiah's total submission to the will of God.

> In Calvin's creed he put his trust;
> Praise heaven, and said that God was good,
> And his calamity but just.
>
> [I, xxxvii, p. 122]

They also explain for Clarel the rigid look of horror he saw on Nehemiah during one of the saint's many naps and remind him of how Nehemiah obsequiously insists upon calling himself the worst of God's sinners. But Clarel cannot comprehend why Nehemiah should so accuse himself or yield such blind obedience to a God who manifests His will in obviously diabolic acts. Experience should lead the innocent into awareness; otherwise man is no different from the animal or the child. Brutal experience that leads back to innocence is a waste.[11]

The blind faith of the Syrian Monk has a sophomoric quality as well, although an element of it remains unconsciously with

Clarel at the end of the poem. His hermit's robe, pinned together with a thorn, covers a pitifully thin body weakened by a long fast in the mountains. He tells the pilgrims that earlier in life he committed a grave sin of doubt, which drove him into the desert to do penance. He remained on the Quarantanian mountain for forty days and there induced a reenactment of the temptation of Jesus, with himself in the role of Christ tempted by Satan. After the harrowing experience, God entered his soul and gave him a contentment his appearance belies (II, xviii, pp. 198-201). In all of this he is another Mortmain: both retreat to a mountain fast, like Jacob, wrestle in a personal battle for faith, return as prophets, and accept pain as inescapable. Unlike Mortmain, however, his prophecy rests on faith.

> 'The grave will test;
> But He, He *is*, though doubt attend;
> Peace will He give ere come the end.'—
>
> [II, xviii, p. 200]

He knows that God still hides behind a cloud of human understanding, but that contentment comes precisely at the moment of recognition and acceptance of it as the great mystery of the universe. Although his sincerity is evident to all of his listeners, the imaginative recreation of the temptation and epiphany scenes appears to Rolfe as only an "ecstasy of fast," and to Vine as simple discovery of pain as the fact of life. The narrator also implies autosuggestion rather than divine communion, citing as evidence the act of flagellation, when the Monk squeezes a stone until blood pours out over his hand. His influence seems negligible in the poem not because of these reactions, but because he is with the pilgrims for only a brief period and because Clarel appears untouched by him. Yet his spiritual battles anticipate the later ones that Clarel will suffer and the decision for or against life that he will be forced to make. The Monk is in this a "later John the Baptist" preparing the way for the young agnostic. But Clarel knows nothing of this at their point of contact and cannot accept the Monk's blind obedience, even though it is, like Nehemiah's, born in suffering. Admirable though it is for both "saints," Clarel cannot follow their lead into faith.

Another protagonist of the heart and unquestioning faith is Brother Salvaterra, the Franciscan who appropriately meets the pilgrims at Bethlehem: like the unpretentious town he is of simple faith. His charming account of the birth and subsequent events of Christ's life advertises his own gentle self, but it presents a religion compounded of sweetness and fairy tales. The Dominican, on the other hand, offered the group on an earlier day an example of a religious whose unquestioning obedience marks his sanctity and one whose cogent arguments defending the Church on a natural level were difficult to refute. His citation of the Church's admonition to a spiritual democracy and his accusation that science limits itself only to the nature of things appealed to Clarel. But acceptance of a personal God of love, ministering providentially to humanity is something more than the refutation of science or the sharing of brotherhood. The Franciscan and the Dominican are exemplary individuals and have discovered in their lives a measure of peace, but their way is not one for Clarel to follow.

The monks at Mar Saba seem to have found their happiness too. They ease the burden for Clarel at their monastery after the terror of the Dead Sea and the death of Nehemiah. But he is not impressed by their sanctity. He finds distasteful, for example, their perpetuation of a myth concerning the Easter fire, despite the fact that Rome long ago declared it a superstition and a fraud (III, xvi, pp. 339-42). The blind abbot, with his hermit's love of jeweled relics, also presents abuses of religion rather than exemplary actions that lead to God. His religious snobbery includes contempt for the Pope in Rome whom he

deemed but Protestant—
A Rationalist, a bigger Paine—
Heretic, worse than Arian;
He lumped him with that compound mass
Of sectaries of the West, alas!
[III, xxiii, pp. 368-69]

The episode at Mar Saba, far from being the Purgatory that the climb from the Dead Valley promised, gives no enlightenment to Clarel. The religion at the monastery may be as old as the structure itself, but it is as dead as the "Death" password demanded by the mad monk, Cyril.

Except for Mortmain's death there, Mar Saba as an influence or a memory is lost on Clarel.

2. If orthodox religion is unworkable for Clarel, why not accept the modern substitutions of business, progress, science, and humanitarianism, as practiced by the Banker, the Presbyterian Elder, Margoth, and Derwent, the spokesmen for the new world?

Melville held ambivalent views on the orthodox Christian Church, even though the characters just now discussed had little to offer the hero. But *Clarel* contains no mixed beliefs whatsoever concerning nineteenth-century thought. While it is true that the final meaning of the poem insists upon Clarel picking up the pieces of his life so that he can begin anew, nowhere does Melville suggest that it be on the terms offered by the age. Clearly, Clarel knows that a cultural failure and the religious vacuum he shares with the rest of the western world are symptomatic of the nineteenth century. Palestine symbolizes this modern consciousness for him, an area, in Sedgwick's words, "parched by lack of faith and wasted by too much celebration."[12] The stars of heaven have disappeared, and chaos rules in their place everywhere. Progress avails nothing, and, as Sedgwick points out, "Science only advances man's ignorance, giving instruments to subhuman materialism."[13] Faith and poetry are dead, even in Judea, where the footstep of Christ should have left a trace for the heart and imagination. This life in the western world, without meaning or promise, in Chase's words, "has withdrawn its richness or ecstasy and is no longer tragic but simply progressive."[14] The promise of life, liberty, and the pursuit of happiness that constituted the

American plan to avoid tragedy was, in reality, an attempt to accomplish what Christ had recommended to the world almost nineteen hundred years before. But the dream brought no more happiness to man than dreams ever can do. The vision of a New Eden discloses a myopic historical perspective and an unwillingness to face empirical reality. The exhortations by prophets of progress, like George N. Curtis, for men to become today the giants they were destined to be, hardly convinced Melville, who loved the individual man as much as Curtis or Whitman ever did, but who mourned even more the fact of his pygmy condition. Accordingly, *Clarel* tells of the crash of the dream and boldly underscores the failure in western civilization after two thousand years of idealism.[15]

Clarel's first bitter disappointment in the wasted "Rose of Sharon" land foreshadows the successive disillusions which he suffers on the pilgrimage. Culture and religion, except in isolated cases, are nonexistent there. The city St. John saw "so bright/With sardonyx and ruby" lies a sunken wreck in a wasted desert. The august site of the Last Supper was, in Christ's time, and is still, within a stone's throw of a garbage dump.

> Pit too they mark where long ago
> Dull fires of refuse, shot below,
> The city's litter, smouldering burned,
> Clouding the glen with smoke impure,
> And griming the foul shapes obscure
> Of dismal chain-gangs in their shame
> Raking the garbage thither spurned:
> Tophet the place—transferred, in name,
> To penal Hell.
>
> [I, xxi, p.86]

Rich traditions linking present with past cause only laughter:

> But here
> The Spahi, with another cheer
> Into a vein of mockery ran,

Toasting the feast of Ramadan,
Laughing thereat, removed from fear.
[III, xiv, p. 322]

The guard, Belex, "Type of the pure Osmanli breed," wears clothes hinting of "the Jew bazaar and moth." Djalea, suspected to be an Emir's son, now earns his keep as a guide for travelers. And where once the visitors were reverent pilgrims, now tourists clutter the shrines. They drink and dance their orgies in monasteries, and some find Nazareth an ideal hunting spot for birds. The Jewish and Christian pretense to the lineage of Palestine rings hollow in the fact of the Muslims' control of the land. The Jews especially have renounced the land, tradition, and their family blood to conform to the outside world's artificial standards.

"Well, so much he,
Averse to Aaron's cipher dark
And mystical. Society
Is not quite catholic, you know,
Retains some prejudices yet—
Likes not the singular; and so
He'd melt in, nor be separate—
Exclusive. And I see no blame.
Nor rare thing is it in French Jew,
Cast among strangers—traveling too—
To cut old grandsire Abraham
As out of mode."
[IV, xxviii, pp. 505-6]

Symptomatic renunciation of tradition and unconcern for dignity carry the day, with the Clarels who dig into the past for beauty and meaning of existence regarded as foolish. Ungar's flight from his country where "honor's out of date" must end in the discovery that nowhere in the modern world will honor be found a negotiable virtue.

Our New World bold
Had fain improved upon the Old;
But the hemispheres are counterparts.
[IV, v, p. 422]

It could hardly be otherwise in an age "So infidel in equipage," in which skepticism dictates freedom from any and all restrictions. Laws are "scribbled by law-breakers, creeds/ Scrawled by free-thinkers," so that men can supplant faith with a knowledge which will set them free. "Faith's receding wave" prepares the way, these thinkers say, for the final liberation of man from the tyranny of God (III, v, pp. 292-94). Yet history runs in cycles to fault such thought. In the great Ciceronian Age, "To bereave/Of founded trust in Sire Supreme/Was a vocation" (I, xxxi, p. 106). That age of sophists so destroyed belief in God that Tully prophesied men would never believe again. And yet it was in this pagan Rome that Christ's mission thrived. Now, the higher criticism of the nineteenth century, particularly in the expressions of Renan and Strauss, presents the rich, humanitarian virtues of Jesus but denies his Godhead: with the aid of Niebuhr, it puts to rest the mythical tales of Zion (I, xxxiv, p. 112). Irreligion holds the minds of men as a consequence; they exult in their license but do not estimate the value of their loss.

"Flamen, flamen, put away
Robe and miter glorious:
Doubt undeifies the day!
Look, in vapours odorous
As the spice-king's funeral-pyre,
Dies the Zoroastian fire
On your altars in decay:
The rule, the Magian rule is run,
And Mythra abdicates the sun!"
[IV, xvi, p. 464]

The autonomy of each man frees him from the commands of State and Church. Democracy grants him the absolute right to

The years before the Civil War involved Melville in a struggle to be free from the lure of the quick dollar. "Bartleby," on one level, surely indicates this. But Melville's wrangling with publishers over royalty rights and an overall concern for dwindling income are noticeably missing after 1860. In the same way, business has no appeal for Clarel. It is virtually absent in the poem as a potent force or influence. The Banker, Glaucon, the Lesbian, and the Prodigal are the only ones directly connected with commerce and they play minor roles. Each of them is a voluptuary, using the marketplace to provide him with the luxuries of the world. The sumptuous house built for the Banker in Thessalonica allows him a beautiful view of Olympus, but he knows nothing of Jove and never heard of St. Paul. His only concern is money: "His bonds he scanned, and weighed his gold" (II, i, p. 144). Cigarettes, rich angora rugs, exotic rose wines, the latest clothes from Paris, all constitute his way of life. The fortune amassed in his lifetime is so a part of him that he will not allow death itself to destroy it. He chooses a likely successor in Glaucon, "The youth with gold at free command." Both are accomplished financial schemers, bon viv- and as shallow as their romantic hatred of the wor- Their refusal to continue to the Dead Sea is o- by Melville to remove them from the is so negligible that their presence a unnoticed by the others. Their symbo- taken by the Prodigal, a third represent-

He traveled for a Lyons hous
Which dealt in bales luxurious

A "toy of Mammon," the Lyonese considers sensual stopover on one of his business trips. Clarel amounts to little more than a nineteenth-c of traveling salesmen jokes, with his sexual sophis lighting Clarel's naiveté. Actually, as he does with Melville uses him less as a representative of busin an advocate of licentious life.

perform as freely as he wishes in society, and enlightened philosophy enables him to penetrate the deepest mysteries. His nineteenth-century egocentric infallibility makes the establishment of other and new churches necessary. The once-prized unity gives way to sects and divisions which ironically bind men in fetters they never knew before.

Besides: how was it even at home?
Behind the mellow chancel's rail
Lurked strife intestine. What avail
The parlor-chapel's liberal?
The hearers their own minds elect;
The very pews are each a sect;
No one's opinion's steadfast sway:
A wide, an elemental fray.
As with ships moored in road unsafe,
When gales augment and billows chafe,
Hull drives 'gainst hull, endangering all
In crossing cables; while from thrall
Of anchor, others, dragged amain,
Drift seaward: so the churches strain,
Much so the fleets sectarian meet
Doubt's equinox.
[III, xxi, p. 359]

In the past, only the aristocrat through disciplined learning came to doubt certain tenets of faith. But "Now the barber's clerks do swell/In cast clothes of the infidel" (II, xxvi, p. 231). The age dispels prophets and sibyls because the full use of reason makes each man self-sufficient.

"Lodged in power, enlarged in all,
Man achieves his last exemption—
Hopes no heaven, but fears no fall,
King in time, nor needs redemption."
[VI, viii, pp. 430-31]

But if business, symptomatic of the age's cultural vacuum, plays next to no part in the poem, natural science does. Not that its spokesmen, Margoth and the Presbyterian Elder, have anything of value to offer Clarel. But Melville's contempt for them as individuals and for their way of life goes beyond their involvement with the young theologian. Their insistence on scientific knowledge harnessing the brutal energies of nature held a certain appeal for Melville because he, too, found nature antagonistic or indifferent to man. But their pygmean findings solve nothing when the great human problems of sin, suffering, and freedom remain unexplained. Scientists who believe they can soar to ultimate truths inevitably learn the moral of "The Bell Tower." In that story, Bannadonna is appropriately buried under his own creation. Woodruff says of him,

> Because he dared to live in a vertical dimension of cosmic idealism and sought mastery over nature, he is struck down by the horizontal dimension of historical time his pride caused him foolishly to ignore.[19]

Melville believed that for all the ingenious discoveries of science, moral and physical evils are not relieved one jot.[20] The mechanical tools they design to afford a man leisure time for contemplation and rest actually rob him of dignity and transfer him into a machine himself. This evaluation of the Industrial Age, like Irving's and Cooper's, can be found in almost all of his works, but nowhere with as much force as in "The Tartarus of Maids."

> Not a syllable was breathed. Nothing was heard but the low, steady overruling hum of the iron animals. The human voice was banished from the spot. Machinery—that vaunted slave of humanity—here stood menially served by human beings, who served mutely and cringingly as the slave serves the Sultan. The girls did not so much seem accessory wheels to the general machinery as mere cogs to the wheels.[21]

Like Benjamin Franklin, scientists are jacks of all trades and masters of none because they exclude imagination, and because they are not poets.[22] Their crass optimism provides the joke of "The Happy Failure." In that story, a young boy travels to an isolated swamp with his uncle, where the uncle uncovers a machine he has been working on for ten years—the Great Hydraulic-Hydrostatic Apparatus. Its purpose is to benefit mankind by emptying all of the swamps throughout the land. The uncle fails in his foolish venture, of course. But the failure comes to a happy ending when, near death in disappointment, he recognizes his foolish ambition and thereafter becomes a better and happier man. He is an isolated case, however, only one in a group of thousands who think the world will be a better place as a result of their scientific contributions.

For Melville, science's basic premise leads back to ignorance; the world contains mysteries undreamed of by scientists.

> But solve the world! Scarce that he'll do:
> Too wild it is, too wonderful.
>
> [IV, iii, p. 418]

Attempts to plumb her wildness only further the work of the Devil, as Ungar says:

> "Arts are tools;
> But tools, they say are to the strong:
> Is Satan weak? weak is the wrong?
> No blessed augury overrules:
> Your arts advance in faith's decay:
> You are but drilling the new Hun
> Whose growl even now can some dismay;
> Vindictive in his heart of hearts,
> He schools him in your mines and marts—
> A skilled destroyer."
>
> [IV, xxi, p. 480]

Man is "disenobled—brutalized/By popular science —Atheized/Into a smatterer—" (IV, xxi, p. 483). Margoth's appearance typifies this: a short, knobby figure, hammer always in hand and a pouch of dug-up earth at his side.[23] The enlightenment of science he preaches is manifest in his animal features and his canine prying and boring into the earth: he appears as an ant from the heights of Mar Saba (III, i, p. 278), and his words of wisdom produce only the echoed braying of an ass (II, xxxiii, pp. 257-58). The makeup of the Presbyterian Elder similarly expresses the cold, harsh reason Science brings to measure the claims of Scripture and history: he carries an ugly thorn cane, a pruning knife, a measuring tape, and, significantly, two horse-pistols. Neither man bothers with conversation, for talk and abstract ideas have no reference to empirical truth. Theology and philosophy confound a man's mind and should be considered as fairy tales.

> It needs we scientists remand
> Back from old theologic myth
> To geologic hammers.
>
> [II, xx, p. 206]

In the poem, the Elder would strip away all ornaments and destroy all temples of the Church unless they can verify Christ's actual, historic presence there (II, x, p. 174). Because the venerable sites of Judea produce nothing, Margoth insists they must be razed to make way for

> Rails, wires, from Olivet to the sea,
> With station in Gethsemane.
>
> [II, xx, p. 207]

Just as he renounces his heritage—"Who's Moses"?—so Margoth challenges God and the ancient world as he boastfully draws a huge hammer over Mortmain's Southern Cross and inscribes

> "I, Science, I whose gain's thy loss,
> I slanted thee, thou slanting Cross."
>
> [II, xxxi, p. 252]

But for all of Margoth's defiance, his meaning and inscription are washed away at once by the rain.

Melville did not oppose science categorically. Many times in the poem the question is raised whether faith and science cannot come together. Melville in fact did not lament over science so much as he believed its rigid attitude prevented a man from arriving at an intelligent point of view.[24] Like Ruskin, however, he predicted that the Spencerean confidence in science and industry would end in dehumanization and deepen man's alienation.

> "Cut off! Cut off! Can'st feel elate
> While all the depths of Being moan,
> Though luminous on every hand,
> The breadths of shallow knowledge more expand?
> Much as a light-ship keeper pines
> Mid shoals immense, where dreary shines
> His lamp, we toss beneath the ray
> Of Science's beacon."
>
> [II, xxi, p. 210]

He considered restrictive science's investigation of nature an end in itself.

> Science but deals
> With Nature; Nature is not God;
> Never she answers our appeals,
> Or, if she do, but mocks the clod.
>
> [II, xxv, p. 228]

Man's curiosity over nature ends in a very short time. Discoveries through science end in technological improvement and human comfort but they touch only the baser side of humanity. A man can remain longer with mystery than he can with pat formulas. This is why Darwin quotes a poet, Shelley, rather than a scientist, when he is faced with the "Mysterious doubt" of the desert. Legends, in fact, fill a greater need in man than science can, contrary to Margoth's arguments, for they appeal to the imagination and allow him to soar.

> Those legends which, be it confessed,
> Did nearer bring to them the sky—
> Did nearer woo it to their hope
> Of all that seers and saints avow—
> Than Galileo's telescope
> Can bid it unto prosing Science now.
> [I, xxxv, p. 117]

Unless it can reveal man's inner self and the meaning of God and the universe, this cult of the "New Zealot to the Sun" must give way to the genuine myth-makers who are at least modest enough to believe they have not solved the riddle of the universe.

> But Science yet
> An effluence ampler shall beget,
> And power beyond your play—
> Shall quell the shades you fail to rout,
> Yea, searching every secret out
> Elucidate your ray.[25]

Margoth and the Elder fall into this cult of scientism, blind to everything they cannot see. This is why they are more a burlesque of reason than reasonable men, and why they never touch Clarel at all.

It is clear that the confident promises of commerce, science, and progress have no substance for Clarel. He fled all of their programs when he left America, precisely because he found them unsatisfactory. Euphoric philosophers and political activists who espouse the coming millenium for the world have no importance either, because they fail to recognize that life, like the tortoise, has a black side as well. "Wise Derwent" is such a foolish optimist, a recreation of Chaucer's Monk—"A priest he was . . ."—who rejects the puritan side of St. Paul and accepts the Apostle's advice, "Rejoice ye evermore." As "A priest o' the club," his "easy skim" suppresses conscience to avoid the pangs of life. This is why the Lesbian is drawn to him at once.

> "Priest, he's a grape, judicious one—
> Keeps on the right side of the sun."
>
> [III, xii, p. 326]

When Clarel is put off by his license, Derwent finds the Prodigal "the pleasantest small fellow," just as he associates Don Hannibal not with the war that left him dismembered but with their last hilarious meeting at *The Cock* in London. Life's joys are for the taking; the ascetic pain of medieval monks has no part in enlightened "modern religion." Melville calls him a "Templar," a "cavalier and monk in one," like the Templars he described in an earlier short story.

> We know indeed—sad history recounts it—that a moral blight tainted at last this sacred Brotherhood (the Templars). Though no sworded foe might outskill them in the fence, yet the work of luxury crawled beneath their guard, gnawing the core of knightly troth, nibbling the monastic vows, till at last the monks' austerity relaxed to wassailing, & the sworn knights-bachelors grew to be but hypocrites and rakes.[26]

As a spokesman for the "broader clergy," Derwent insists that "All turns or alters for the best," as though he could learn no lesson from Voltaire's Pangloss. He is the "Pontiff of optimists extreme," ready with an easy quip or with an explanation of indisposition for the jeremiads and lamentations of his neighbors. He glides like quicksilver over doubt and complexity: "be not extreme, midway is best." He describes the rock of terror as "queer," Mortmain's prophecies as "mad," and Salvaterra's sanctity as "unmanly." He dismisses Sodom and Gomorrah with "Ah, Genesis," Rolfe's biting song on the modern loss of divine light with "Fine, very fine," and the Habbibi and mad Cyril incidents with a dancing jig. Ready to laugh at any jest, he finds no humor in Don Hannibal's invitation to share a coffin. His religion embraces all peoples and theories, except those of gloom and damnation.

> Things all diverse he would unite;
> His idol's an hermaphrodite.
>
> [III, xvi, p. 342]

This manipulation makes him a clown, for only a robust circus man can "harmonize for all/Moses and Comte, Renan and Paul." He is like King Abruzzi in *Mardi*, who wishes to live only in sunlight. He fits the style of the cultivated Marquis de Grandvin.

> In best of worlds if all's not bright,
> Allow, the shadows chased by light,
> Though rest for neither yet may be.[27]

He is another Reverend Falsgrave, "trying to cheerfulize Christ's moan." His faith that fits like "an over-easy glove" and has no place for Job forces Clarel to the reluctant conclusion that Derwent's charm is the sum of his nature, a quality he has no need to acquire.

Once Derwent comes on the scene he is involved in all of the issues and actions that follow. His personality is engaging, except to the extremists, Mortmain and Ungar. Melville knew that attraction of such latitudinarians, like Henry Ward Beecher and Washington Gladden, was based more on their manners, educated speech, and cultural awareness than on a theology rooted in sin and redemption. Derwent fits this style as he gently avoids controversy by becoming all things to all men. His buoyant outlook keeps his eyes on the sky, making him a fool no different from Margoth, who peers intently at the earth. Melville believes that neither character evaluates man and nature correctly. What Derwent and other idealists fail to consider is the fact of man's fallen nature. The fall in the Old Testament was for Melville the cardinal fact of man's existence.

> In my eyes, it is the only metaphysical truth in that book even though it appears in the form of allegory.[28]

The fall is the actuality of the natural universe. Accordingly, Original Sin is the proper metaphor for awful reality, a symbol of the blight that man must recognize and live with. Ahab's fatal mistake lies in his attempt to impose meaning on something that operates outside this limitation. Conversely, the quests of Pierre and the Confidence-Man lead nowhere because faith in a benevolent ideal manifests an ignorance of life's meaning.[29]

This is not to say that Melville held only a pejorative view of life. On the contrary, whatever richness life had to offer he felt men should take, so long as they retained their dignity. But to dream that all is richness ill prepares one for the awakening to reality, as he wrote to Sophia Hawthorne in 1852.

> For though we know what ought to be; what it would be very sweet and beautiful to be; yet we can't be it. That is most sad, too. Life is a long Dardanelles . . . the shores of which are bright with flowers which we want to pluck, but the bank is too high; and so we float on & on, hoping to come to a landing-place at last—but swoop! we launch into the great sea! Yet the geographers say, even then we must not despair, because across the great sea, however desolate and vacant it may look, lie all Persia & the delicious lands roundabout Damascus.[30]

In Ishmael's quest Melville lauds man's attempts to find transcendent light in the darkness of life: "And so, through all the thick mists of the dim doubts in my mind, divine intuitions now and then shoot, enkindling my fog with a heavenly ray."[31] But to determine one's life by intuitions of divinity is as foolhardy as to doubt that there are such intuitions. Things must be taken for what they are, examined and accepted in all of their ambiguity.

> I love to sail forbidden seas, and land on barbarous coasts. Not ignoring what is good, I am quick to perceive a horror, and could still be social with it—would they let me—since it is but well to be on friendly terms with all the inmates of the place one lodges in.[32]

Melville's contempt for the Transcendentalists, meliorists, and for optimists generally, appears in the foolish ideals and behavior of the New Apostles in *Pierre.* They lack a knowledge of this world and its inscrutability, and, like Scribe in "I and My Chimney," offer to men "a false hope and a distorted reality."[33] Idealism, in any form, fails to account for the "empirical world of actuality." Oliver, in "Cock-A-Doodle-Do," and Mark Winsome and Egbert, in *The Confidence-Man,* preach the same mystical nonsense.

The myopic vision of optimists leads them to believe that man can be regenerated. Christian idealists rest their hopes on this dream, and yet the world is no more Christian now than it was before the coming of Christ.

> "The world but joined the Creed divine
> With prosperous days and Constantine;
> The world turned Christian, need, confess,
> But the world remained the world, no less:
> The world turned Christian, need confess,
> Hearts change not in the change of gods.
> Despite professions, outward shows—
> So far as working practice goes,
> More minds with shrewd Voltaire have part
> Than now own Jesus in the heart."
>
> [IV, xviii, p. 470]

The nature of man cannot be changed, no matter how high he gazes into the skies: he cannot see beyond the limitations of his eye. Nor can he be reformed by sweeping movements to a perfected civilization. The society that turns against Jimmy Rose after he loses his money is no better and no worse than the man-of-war world Redburn and White-Jacket are introduced to or the one that crucified Christ. Poverty and physical ills should be cured wherever possible. But to go beyond this and attempt a remedy for man's soul because heaven lies within man's reach, expresses the same shallowness that Derwent demonstrates in his gloss over the failure of Christianity. Mortmain has no such notions of perfectibility. Like Ungar, he acquires this knowledge through pain. Despite the harsh gift of bastardy that life offers at birth, "peace and goodwill was his acclaim." At an early age, he dedicates his life to a pursuit of the "uncreated Good," so that humanity can prosper. But in him "Precocities of heart outran/The immaturities of the brain" (II, iv, p. 156). His painful discovery that "Malice divides with ignorance," brings him full circle, his life amounting to nothing more than a quixotic effort to fling "a rainbow o'er that wreck."

All reformers face the same fate: "Experience with her sharper touch/Stung Mortmain" (II, iv, p. 156). The amputated condition of Don Hannibal attests to this knowledge; and Ungar's scarred evidence of the romantic Confederate mission that failed expresses an older, cynical reformer. Social and political experts cannot alleviate human suffering. They forget that liberty from himself can never be given to a man. This is the only positive reform that could aid him, and it is impossible of attainment. This is the heavy moral of "The Bell-Tower" and, specifically, of the epigraph:

> Like Negroes, these powers own man sullenly; mindful of their higher master; while serving, plot revenge.
>
> The world is apoplectic with high-living of ambition; and apoplexy has its fall.
>
> Seeking to conquer a larger liberty, man but extends the empire of necessity.
>
> from a private manuscript[34]

Man is what he is, visited by desires for freedom and bound by unfreedom. No evidence can be cited to prove what happiness is available, or that it results from unrestrained freedom. On the contrary, man tires quickly in a free condition where all people and things are leveled. This is why he needs and respects law: law preserves him in an acceptable order that dissipates at once when it is removed.

> At this, some riders feel that awe
> Which comes of sense of absent law,
> And irreligious human kind,
> Relapsed, remanded, reassigned
> To chaos and brute passions blind.
>
> [II, xxiii, p. 217]

In the political currents of the twentieth century, these conclusions would have Melville appear an ultra conservative. Yet he was a consistent democrat in spirit, not unlike the Dominican's definition:

> In this gown
> I sat in legislative hall
> A champion of true liberty—
> God's liberty for one and all—
> Not Satan's license. Mine's the state
> Of a staunch Catholic Democrat.
>
> [II, xxv, p. 226]

Nathalia Wright also considers him a democrat, although his "world has an aristocratic cast. When invoking the spirit of equality his aim was not to degrade but to ennoble, to exalt the common multitudes, and to infuse the veins of all creatures with one royal blood."[35] This is surely the meaning of "Knights and Squires" in *Moby-Dick*.

> Men may seem detestable as joint stock-companies and nations; knaves, fools, and murderers there may be; men may have mean and meagre faces; but man, the ideal, is noble and so sparkling, such a grand and glowing creature, that over any ignominious blemish in him all his fel-

> lows should run to throw their costliest robes. . . . But this august dignity I treat of, is not the dignity of kings and robes, but that abounding dignity which has no robed investiture. Thou shalt see it shining in the arm that wields a pick or drives a spike; that democratic dignity which, on all hands, radiates without end from God; Himself! The great God absolute! The centre and circumference, our divine equality![36]

Democracy is the formula that mystically unites Vere the Captain and Billy the deck-hand in an Abraham-Isaac relationship that results from mutual cognizance of human obligations, suffering, and love. The burden of Melville's brand of democracy tasks each individual, as it does Vere and Billy, because it rests on creative rather than instinctive acts, more often than not insisting that desires, pleasures, and instincts be set aside. The popular democracy that insists upon the release of all urges as a primitive and healthy program for harmony of self and society, he insisted, results in murder, flogging, starvation, malice, and other abuses. Man deserves more than this and can receive it through a proper balance of instinct and reason, of law and freedom. In this Melville blended a memory of idyllic life in the Marquesas with the Calvinist heritage he never renounced.

In addition to a perfective assessment of man, idealists insist upon a return to nature for sustenance and virtue. When man divorces himself from her, they argue, evil is created: in a world of indefectibility, where human instincts are harmonious with nature, evil cannot exist. Emerson's famous essay on nature provided such a religious-union formula for the better part of the nineteenth century. To Melville, however, a dissenter in virtually every aspect of the Transcendental approach, anyone who believes this and acts accordingly prepares his own disaster.

> Come out of the Golden Gate,
> Go round the Horn with streamers,
> Carry royals early and late;

> But, brother, be not over-elate—
> *All hands save ship!* has startled dreamers.[37]

The herb-doctor's sarcastic comments on the fictitious book "Nature in Disease" sum up in hyperbole Melville's views of nature as only benificent.

> "A title I cannot approve; it is suspiciously scientific. *Nature in Disease?* As if nature, divine nature, were aught but health; as if through nature disease is decreed! But did I not before hint of the tendency of science, that forbidden tree? Sir, if despondency is yours from recalling that title, dismiss it. Trust me, nature is health; for health is good, and nature cannot work ill. As little can she work error. Get nature, and you get well."[38]

Nature to Melville is not contrary, as the herb-doctor implies here with his casuistry. It comprises good and evil in a balance that works out neutrality or indifference. The Maldive shark and the dove are created by the same god. Nature includes the desert and the oasis. But, unfortunately, man naively accepts the good of nature as normal and rages over the bad as unusual. Melville emphasized the opposite as true, but only as a counter to the transcendent views that carried the day. In his works he sees nature in the iceberg, the destructive whale and vicious shark, the avalanche, and the bitter waters of the Siddim. This side of nature is presented in *Clarel* over and over again. It appears in the eagle that steals Mortmain's cap. It visits death on Ruth and Agar through a raging fever. It deludes Nehemiah and drowns him in his sleep. It is constant, following inexorably the physical laws of the universe. Its resources stir up avarice among men and provoke them. Failure to recognize this black side of nature imperils man and brings him to disaster. Once recognizing it, however, man can live in its order, even where he cannot understand its meaning. Olivet and the Dead Sea both share in the mist and the sunshine of nature, and yet no man can comprehend why. Melville is saddened over nature's indifference, but he knows that human contentment comes only from imitating her neutrality.

3. Why not bolt from reason and gratify his sensual desires, as Glaucon and the Prodigal do?

One possible way out, and an easy one, from the fact of life's grimness is to heed the hedonist's advice: "Gather ye rosebuds." A cup of ale, a willing woman, a song and dance work wonders for the man with a "damp, drizzly November" in his soul. Whenever the "hypos get the upperhand," a man can dissipate them with a laugh and careless abandon of the senses. But Clarel's "monkish thong" binds his deepest sensual desires so that there is no real battle with the flesh. Nevertheless, on three occasions he is tempted to throw over his puritanism. Only the Prodigal's invitation troubles him; the first two repel him at once.

Shortly after the pilgrims leave Abdon's Inn, Clarel talks with Glaucon. He has already heard the Smyrniote's lush song and his call for pink as the color for life. Perhaps if his ignorance of Homer had not been so blatantly revealed, Clarel as a scholar could have listened with some patience to his cavalier views on sex and marriage. But a shallow sensibility that renders Glaucon blind to Olivet and deaf to "death" dismisses him from Clarel's mind as worthless.

The Lesbian similarly antagonizes Clarel. He rallies all the pilgrims at Mar Saba in a revelry that becomes a little allegory of "eat, drink and be merry, for tomorrow we die." Cut off from society, Mortmain, of course, refuses to join the feast. Ordinary chores take Djalea from the party, or at least he uses that as an excuse. But Clarel deliberately refuses to join the "bacchic throng." Melville indicates a certain prissiness in the student here, for the party seems inoffensive enough, one that follows naturally from the dread experience of the overnight vigil at the Dead Sea. This accounts for Rolfe joining the group and accepting the Lesbian as "an excusable poor sinner." Rolfe implicitly indicates that Clarel should not take seriously one who is obviously not broken "with fast and prayer," for his licentiousness comes naturally to a man from Lesbos:

> His home was, a lax Paradise,
> An island yet luxurious seen,
> Fruitful in all that can entice.
>
> [III, xi, p. 314]

But Rolfe's protests over a man who falls outside "Observance of the stellar sphere" fail to impress Clarel. To him, the Lesbian's actions are a contemptible mockery of the holy Mar Saba. Frolicking songs of wine and women profane the sacred air. Like Glaucon's appeal, Clarel refuses to hear the Lesbian's call for sensual delight.

A third temptation stirs Clarel, however. In this case it is the Prodigal from Lyons who upsets him. The Prodigal comes at a propitious time, for the anxiety built up in Clarel over a return to Ruth is compounded by a deep fear that he is about to make a fatal mistake in marriage, and by a concern for death that borders on fixation. At such a time, the Prodigal represents the last call of the satyr to Clarel, his voluptuous appeal disguised as a possibility for Clarel to find the long-sought companion. The Lyonese tells him of the ideal mate he had on one of his jaunts in Peru, and how "the holidays flew" when they were together. The homosexual hint is Clarel's construction, however, for this wandering Jew has eyes only for beautiful, sensuous women. He recognizes Clarel's fear of the joyous life and his readiness to dwell on death and the doom of God. For the Prodigal, this preeminence of "Cape Horn over Damascus" sums up Western man's incapacity for joy. Fortunately, he has no Cape: some men are born under lucky stars and are not troubled with weighing things forever. Even the doleful things of Solomon have no reference to his life: instead of wisdom and lamentation in the Books of the Maccabees and Solomon he finds juicy accounts of sex. He advises Clarel to ignore

St. Bernard's gloomy commentaries on these books and to feast his eyes on the grapes and houris of Hafiz.

> Come, look at straight things more in line,
> Blue eyes or black, which like you best?
> Your Bella Donna, how's she dressed?
>
> [IV, xxvi, p. 497]

Sex is for the taking. Man cannot change the fact of his flesh. Nature herself makes a man responsive; when he ignores the body's call man thwarts nature's design.

Although Clarel ignored Glaucon and the Lesbian, the Prodigal's words cause him that night to dream of the conflict between Shushan's lure and the ascetic discipline of his own life. The dream affords him no resolution, so that the deepest impulses roused up by his roommate still disturb Clarel when he awakens. But the Prodigal offers only an illusion, Clarel concludes. In his waking hours a man comes to know bitterly that nothing in the senses can bring lasting ease.

> But who will bring to *me*
> That living water which who drinks
> He thirsteth not again! Let be:
> A thirst that long may anguish thee,
> Too long ungratified will die.
>
> [IV, xxviii, p. 503]

The solution of the hedonist fails to touch the spirit of man. The unresolved debate of the body and the soul is eternal.

Clarel occupied a considerable period of Melville's life in thought and composition. It is no surprise then to find echoes of previous writing, data of the poet's life, and summary judgments of the problems that were raised throughout the decades of his writing. The poem, more than any other single work, presents the ambiguities of choice that haunt a man in his pursuit of certitude and happiness, and concludes with the awful fact that truth is ephemeral and happiness unavailable. Translated into dramatic personal experience, this accounts for Clarel's final placement on the "natural street," the Via Crucis, at the end of the poem. But if the ambiguities defy explanation, the three possibilities just now discussed do so on a very low key. Failure by Clarel to utilize any of them satisfactorily produces neither intellectual confusion nor emotional setback. On the other hand, the alternative five possibilities, which will be discussed in the following chapter, contribute to the final tragedy.

IX

The Pain of Wisdom

"Humanity, thou strong thing, I worship Thee, not in the laureled victory, but in this vanquished one."
"The Encantadas"

"Praise be to God for the failure."
"The Happy Failure"

In *Clarel* the use of spokesmen for ideas obviated the interpolations, rhapsodies, and other artistic breaks in narration which comprised the prophetic quality of Melville's great prose. Except for Rolfe, each character clearly presents a point of view that reflects his life, and does so without the poet's attacks or support. But in the broad areas just discussed, with only the sincere Christians excluded, the spokesmen are freighted with notions of the new world that are repugnant to the author and, as a consequence of his art, to the reader as well. The poem does not suffer from this obvious bias because greater attention is given to the main theme, which deals less with the complexities of the age than it does with the personal problems of the hero. The two, of course, cannot be separated, as will be seen hereafter, particularly in the cases of Mortmain and Ungar. Even so, all of the spokesmen are important in the poem to the degree that they mirror the anxieties troubling Clarel and are honest in facing up to them. Everyone and everything revolve around him. At first glance, Ruth appears to be by far the most important single person in this regard, her presence affording Clarel immediate pleasure and hope for permanent happiness. Of the five, important, alternative ways of life to be discussed in the following pages, the other four are meaningless compared with the irresistible attraction she has for Clarel at the outset. In fact, the logic of the poem insists that the other seven possibilities on the pilgrimage would never have been raised for Clarel if Nathan's death had not suspended the consequences of his declaration to Ruth. It is because of this immediate and spontaneous commitment to her by Clarel and because she is intimately involved in the tragedy that Ruth poses for him one of the major decisions of his life. Ironically, fate's intervention robs him of that choice, thus leaving the question unanswered:

4. Romantic love for Ruth, with maternal nourishment from Agar, can provide immediate comfort, but can it sustain the "traveler" for a lifetime?

When Clarel commits himself to Ruth, he wants desperately to believe that the love of man and woman promises bliss or, at least, a contentment to still the insistent voice of loneliness. But Melville intended Ruth's appeal to him as only a siren's song, a promise that could not be met. For this reason, despite its critical part in the plot, the love affair enters into the poem in sketchy and unconvincing fashion. One critic suggests that Melville himself was constitutionally unable to derive pleasure or happiness from marriage; that, as a consequence, nowhere in his writings is the subject treated as a desirable end.[1] This is not difficult to support, for random sampling reveals such an attitude toward marriage. It is the finality of adventure, an accommodation to the prosaic demands of daily life: "Here, putting an end to his rovings, he marries."[2] All too soon in marriage, the ecstatic lovers settle into habits of relationship that erase arduous memories, as they do for Rip Van Winkle and his wife.

> But good or bad, time has a persistent, never-halting way of running on, and by so doing brings about wonderful

> changes and transformations. Ere long the bride developed into the dame; the bridegroom into that commonplace entity, the married man.[3]

The devoted couple of "Poor Man's Crumb's" are husband and wife in heroic fidelity, but almost less than persons in the daily struggle for survival. In the novels Ahab alone is married, and he only recently to a bride whose attraction is negligible next to the pull of the whale. Pierre is spiritually married to Isabel, a relationship that ends in disaster when the spiritual descends to the erotic. The wife of the narrator becomes an enemy as the marriage wears on in "I and My Chimney"; the wife is a wasted, dying thing in "Cock-A-Doodle-Do," subservient to a rooster. Hunilla stands as the exception, an exemplar of married love, but her image is doubtful because time has not tested the relationship. The courtship of Clarel and Ruth is not unique in this aspect, for the overriding presentiment and actuality of death follow the pattern of unhappiness of marriage readily discerned in Melville's other works.

However, at his entry into Jerusalem Clarel does need Ruth and his love for her is genuine if not ecstatic. But it is less insistent than the craving he has for any mate—male or female—who can bring him friendship. In this need, his mental and spiritual condition when he meets Ruth is like the depression of Ishmael in New Bedford, when he makes his first move back to the human race through "marriage" with Queegqueeg. Ruth's death, after her tacit promise to fulfill Clarel, parallels Yillah's disappearance from Taji. He also takes on a new view of life after his first impulse of love, but his dive into the depths of the universe's mystery and his absolute independence make Yillah only incidental in the long, Pacific search. As friend or lover, Ruth represents for Clarel the highest expression of human love attainable at the time, but, unlike Yillah, on a natural level alone. She comprises grace, innocence, and fertility; she is "a priestess of sweet charity." He sees in her virgin eyes the "Pure home of all we seek and prize." With her he can "win Eden back," and make Christ the Crucified and all other symbols of pain "Seem foreign—forged—incongruous."

But fate interrupts, and death interposes with its insistent motto: "Biers need be borne." Lovers' "flushful hope's aurora" takes on as illusory symbols the shell, the hummingbird, and flower, while the truest symbol—the death moth—hovers always overhead. Clarel misreads his forced separation from Ruth and foolishly believes that life will continue in romantic perfection upon his return. What comes in between the separation and reunion is the Dead Sea.

The separation gives Clarel an opportunity for second thoughts. The virginal Ruth touched a part of him that longed for spiritual perfection. In the short time of their acquaintance, he knew no other part of her nature. But in the distance of Mar Saba, he begins to fear the carnal side of woman corrupting his pure love.

> Possessing Ruth, nor less his heart
> Aye hungering still, in deeper part
> Unsatisfied. Can be a bond
> (Thought he) as David sings in strain
> That dirges beauteous Jonathan,
> Passing the love of woman fond?
> And may experience but dull
> The longing for it?
>
> [III, xxx, pp. 395-96]

Disclosure of any lower order threatens the purity of relationship.

> Can Eve be riven
> From sex, and disengaged retain
> Its charm? Think this—then may ye feign
> The perfumed rose shall keep its bloom,
> Cut off from sustenance of loam.
> But if Eve's charm be not supernal,
> Enduring not divine transplanting—
> Love kindled thence, is that eternal?
>
> [III, xxxi, p. 397]

Sexuality in Ruth shatters the dream for Clarel. St. Francis, St. John, the Blessed Mother, all knew a love free of impure self: "Marrying none is in heaven." Because he insists upon the same purity, Clarel fears a marriage where a wife, like Job's, can mock ideals, where a husband loses integrity in the symbolic removal of Adam's rib in marriage. Clarel wants Ruth, but he desires chastity more. The possible loss of this precious element through sexual union associates in his mind the image and name of Ruth with death, but on a level below consciousness. At Mar Saba, when Cyril the mad monk demands the countersign, he suggests "Death" to Clarel for he sees it in his face. Clarel immediately calls upon Ruth's memory to "Abash these base mortalities," but all that he conjures up is Ruth, like Beatrice, chastising his mortality (III, xxiv, pp. 373-74). Later, in Bethlehem, Derwent calls out the name of Ruth, Naomi's daughter, and thereby startles Clarel. But instead of a warm glow that suffuses the lover at such a moment, what comes to him is the painful remembrance of a funeral of a young Armenian virgin (IV, xvi, p. 461). This Ruth-death association accounts for the vision he has after Ruth's death, which includes Nehemiah, Celio, Mortmain, Nathan, and Agar in physical features exactly as he remembered them. But because he never really viewed Ruth as she was, a woman of earthly form, her appearance resembles the Pearl maiden, ethereal and inaccessible.

> But Ruth—ah, how estranged in face!
> He knew her by no earthly grace:
> Nor might he reach to her in place.
> Any languid vapors from them go
> Like thaw-fogs curled from dankish snow.
>
> [IV, xxxii, p. 518]

Ruth cannot fill Clarel's need for a mate because her carnal gift in marriage will destroy his Platonic conception of love. As a result, more than any other character in the poem, she functions exclusively as a symbol. Her death in Jerusalem, at the beginning of Lenten mourning, reenacts for Clarel the passion and death of Christ. Her pure image, or symbol, unconsciously fuses with his notion of Christ, and thereby incites unconscious expectations of her resurrection on Easter Sunday; like Celio, Clarel demands living evidence of a benevolent God. But Ruth remains in the tomb, a dead token of the laws of the universe. Her failure to rise completes his illusion of her as pure spirit and dashes any vague hope in a God of love and providence. Ruth's death also lays to rest the power of the Hebrew religion, which she also symbolizes, and the promise of immortality Clarel allowed himself to associate jointly with her being and Christianity. It cancels out all religious and social prescriptions for life proffered by outsiders. He achieves this wisdom appropriately by Epiphany Sunday; help will come from nowhere outside himself. At the point of discovery, he comes full circle, from despair at Jaffa to bereavement for Ruth and to deeper anxiety over his alienation. But in the movement he sheds the romantic melancholy of the student in escape and assumes total responsibility for his life on a daily basis. This mature self-identification flows from Ruth's gift of love and her factual death, each necessary to the other in tragedy, and both paradoxically requisite in the making of a hero.

5. If all three—religion, the new world, and romance—are without meaning for him, why not cut himself off completely from their influence and join the misanthropes, Celio, Mortmain, and Ungar?

Ruth's death does not break Clarel's heart. Melville had no Romeo-Juliet theme in mind when he wrote the poem. Love on a natural level could not satisfy him or Clarel. Ruth's death merely removes from Clarel the temptation to quit his search for ultimate truths. Married to Ruth, he might have become another Rip Van Winkle or John Marr, settled in the habit of relationship; he probably would be the grocer of Melville's little poem, buried in a prosaic life when his deepest wishes called for heroic adventure:

In La Mancha he mopeth,
  With beard thin and dusty;
He doteth and mopeth
  In library fusty—
'Mong his old folios gropeth:
  Cites obsolete saws
  Of chivalry's laws—
  Be the wronged one's knight:
  Die, but do right.
So he rusts and musts,
While each grocer green
Thriveth apace with the fulsome face
Of a fool serene.[4]

Melville loved all men who dive, even the foolish knight of La Mancha. Were Clarel to quit his search for a "grocer green" marriage, Melville would have scorned him as he does Derwent. Instead, Clarel continues and comes to a wisdom reserved for such divers. Along the way, however, he almost stumbles into the monomania of Celio, Mortmain, and Ungar. They shun the grocer's green life and attempt to "Be the wronged one's knight," like Quixote. All three are so dynamic and well-meaning in their unwillingness to live with evil that Clarel comes dangerously close to accepting them as exemplars.

Like Clarel, Celio, Mortmain, and Ungar, Melville was appalled by the evil in the world. Earlier discussion disclosed how he registered this repugnance; how the Manichean element so colored his sensibility that Moby-Dick, on one level, could become for him a mammoth symbol of evil; and how Claggart's motivation, or lack of it, fascinated and repelled him, as did Jackson's diabolic influence over the crew of the *Highlander.* Melville filled Celio, Mortmain, and Ungar with this *idée fixe,* and presented them to Clarel as working examples of the right way to hate evil but of the wrong way to attack it.[5] Their actions, accordingly, are intense but pitiful, their lives inevitably cut off from commonality because of overreaction to evil. Even when they start with the purest motives, such men—like Taji, Ahab, and Pierre—insist upon changing universal laws to suit their own ends, when life cannot be reshaped to meet their demands. Men must compromise their deepest desires and accept unbending cosmic precepts.

Clarel's confrontation with the three monomaniacs begins with Celio, although Clarel never exchanges a word with him. The understanding between them extends beyond any communication words could have afforded, however. Despite the fact that Celio comes to his state of exile from a background of Catholicism, and Clarel to his out of Protestant agnosticism, the two recognize in each other kindred souls, mates in distress. But the "boundless sea" of existence resists successful gams, in Melville's assessment of life, and Celio goes to his death completely alone, unmourned except for Clarel.

Celio has the mark of a vengeful God in the hump he carries on his back. The mark on his soul, however, troubles him more. He cannot rest content in the knowledge that Christ's life and death could effect no change in man's behavior.[6] Even worse for his own peace, because he cannot find genuine Christianity in the Catholic Church he renounces her and all religion. But without some anchored faith he has little chance of survival.

> At sea, in brig which swings no boat,
> To founder is to sink.
>
> [I, xii, p. 39]

Like Pierre, he demands to know why human actions contradict the ideas that Christ taught.

> 'Tis eighteen cycles now—
> Enigma and evasion grow;
> And shall we never find thee out?
> What isolation lones thy state
> That all we else know cannot mate
> With what thou teachest?
>
> [I, xiii, p. 43]

But men alone are not culpable: the pastoral promises of Christ were all delusions. Had He not spread assurances of redemption, the world could have moved along in stoical resignation. Christ's bleeding face of martyrdom has no relevance, particularly in a modern, corrupt world, where the evil face of Medusa fascinates and paralyzes the race. God should have foreseen this. Instead, He offered His Son to the world as a dove and failed to destroy the shark. After eighteen hundred years, Christ's mythical stories haunt civilization but are powerless to turn it to good. This is the cause of Celio's despair: Christianity's failure to convert man to goodness shows no salvation is possible.

Melville pictures Celio hobbling through St. Stephen's Gate, a nineteenth-century martyr to lost ideals. But whereas St. Stephen suffered death as testimony to Christ's word, Celio suffers and dies outside the gate, a witness to the collapse of Christianity. Even with his misanthropic gesture, however, Celio retains pity for mankind, as seen in one poignant episode. In it, a funeral cortege winds outside the gate and Celio mistakes it for a searching party out to fetch him. After he discovers its purpose, which has nothing to do with him, he cries for the corpse and for the mourners. This compassion burns so deeply in him that he cannot compromise for even a part of Christ's divine plan of perfection. He wants all of it for man, or nothing. If one cannot have the Christian life in full, nothing remains but chaos and death. Accordingly, he huddles against a wall, like Bartleby, and dies. His earlier cry to "Bice" echoes over the hills ironically, for no Beatrice of theology and grace comes to aid him. Like Christ, Melville implies, Dante only elaborated the religious myths that despairing men cling to.

Celio, Redburn, White-Jacket, Pierre, Bartleby's lawyer, and other compassionate Melville characters grieve over the human race in suffering and loss of perfection. Not one of them discovers permanent relief for mankind, nor takes consolation in the promise of life after death. When they despair like Bartleby, or transcend the problem like Mark Winsome, because they cannot abide the fact of earthly limitation, Melville pities them but marks them as failures or cowards: it is no major accomplishment to recognize disorder in the world. The greater task remains after the discovery: how can a person live here and now and prepare for future contingencies when hope is erased and pain increased? Celio, for one, dodges the question when he forages through the past and ignores present and future possibilities for action. He suffers greatly and unjustly. But his protests have little to offer Clarel, who insists upon all of life examined, experienced, and translated in earthly terms of time, space, and persons. Like Socrates before him, he believed the unexamined life is not worth living.

Mortmain repeats Celio's Gethsemane message: the bitter cup of life must be drunk. For him, Christ's chalice sums up the Christian religion in that life holds no happiness for man; the death of Christ after the drinking of gall sets the example for all mankind to follow. This is the meaning of the black skull cap Mortmain wears, a constant reminder of the death of the human spirit. Like Celio, he sees evil everywhere.

> "Then where?
> A Thug, the sword-fish roams the sea—
> The falcon's pirate in the air;
> Betwixt the twain, where shalt thou flee . . ."
>
> [II, x, p. 176]

Ghosts of Sodom haunt the world, and men work out their malice influenced by the star called Wormwood. War and bloodshed underline all their actions and prepare them for "hell's hot kingdom." History proves false the humanitarian dreams of Derwent and all other romancers. It proves that man's malicious designs must be yoked by authority.

> "Man's vicious: snaffle him with kings;
> Or, if kings cease to curb, devise
> Severer bit. This garden brings
> Such lesson. Heed it, and be wise
> In thoughts not new."
>
> [II, iii, p. 154]

But because this theme shocks society, stories of perfection and of civilizations in peace are invented.

> We've touched a theme
> From which the club and lyceum swerve,
> Nor Herr von Goethe would esteem;
> [III, iii, p. 285]

His return from the mountain vigil signals a new role for Mortmain in the group. Before the return, he expresses his bitterness in tirades against Derwent which actually amuse the other pilgrims. After his retreat on the mountain, the others cringe in the exposure of evil he presents. From the moment of his reappearance until his death, he presses upon them the blackness of his skull cap.[7] His scream of "Dies irae, dies illa"! after the masque at the monastery, echoes his other jeremiads as though he himself were a god of vengeance hurling down promises of hell. Like Bartleby, he has pierced through "the mystery of iniquity" to arrive at scorched self-identity and final isolation. Accordingly, he holds no further conversation at Mar Saba. He ferrets, instead, among the bones of ancient monks and acknowledges to Cyril the proper countersign "Despair." His renunciation of the human race appears complete in his willed death, which is attributed to no physical cause.

> With eyes still feeding on the Tree,
> Relapsed he lingered as in Lethe's snare.
> [III, xxviii, p. 389]

And yet, this is not complete despair, as though Mortmain could not accept the logic of his own nihilism. His last words, as he sits staring at the tree, are words of hope, not in the God he has sought but in the mystery of "the angel-tree" that hints of immortality.

> "Yet hear me in appeal to thee:
> When the last light shall fade from me,

> If, groping round, no hand I meet;
> Thee I'll recall—invoke thee, Palm;
> Comfort me then, thou Paraclete!
> The lull late mine beneath thy lee,
> Then, then renew, and seal the calm."
>
> [III, xxviii, p. 389]

He calls on the "Paraclete," the comforter, a synonym for the Holy Spirit, and thereby registers dependency upon something outside himself as a final action. This is the suffering of an agnostic to the end whose reward is the eagle's feather on his lips, similar to Nehemiah's pencil of light as a sign of honest endeavor. Although the Crag of Agonies becomes him, he has no heart of stone: his "thrill" at Nehemiah's death and his earlier work for humanity manifest a compassion that ties him to the human race. Accordingly, although the Saba friars cut him off from Christian burial outside the monastery walls, Rolfe invokes a communal prayer of nature and fellowship at his death. Clarel, too, sees evidence of affirmation from the "negative" Swede in his death-stare at the palm tree: "Fixed seemed it in assent indeed" (III, xxx, p. 395). The rage has disappeared in final acceptance and reconciliation.

> Till Clarel—minding him again
> Of something settled in his air—
> A quietude beyond mere calm—
>
> [III, xxxii, pp. 398-99]

His earlier stare and fixation on evil place Mortmain among other Melville characters whose pained eyes seem to focus on a dread event of the past. Jackson on the *Highlander,* whose contact with evil leaves him "gnawed within" and "scorched without," hardly sees the everyday objects about him. Ahab's fixed gaze on the sea, like Bartleby's and Daniel Orme's,[8] expresses a horror beyond communication. Bulkington, too, registers a look of sorrow: ". . . in the deep shadows of his eyes floated some reminiscences that did not seem to give him much joy."[9] Benito Cereno carries in his eyes a mirror of terror: " . . . but directly the sane memory of the past seemed replaced by insane terrors of the present. With starting eyes he stared before him in vacancy."[10] Billy Budd's friend, the Dansker, reflects similar dread in his eyes, a hint that he has seen the fall of man before and is now witnessing its reenactment in Claggart's destruction of Billy. Mortmain is different from the others, however, for he seems at the last moment to resolve this enigma of evil and humanity, as though he knows that life has value despite the pain and absurdity. The ambivalence that Melville himself carried to the end of his life is the nature of Mortmain, leaving Clarel awed and puzzled. Melville leaves Mortmain like an object disjoined, "where vulture unto vulture calls," but in a state where "tired spirit sleeps." He suggests emotional tranquility for him but without intimation of transcendent redemption. Mortmain in this is the author's Everyman—anticipating the Epilogue—one who made his own "Uncreated good" out of a life of search and suffering.[11] The intensity of his pain lies beyond human understanding. The constriction of his spirit that results from personal cosmic battle renders him finally unintelligible to Clarel. As admirable and consistent as his life has been, his final isolation beyond words and significant gestures—except the last look at the tree—cannot help Clarel in the resolution of his own problems.

Celio's death introduces Clarel to tragedy in the Holy Land. Nehemiah's death makes less of an impression because dreamy acceptance of the Christian myth by anyone precludes sound judgment of the human predicament. Mortmain's death, however, reinforces for Clarel his own identification with man's tragic state and leaves him

> feeling pain
> That such a heart could beat, and will—
> Aspire, yearn, suffer, baffled still,
> And end.
>
> [III, xxxii, p. 399]

The waste of Celio and Mortmain perplexes Clarel because their lives were dedicated to good and should have made some impression on the world. Nevertheless, he implicitly agrees with Rolfe that such prophets lack the necessary balance for survival.

> "If mad
> 'Tis indignation at the bad,"
> Said Rolfe; "most men somehow get used
> To seeing evil, though not all
> They see; 'tis sympathetical;
> But never some are disabused
> Of first impressions which appal."
> [II, xxxvii, p. 267]

Both rebels see life as ugly and men as unloving. Their cynical observation is as wrong, Melville indicates, as the Transcendentalist's denial of the black side of nature: to close one's eyes to light demonstrates the same sophomoric ignorance. A proper tension between the two must be struck for the preservation of sanity, after recognition of all that life has to offer.

The vision of Ungar is equally myopic and is expressed in the first words he speaks to the group: "A gun/A gun's man's voice—sincerest one" (IV, ii, p. 413). This "wandering Ishmael from the West" also lacks the perspective that could bring him peace; but, like Christ, such men have no choice or future, as Rolfe observes:

> This type's assigned
> To One who sharing not man's mind
> Partook man's frame; whose mystic birth
> Wrecked him upon this reef of earth
> Inclement and inhuman.
> [IV, x, p. 437]

These men with "Calvary-faces" insist that Plinlimmon's philosophy cannot be the foundation of modern ethics, and when they discover that few heed their cries they turn in anger and strike men off as unworthy. Extreme sensitivity over a lost ideal wedges Ungar into just such a position, leaving him broken in trust.

His very virtues, in the blench
And violence of fortune's wrench,
Alas, serve but to vitiate?
Strong natures have a strong recoil
Whose shock may wreck them or despoil.

[IV, v, p. 422]

He hates his monomaniacal state but cannot change it.[12] He cannot accept man's "ever-bubbling wickedness," which comes at birth and lasts till death. He derides all the Derwents who visualize a new Eden, for human nature does not change, no matter how resounding the words of advocates of progress and reform. Left on his own, man can do nothing. And he is on his own willfully and perversely, cutting God out of his life in a substitution of modern world's humanism.

Ungar's desperate try to perfect civilization occurred during the Civil War. As a Confederate officer, he fought for the ideals of the South, despite his hatred of slavery. Union victory smashed the quest and left him empty of dreams and almost bereft of hope. War scarred him on the temple and neck, leaving him as dramatic evidence of its violence and futility.

Ungar is Mars in funeral
Of reminiscence—not in pledge
And glory of brave equipage
And manifesto.

[IV, xvii, p. 466]

His eyes, like "sad woods they be, where wild things sleep," see only the effects of war and the viciousness of humanity. His condition has another dimension, for his lost cause parallels Christ's failure. Worse, as a symbol of military violence it underscores the fact of Christ's lost mission at the same time that Ungar wishes Christ's Sermon on the Mount were possible: like Celio and Mortmain, he cannot accept anything short of Christian perfection. This accounts for his diatribes against "the bland substitutes" of the nineteenth century that are couched in slogans of democracy.

In this connection, Ungar insists that democracy can succeed only so long as Adam's fall is denied. Yet he sees the "Dead level of rank commonplace" as the very mark of the fall. The democracy un-Christianized he finds everywhere rests on a contradiction of terms: democracy itself presupposes an exchange of love, but nowhere in the modern world is there evidence of such mutuality. Democracy is a philosophical theory which founders in practice. America, its only possible area for success, testifies to the corruptibility and impossibility of such a system. If America cannot make it work, nowhere in the world will democracy survive. The lesson from this is clear: only when man admits his sinful state and is born anew will he find order in his life. Then God will enter his soul and yoke him to His law in this life and determine his future in heaven or hell.

The sorrow that Ungar experiences stems from "the tortured state of all the Ungars in this world, who in their heart of hearts revere the Lord, though their tongues mock and revile. . . ."[13] He finds the evidence of God's absence overwhelming but cannot believe it possible.

> "Transcended rebel angels! Woe
> To us; without a God, 'tis woe!"
>
> [IV, xxi, p. 479]

Defeated in war, oppressed by malice everywhere, afflicted by spiritual depression, he nevertheless continues to assault evil at every turn. This is Rolfe's meaning in his assessment of the man to Clarel.

> "Dusked over. 'Tis an iron glove,
> An armed man in the Druid grove."
>
> [IV, xvii, p. 466]

In these attacks, Ungar singles out the modern world as vicious and urges his companions beyond the dehumanization processes of progress, science, irreligion, and democracy.

"Look up: the age, the age forget
There's something to look up to yet!"
[IV, vii, p. 430]

Brother Salvaterra recognizes this ambivalence of hate and hope in Ungar and suggests that the cross he bears is the sword he carries. Melville regrets that the sword cannot bring Ungar the redemption attributed to the cross and implicitly wishes that ideals for all such men could be attained. But he regrets even more the fixation over the lost ideal that drives Ungar and brackets him with Celio and Mortmain in an unholy trio of monomania.

Melville, too, in his earlier years aspired to a perfected state for man where poverty, sickness, and gross social inequities would disappear or diminish. This deep compassion pervades *White-Jacket;* and Redburn's dilemma over the starved corpses reflects the author's hatred of man's indignity to man. Democracy and man's nobility were religious and consistent with Melville throughout his life.[14] The poems on the Civil War, and particularly "The Supplement" to *Battle-Pieces,* repeat Melville's hatred of war and his love for man. The "Knights and Squires" chapters already alluded to similarly champion a spiritual democracy in which all men can be happy. But this early idealism or hope for regeneration changed in Melville's later years. The wonderful philanthropy of *White-Jacket* gave way to a social skepticism. Thus the measured command of Captain Vere substitutes for the unbridled freedom Taji demands. Melville still believed democracy should be sought, but only in a limited sense: man's depraved condition presupposes the fall and precludes any possibility for lasting happiness. An order must be superimposed because men are unpredictable in a state of liberty.

Accordingly, working democracy for Melville is actually restricted to the exceptional man of lowly circumstance. While his concept of democracy included all men as equal before God, it did not allow for all men to minister to the needs of other men.[15] *Clarel* and *Billy Budd* clearly indicate this distrust of majority rule and a corresponding confidence in those who are eminently qualified as rulers to take over the government.[16] The older Melville feared that democracy pushes man whole eons back to nature. He still pitied man and loved him in his potential, but, like Shakespeare, his humanism was skeptical of democracy.[17] Even in *White-Jacket* he observed that democracy requires officers. As the years brought him wisdom, Melville gave his officers greater command.

The failure of Celio, Mortmain, and Ungar to succeed saddened Melville, but he wished their failure to serve as a lesson for Clarel. His own dashed hopes of man's perfection left him crushed, particularly in the Civil War holocaust. But he discovered that the urge for survival in a world of empirical reality precedes lamentation over a lost cause. One must rally and assume a new set of values when the old ones are found unworkable. To do otherwise is to bring on insanity. The individual is a precious commodity, but he must give way to other individuals in the societal demands which life places on him.[18] The individual cause, whether it evolves from an original pure ideal or not, cannot control society. It cuts man off and contradicts human nature, as Stern observes:

> . . . idealistic vision results in personal vision; personal vision results in separation of self and community; separation results in a sterilizing and frantic quest for the attainment of vision according to the dictates of self; the quest results in obliteration of self and murder.[19]

In this sense, Celio, Mortmain, and Ungar are only counterparts of Taji, Ahab, and Pierre. Melville created the three early heroes out of his own deep beliefs and wishes. Twenty years later, he was content with the more modest goals of Babbalanja, Ishmael, and Plinlimmon. He knew that the secret lying at the bottom of the whirlpool, in the head of a whale, and in a sarcophagus was not to be uncovered. Celio, Mortmain, and Ungar fail to know this truth, and in their ignorance reflect Melville's earlier rage. Clarel must profit by their mistakes.

6. Since such antisocial attacks avail one no happiness, perhaps it is better to die to society and its sorrow by imitating Vine and Agath?

Agath and Vine also have a lesson to teach Clarel. They are both men of sorrows, turned inward, away from life's struggle. They do not rage, capitulate, and die, like Celio and Mortmain, because what they sought is unattainable. Instead, they refuse to look any farther for ports in a landless sea. They know all of the world's evil and are content merely to survive. Melville pities them as symbols of the human situation, but he wishes Clarel to learn and accept only half of their bleak assessment of life.

Years before, the ship that Agath captained—*The Peace of God*—foundered because of the sorcery of a Moor. The incident choked off his orthodox Christian beliefs and left him

> Bearded and pitted, and fine vexed
> With wrinkles of cabala text . . .
>
> [III, xii, p. 322]

As a result, he knows now that Ahab's Fedallah, like his own Moor, waits below for every man, ready to take over the tiller at the first opening. If anyone ignores this fact and accepts Christian optimism for a text he must do so within protective walls or Ammonite robbers will beat him to death (III, xii, p. 325). To him, "The bleeding man upon the tree" is a cosmic symbol signifying the pain that fate holds for everyone. He appropriately displays a tattoo of the crucifixion as a constant reminder that life offers little but pain and death. The story he tells completes the meaning of his ensign, with the moral that anyone who lingers in the Christian hopes of peace will change at the first shot of a man-of-war's cannon.[20]

At Vine's request, Agath tells of his experience off the coast of South America. The account is actually of Narborough Island, a sketch Melville drew in "The Encantadas." Agath presents the island of stones, dust, and overall aridity as symptomatic of the world and of man's hopes. It complements his keen-sighted vision of Jerusalem as a wreck. He has lived with evil so long that Jerusalem—or any other city—holds no messianic memory or promise for him: everything of value has foundered. Similarly, his scream at the sight of a scorpion comes out of a fear-driven consciousness. As with Benito Cereno, living with evil has robbed him of any defense to ward it off. He will plod on, like the tortoises in his Narborough story, just as he accepts Nehemiah's ass for the journey, without selection, hope, or anticipation of change. He is gentle but deaf to Derwent's cheery "luck to thee" when he leaves, because

> schooled by the inhuman sea,
> He feels 'tis vain to wave the hat
> In God-speed on this mortal strand;
> Recalling all the sailing crews
> Destined to sleep in ocean sand,
> Cheered from the wharf with blithe adieus.
> [IV, xiii, pp. 445-46]

Vine has been schooled in sorrow, too. But his nature is more complex than Agath's, and his resignation to a life without hope at least makes existence tolerable. Thus he drinks with the revelers at Mar Saba, where Agath cannot; and the scorpion that chills Agath leaves him indifferent. His stoicism has a maturity that the mariner's lacks. Because of this he exerts a strong and dangerous influence on Clarel.

Melville had two things in mind when he conceived of Vine. First, Vine was to be the living Christ, walking through the Holy Land eighteen hundred years after His death. Second, Vine was to play his role as merely another member of the pilgrimage, one from whom Clarel was "wishful to learn."

The alter-Christus figure emerges clearly. Melville deliberately framed Vine in Christ-settings to emphasize Jesus's lost cause. Vine first appears in a pastoral setting at the Sepulchre of Kings, deep in introspection. Afterwards, Clarel finds him sitting at the waters of Siloa, although now Siloa is "but a rural well." The seated image appears again with Vine gazing sadly over Jerusalem, while he murmurs a lamentation from Jeremiah. Clarel attempts to speak to Vine at Gethsemane, but Vine, like Christ, seems carried off into another world. Vine's name consistently takes on Christ's meaning of "I am the vine and you the branches," but for ironic effects. Thus after his cry over Jerusalem, Vine picks up a weed and scatters the seeds on the sterile ground. On the first night at the Dead Sea, Vine crouches over the waters and recovers a piece of driftwood that might have been at one time "a palm-shaft green." In disgust, he hurls it back into the water, "as one whose race of thought long since was run. . . ." The driftwood ironically returns in a different form, for it is he who discovers the drifting body of Nehemiah in the same waters. Pain and death become him as does the crown of thorns he plaits all the while Margoth lectures to him on science. The wood image completes the Vine-Christ parallel toward the end of the pilgrimage when Vine sees the palm tree at Mar Saba. As though he has not already given up on life, the tree awakens the memory of the past and a lost Garden of Eden: the tree becomes to him a "Tropic Seraph." But it is only an idle, momentary longing, which he puts away when he remembers the "reversion" and "subverting" of fate.

Vine as Christ stands a witness to the failure of Christianity or as a continuing symbol of Gethsemane as the permanent abode of Christ. Like Christ, who asked His Father to remove the chalice of bitterness, Vine envies Derwent's skimming over life and regrets his own endless diving. Whereas Christ grieved only over the immediate passion of His human nature, Vine mourns because his chalice when drunk leaves nothing but bitter dregs. Man's passion goes on forever with no hope of resurrection to eternal life. This is why Vine answers wistfully "In pace" to Derwent's professional "Resurget" over Nehemiah's corpse. But the peace Vine sees in the dead evangelist is only an end to the pain of life. Vine as Christ journeying through Palestine is Melville's most pessimistic comment on Christianity, or on Christ's lost leadership.

On a second level, Vine is only another human being on a pilgrimage, one whose presence in a group of seekers contradicts his words and gestures. Melville singles him out in an analysis of description, clustering images about him that make up his character, where discursive statement and occasional description tell of the other pilgrims. These images total non-life, which excludes death as a part of the process of life; this explains his envy for the drowned Nehemiah. Because death for Melville remains in mystery, possibly a dramatic, inexplicable stage in a regeneration of nature, he heaps the sterile images on Vine to limit his influence on Clarel, who must affirm life or die. Accordingly, Vine builds the cairn of stones as a "monument to barrenness," and masochistically pelts his own shadow with stones. He admires the Monk's devotion to the "passion-flower" of Calvary because "all the world is elegy." Branchless trees and silence become him as signs of a sterile soul beyond shock and change. His longing for non-being renounces all time but the past.

> For my part, I but love the past—
> The further back the better; yes,
> In the past is the true blessedness;
> The future's ever overcast—
> The present aye plebian.
>
> [III, xxvi, p. 379]

This is why he is at home in Mar Saba, a "Lithographed" ancestral footstep. Only there, and in solitude, does he break into the moment of hope mentioned above, when he longs for the immortality of the palm tree. Even then, he places it in a world of fancy, like the undying amaranth he hymned at the revel.[21] As such, he moves outside life, "A shadow . . . brushed by light" (III, xxvi, p. 379). He has mortified a voluptuous nature for so long that he is inured to pain and joy. Clarel's naive declaration of manly love at Gethsemane is actually an invitation to life, which Vine is incapable of accepting. Love, communication, change, and hope are abstractions in a world of unchanging nothingness. This is why he respects Agath, another man of sorrows, who has learned this fact.

Vine's watchful eye,
While none perceived where bent his view,
Had fed on Agath sitting by;
He seemed to like him, one whose print
The impress bore of Nature's mint
Authentic; man of nature
If simple; naught that slid between
Him and the elemental scene—
Unless it were that thing indeed
Uplooming from his ancient creed;
Yet that but deepen might the sense
Of awe, and serve dumb reverence
And resignation.

[IV, ii, pp. 413-14]

Like the portrait of the Cenci, Vine combines good and evil in the guise of aloofness or apathy.[22] His endless hours of rumination convince him that life must be faced, without joy or expectation. Clarel takes away from him the "new sense . . . of fate's pertinence," but he must go beyond suffering and nothingness as the end and meaning of life.

7. Perhaps no one answer can be found, no one way of life is best. Therefore, is not Rolfe's eclectic approach to life best, his endless questions complementing a continuous participation?

Rolfe presents yet another facet of life for Clarel to study, although his personality looms so large that an intimate relationship, such as the one Clarel hoped for in Vine, is impossible. Of all the pilgrims, Rolfe is the only obviously heroic figure. He is another Jack Chase, Marnoo, and Jack Roy, the perfect blend of "A genial heart, a brain austere." He has the overview of the Dutch painter, Jan Steen, who calls for all of life—"wine and brine"—as he puffs serenely on his skull-bowl pipe.

> "All's picturesque beneath the sun;
> I mean, all's picture; death and life,
> Pictures and pendants, nor at strife—
> No, never to hearts that muse thereon.
> For me, 'tis life, plain life I limn . . ."[23]

Rolfe supplements "Plato's theme with daedal life in boats and tents" (I, xxxi, p. 99). He reminds Clarel of what Adam must have looked like. He is a traveler like Typee, spinning yarns about Lima, England, Rome, and Tahiti. He is an historian, recounting legends of St. Helena, the Catholic Church, the Turks, and Chinese. He has an ear for local stories, filling in the other pilgrims with details he alone knows. His good fellowship even draws a word of praise from Vine. He respects the profound findings of science short of its denial of God and legend. His charity includes forgiveness for the Lesbian's licentiousness and for the bad manners of the Presbyterian and Margoth. He demands tolerance for the Turks and for all non-Westerners traditionally scorned by the Anglo-Saxon West. He pities the monomaniacal Mortmain and overlooks the absurdities of Derwent.

In addition to his broadmindedness and obvious intelligence, Rolfe is a dreamer. He loves the myths that men weave out of their secret wishes. The poignant story he tells of Arculf and Adamnan carries him back imaginatively to the "good old days" when man firmly believed in something. The simple tales of Bethlehem recall for him the Polynesian Islands and innocent natives there. The charm of the Catholic Church vested in its ritual and tradition carries for him the same appeal of Egyptian and Grecian mythology. Like Melville, he hates Niebuhr and higher criticism for subjecting the tales of Jesus to skeptical scrutiny: he would rather have a man with some faint hope even where his reason dictates otherwise. The grave waits inevitably, of course, and dreaming will not remove the awful fact. But he would ease the grimness with thoughts of fountains dancing and lush palms planted at the head of his grave, for no one knows about immortality.

Rolfe differs from Derwent in facing up to the facts of life. Like Vine, he knows evil exists as a fact:

> "Evil and good they braided play
> Into one chord."
>
> [IV, iv, p. 419]

This is why he prefers the Latin cross of pain to Derwent's bloodless Grecian symbol. The palm tree at Mar Saba flashes across his mind idyllic memories of the South Seas, but he knows Judea controls him. He applauds Jesus's Sermon on the Mount but recognizes that man's weakness proves it impractical. Like Vine, he sits on a hill and gazes mournfully over a dead Jerusalem, while his imaginative vision encompasses a "glorious" modern world he knows is even more "a stony metropolis." Although he generally adheres to a Protestant religion, he sees the Protestant Church now at the end of the road because it ignores demands of the heart. His own pilgrimage—it is not his first—attests to this series of contradictions. And he is a genuine pilgrim, even if the goal he seeks is as impossible of attainment as are philosophers' absolutes. He affirms to the others that man must believe in God, yet confesses to Clarel that he can find no sure evidence of the Creator's hand.

Such is the eclecticism he prescribes as cures for Ungar and Mortmain. But his "manysidedness," which makes him all things to all men, cannot serve Clarel.

> and here, all sects, behold,
> All creeds involving in one fold
> Of doubt? Better a partisan!
> Earnest he seems: can union be
> 'Twixt earnestness and levity?
> Or need at last in Rolfe confess
> Thy hollow, Manysidedness!
>
> [III, xvi, pp. 344-45]

What Clarel objects to is the pragmatism Rolfe has worked out for his own sanity, a compromise which has to embrace the modern world.

> "Yes, God is God, and men are men,
> Forever and for aye. What then?
> There's Circumstance—there's Time, and these
> Are charged with store of latencies
> Still working in to modify."
>
> [IV, xxi, p. 481]

Rolfe's views throughout the journey are honestly said. Ungar, in this connection, at first fears Rolfe as a gossip with his multiple arguments but then recognizes the other man's sincerity and pours out his deepest troubles to him. Such sincerity cannot substitute for belief, however. This accounts for Clarel's refusal to take Rolfe seriously, for Clarel desperately needs a consistent point of view.

Many readers of *Clarel* identify Melville with Rolfe in his actions and aspirations.[24] But the movement of the poem does not allow for any single spokesman of the author's views. The prismatic design has elements of Melville's nature and beliefs glinting in different characters at different stages of the poem. Rolfe is not *the* teacher for Clarel. He is only one of the instructors, and his lesson is not completely acceptable. For Melville, Rolfe must have seemed a reincarnated Jack Chase. He does have the flair that Melville applauded, the magnetism that he himself had in the 1840s. But for the older Melville his chameleon thinking is not adequate in a world of sorrows; it cannot relieve Clarel's anxieties. Vine's sorrowful judgments cleave closer to the truth. Or a blend of Vine and Rolfe might offer to the young student the exemplar he requires:

> The student glanced from him to Vine:
> Peers, peers—yes, needs that these must pair.
> Clarel was young. In promise fine,
> To him here first were brought together
> Exceptional natures, of a weather

Strange as the tropics with strange trees,
Strange birds, strange fishes, skies and seas,
To one who in some meager land
His bread wins by the horny hand.
What now may hap? what outcome new
Elicited by contact true—
Frank, cordial contact of the twain?
Crude wonderment, and proved but vain.
If average mortals social be,
And yet but seldom truly meet,
Closing like halves of apple sweet—
How with the rarer in degree?

[I, xxxi, p. 100]

The blended perfection is not to be found in Rolfe. His ability to encompass all things makes him an impressive figure, but it does not take him too far beyond Derwent's shallow vision. He brings joy with him. He can dance and drink with the other revelers and pursue the most profound philosophical argument. He can sail ships and ride a horse like an Indian. But his "manysidedness" glosses over the tragedy of life. This is why Vine has a stronger hold on Clarel. Rolfe's cognizance of the greater needs of the heart over the head fails to convert him fully to the heart. His inability to resolve the ambiguities can only add another burden to the scattered thoughts of Clarel. In Bethlehem, responding to Rolfe's question, Clarel stresses his deep need for conviction:

"I would
I were his mate," in earnest mood
Clarel rejoined; "such faith to have,
I'd take the rest, even Crib and Cave."

[IV, xviii, p. 465]

Clarel would sooner accept Djalea's serenity than the Rolfean eclecticism he rejected in America, a pluralism he was constitutionally unable to adopt. Rolfe's large nature lacks the consistent point of view that Clarel sought in the Holy Land. Rolfe glitters at every moment, but time and distance cast the strongest lights into shadow, as Melville says of the Marquis de Grandvin, his most urbane personage.

> Are there natures strong to draw and enthrall, yet whose influence is like that of the magnet, only operative as a bodily presence? Yes, withdraw the magnet and all is over. . . . Shall nothing be crystallised into permanence? Nothing at last remain of our Lord Bountiful but the empty larder and void dusty bin?[25]

Rolfe's natural perfection has this great attraction but it pales to insignificance next to a higher ideal Clarel must attain.

8. No one answer can be found. It rests only with Allah, as the Druze says on the pilgrimage. One survives. Nothing else matters—questions, harangues, cajolings—for man cannot change the inexorable movement of fate.

These seven alternative attitudes, prescribed by the words and actions of the respective characters, constitute for Clarel all that life has to offer, and no one way is adequate. If such elements were subject to change, probably the Rolfe-Vine fusion could provide a necessary defense to wage continued war against the universe. Rolfe and Vine are similar in sensibility but poles apart in final attitudes. Rolfe demands that one rebound continuously, even if only to dream that Polynesian memories will come true. Vine continues his pilgrimages, but only as a means to occupy weary time, for man's questing can never provide answers, can never bring peace. Rolfe strives to evaluate all experience objectively and remain open to change. Vine is beyond such examination and can only remain the pejorist.

Because no one of these solutions is adequate for him, when he is last seen Clarel "Vanishes in the obscurer town," alone and close to despair after the reluctant departure of Rolfe,

Vine, and Derwent. His depression is offset only by the physical presence of other strangers who plod ahead on the Via Crucis. He walks alone but resolutely behind the crowd. In this he most clearly resembles Djalea, who, implicitly, has since agreed to conduct another group to the Dead Sea and beyond. This stoicism rests on acceptance of life as a set of obligations, an attitude which enables the Druze to adjust to any change or emergency. This is why he shows no concern when Mortmain shocks the others with his decision to remain alone on the Quarantanian mountain.

> "Well, let be. Why chafe?
> Nights here are mild: one's pretty safe
> When fearless. —Belex! come, the road."
> [II, xv, p. 191]

Agath's sighting of Jerusalem as a wreck commends "the Timoneer" to the guide as keen-eyed, but Djalea himself is beyond lamenting the wreckage. Jerusalem as a symbol of a foundered world might have meaning for him if there were tools available for its recreation. So, too, even though he applauds Mortmain's heroics, Djalea wonders why reformers grieve over lost ideals when grief cannot retrieve them. The Sermon on the Mount, and the story of the Good Samaritan, and hopes for an end to wars keep men like Derwent in a state of euphoria. Djalea will not scorn them, he will gently tolerate their ignorance.

> The armed man's eyes
> Turned toward him tolerantly there
> As 'twere a prattling child.
> [III, viii, p. 308]

The guide detects nobility in Vine and respects him as one who also has plumbed life's mystery. But Vine cannot impose the needed order in society, lying on the ground or musing on rocks over the fallen universe. His assessment of man's condition is the correct one, but withdrawal from the struggle lessens his nobility. Djalea shares the other man's distaste for language and extraversion, but he avoids obsessive introspection that leads to nothingness.

> There, all aside,
> How passionless he took for bride
> The calm—the calm, but not the dearth—
> The dearth or waste; nor would he fall
> In waste of words, that waste of all.
>
> [III, v, p. 295]

Djalea shares Rolfe's capacity for rebounding in the face of sorrow, although he will not share Rolfe's exuberance. This accounts in part for his leaving the revelry at the monastery. Rolfe's Tahiti reveries also have no relevancy for him. Tahiti exists only in the imagination, as does the story that an innocent John found wild honey in the desert.

Like Clarel, Djalea learned very early that the cross and the Via Crucis symbolize the pains and contradictions of life: his own birth as an Emir's son and his present ignominious position as guide prove the point. In his youth, he learned that the gun in hand prevents further disgrace: calamity comes most frequently to the unprotected. On the other hand, the pipe he smokes brings him pleasure and serenity that offset the trouble that lies in wait.[26] The gun and the pipe are emblems of his life, clear signs that

> Never the attending Druze resigned
> His temperate poise, his moderate mind . . .
>
> [IV, xvi, p. 458]

Empirical realities, of course, force a man into work for pay and defense of his life, but they cannot destroy the riches of his inner self.

> Djalea in face
> Wears an abstraction, lit by grace
> Which goverened hopes of rapture lend:

On coins *his* musings likewise bend—
The starry sequins woven fair
Into black tresses. But an air
Considerate and prudent reigns;
For his the love not vainly sure:
'Tis passion deep of man mature
For one who half a child remains:
Yes, underneath a look sedate,
What throbs are known!

[IV, xxix, pp. 506-07]

Because sensual gratification is as natural to man as the fulfillment of duties imposed on him, Djalea gives both their proper position and orders his life around this fact. This is life, so ordained by God, whose mysterious being cannot be plumbed: "No God there is but God." Perhaps He will listen to the human cry, "Allah preserve ye, Allah great!" But until He does one must persevere in the daily rounds of obligations and revel in the small joys of experience. There is no retreat: the pilgrimage through the desert must be made time and again.

Melville did not intend Clarel as the counterpart of Djalea. The sensual side of the Guide, as well as his practical handling of money and people, are not detected in the young student. He might come to a new evaluation of them at a later time, but his distraught condition at the end of the pilgrimage precludes any present awareness. Nor does he have the slightest measure of composure that Djalea shows at every turn. But, like him, Clarel remains "the traveler" he was when first he entered Abdon's Inn. In this way, he completes the Wandering Jew theme woven throughout the poem, which is highlighted at Mar Saba in the dramatic presentation of Cartaphilus, "the Jew/Who wanders ever. . . ." (III, xix, p. 349). Abdon, Nehemiah, Celio, Vine, Mortmain, Rolfe, Ungar, the Prodigal are all restlessly moving in the dim hope of finding the Promised Land. Djalea alone knows that this Sharon does not exist and that man's burden is precisely this endless wandering. When Clarel accepts this fact of life, he will share Djalea's composure; his final movement indicates that he will.

He comes to the Holy Land an orphaned traveler, seeking a *fidus Achates,* or, at least, a guide to help him identify his problems. He ends in the same wandering condition. But he learns in between that commitment, or existence, must be in solitude, and not in relationship with other people or things, as Vine's rejection at Gethsemane implied. Melville stamps all of his life's thinking with this fact. His earlier sketch, "The Piazza," dramatizes the total inability of one man to relieve another of his sorrows. The essential self for Clarel is his concern, for any meanings in life will be known only as they have direct and intimate bearing on him. The doubloon image of *Moby-Dick* operates precisely for Clarel, for it suggests that the self is an undetermined thing owing neither its existence nor its principle of action to the world outside.[27] Taji sums up this existential state, saying that in each individual exists potentially all who ever existed: "And like a frigate, I am full with a thousand souls."[28]

Clarel is another Ishmael filling out the catalogue of Melville's Isolatoes. His loneliness is more acute, for he does not even have a coffin souvenir of friendship. He is another Hunilla or Israel Potter, a symbol of humanity's grief, powerless to change his lot, enduring, dignified in passive nobility. His preference for life advances him beyond Bartleby, for he refuses to lie down and die. He knows that evil exists as a horrible force and must be accepted as such. But life imposes an obligation of continuity, forebearance, and silence in the face of evil. When Agath is terrified by a scorpion, Rolfe observes that this fact of awful discovery and continuation must be known if one is to live in a world of scorpions, while Belex smokes away and Djalea combs his horse's mane, both undisturbed by this "small epitome of the devil." The innocent may overlook this fact of evil in the world and the coward will flee from it, but it remains constant in the world despite them, as Melville pointed out elsewhere.

> A primary law binds the universe. The worlds are like apples on the tree; in flavor and tint one apple perchance may somewhat differ from another, but all partake of the

> same sap. One of the worlds we know. And what find we here? Much good, a preponderance of good; that is, good it would be could it be winnowed from the associate evil that taints it. But evil is no accident. Like good it is an irremovable element. Bale out your individual boat, if you can, but the sea abides.[29]

Heroic, balanced natures recognize the nature of this world and adjust their lives and institutions for proper bailing:

> With certain evils men must be more or less patient. Our institutions have a potent digestion, and may in time convert and assimilate to good all elements thrown in, however originally alien.[30]

Ishmael achieves this wisdom at the try-works and is able to resist Ahab's manic influence. Innocents must confront evil if man is to survive, and cowards do battle, if he is to have dignity. This was the truth Shakespeare gave to the world:

> Never the lines had lightly scanned,
> Steeped in fable, steeped in fate;
> The Hamlet in his heart was 'ware,
> Such hearts can antedate.
>
> No utter surprise can come to him
> Who reaches Shakespeare's core;
> That which we seek and shun is there—
> Man's final lore.[31]

Robert E. Lee arrived at this knowledge of good and evil and accepted all adversity through such wisdom:

> Comrades and cause, station and riches lost,
> And all the ills that flock when fortune's fled.
> No word he breathes of vain lament,
> Mute to reproach, nor hears applause—

His doom accepts, perforce content,
  And acquiesces in asserted laws;
Secluded now would pass his life,
  And leave to time the sequel of the strife.[32]

Loneliness in calamity marks Lee, Shakespeare, Clarel, and all the Ishmaels of the world, and signifies the true human condition.

The Ishmael condition, then, obviates hope for serenity. Babbalanja's decision to remain at Serenia denies this and thereby creates a life of illusion. Clarel's decision to continue, even though it arises from a different temper, recognizes that the hero must accept life for what it is and not for what he would like it to be and yet believe there might be something beyond his knowing. This is the meaning of "Of Rama" (I, xxxii, pp. 107-09), a separate canto Melville inserted because of his own inability to quit the search. This ambivalence can be detected at every turn of his life and writing. In one of the sad letters to Hawthorne he called life wild, but he also called it "glorious." Rolfe says on two occasions, "I am what I am," echoing "Rama," yet he persists in Polynesian dreams. Clarel despairs at Siloam's cemetery, but cries out over Ruth's corpse:

  "Spurn—I'll endure; all spirit's fled
When one fears nothing.—Bear with me,
Yet bear! Conviction is not gone
Though faith's gone: that which shall not be
It *ought* to be!"

[IV, xxx, pp. 513-14]

Before this awful moment, he saw Celio, Nehemiah, and Mortmain each give way to death in deliberate choice over a life not worth further effort. Now given the same evidence in a circular journey of futility, with death a pervasive force, Clarel chooses life instead, with all of its pain. In his "nevertheless," "even so" assertion, he creates his own self as the circumference of possibilities and thereby routs death, or fits it into his comprehension of life. He puts the lie to the mad Cyril's vision of death in his face and silences Mortmain's elegy over a dead world. He knows the cost of such choice, for "Doubt bleeds nor faith is free from pain" (III, xxi, p. 364), as Job and Hamlet both knew. He echoes Ahab's words on the price one pays for existence: "From storm to storm! So be it, then. Born in throes, 'tis fit that man should live in pains and die in pangs!"[33] The goal he seeks is no closer at the end than at the beginning; but, as Wright concludes, this endless pursuit lies at the heart of Melville's thought: "One is always traveling but never arrives."[34] In a movement, however, the "oughtness" of life is Clarel's salvation and Melville's consolation. It echoes the little motto Mrs. Metcalf says her grandfather pasted out of sight on a side wall: "Keep true to the dreams of thy youth."[35]

This death of innocence and birth of a finer substance out of pity for man runs like a Grecian thread throughout Melville's works. Man's inevitable tragedy stalks Redburn's steps and makes White-Jacket genuinely compassionate. In one of his finest poems Melville presents the hero in the mixed world of good and evil:

> But seldom the laurel wreath is seen
>   Unmixed with pensive pansies dark;
> There's a light and a shadow on every man
>   Who at last attains his lifted mark—
>   Nursing through night the ethereal spark.
> Elate he never can be;
> He feels that spirit which glad had hailed his worth,
>   Sleep in oblivion. —The shark
> Glides white through the phosphorous sea.[36]

Clarel continues this Grecian demand for nobility in the face of castrophe. As a hero, Clarel resigns himself to the inscrutable laws of the universe. Like the Druze, he will not try to justify the works of God, but neither will he rest in His mercy. He finds no substance in the Emersonian belief that good will eventually replace evil until man returns to paradise; he knows

> That little avails a pilgrimage
> Whose road but winds among the flowers.
> [II, xiii, p. 185]

He observes that life begins in dust and ends in stone. In between are the bitter waters, craggy mountains, and arid deserts of existence. There is no escape from this world.

Melville's ambivalence carries over with greater force into the Epilogue. The poet feels Clarel's despair so keenly that he consoles the hero with a vague promise of the soul's immortality. He remembers St. Paul's rebuke of death and applies it in the very last lines to Clarel, in what Braswell calls a kind of pantheistic "strained type of immortality."[37]

> Emerge thou mayst from the last whelming sea,
> And prove that death but routs life into victory.
> [IV, xxv, p. 523]

In the same way, although every philosophic argument convinces one that life ends at death, faith in "the persistent flow" of life's rhythm supplies the heart with reasons the head could never know:

> But Faith (who from the scrawl indignant turns)
> With blood warm oozing from her wounded trust,
> Inscribes even on her shards of broken urns
> The sign o' the cross—*the spirit above the dust!*
> [IV, xxv, p. 522]

But if the Christian sign of the cross, or Christ Himself, cannot redeem Clarel and humanity, regeneration through nature may carry man's spirit above the dust, so that

> Even death may prove unreal at the last,
> And stoics be astounded into heaven.
> [IV, xxv, p. 523]

Melville expressed these same anguished hopes for immortality through nature in another poem which mourned the fact that all dies:

> For me, within the brown arcade—
> Rich life, methought; sweet here in shade
> And pleasant abroad in air! But, nay,
> A counter thought intrusive played,
> A thought as old as thought itself,
> And who shall lay it on the shelf!—
> I felt the beauty bless the day
> In opulence of autumn's dower;
> But evanescence will not stay!
> A year ago was such an hour,
> As this, which but foreruns the blast
> Shall sweep these live leaves to the dead leaves past.
> All dies!—[38]

But "like the crocus budding through the snow—" and the violet replacing the hemlock in *Clarel*, and Rip Van Winkle's lilac supplanting the willow, nature's renaissance offers a hope of immortality that cancels the blankness of the prairie and the chaos of the ocean.

> "Dies, all dies!
> The grass it dies, but in vernal rain
> Up it springs and it lives again;
> Over and over, again and again
> It lives, it dies and it lives again.
> Who sighs that all dies?
> Summer and winter, and pleasure and pain
> And everything everywhere in God's reign,
> They end, and anon they begin again:
> Wane and wax, wax and wane:
> Over and over and over amain
> End, ever end, and begin again—
> End, ever end, and forever and ever begin again!"[39]

This is as much consolation as anyone can offer. This poem, the ambiguous message of *Billy Budd*, and all of *Clarel* witness in Melville the final triumph of heart over head. The spiritual regeneration he hoped for appeared dim to him but never disappeared altogether. As Lewis points out, "Melville . . . had penetrated beyond both innocence and despair to some glimmering of a moral order which might explain and order them both, though his vision remained slender, as of that moment, the center of light not yet known, but only believed in and still ambiguous, at that."[40] The thin pencil of light is nothing next to the avalanche at Nehemiah's death. But however overpowering the slide appears to be, the "miraculous" light of the rainbow does hover over the saint's body. Until the day when even such signs are gone, Melville will hope for greater light. Until then, like General Lee, Djalea, and Clarel, he will face life with whatever it has to offer, strengthened by his own enduring nobility, and persevering in the knowledge that "No God there is but God."

X

Conclusion

> He took the attitude of absolute independence toward the world. He said, "My books will speak for themselves and all the better if I avoid the rattling egotism by which so many win a certain vogue for a certain time."
>
> Titus Munson Coan, [The Boston] *Literary World* (December 19, 1891)

The failure of *Clarel* to gain an audience in the nineteenth century symbolizes the loss of reputation Melville suffered after the 1850's,[1] a condition that caused him great distress at the time. Thus the attachment of fame to toadying patronage that he made in a letter to Hawthorne in 1851 was partially whiplash to earlier devastating criticism and partially a necessary assertion of self-confidence in the final days of work on *Moby-Dick*. Over the years thereafter, this forced detachment became less a reaction of pique and more a real posture of indifference to criticism and sales of his works. By 1876, therefore, he was not deeply concerned over the success of the poem, as can be seen in the *Note* he included at the beginning of the edition, and in the wry comment he made in a letter to James Billson: "*Clarel,* published by George P. Putnam's Sons, New York—a metrical affair, a pilgrimage or what not, of several thousand lines, eminently adapted for unpopularity."[2] This assessment was substantiated over a long period of unpopularity, a situation that has changed in recent times, but only by comparison. The consequence, unfortunately, has been the submergence of a major work so that the general Melville reader, unfamiliar with the poem, is left with a glimpse of the author's profile.

The overall reaction to the poem discloses a recognizable pattern. The nineteenth-century reading, except for a few, isolated, but qualified approvals, ran from "inferior," to "bad," to "unintelligible absurdity." The poem was attacked because of its Godlessness; because it fulminated against all that was good in a progressive, scientific age; because its barren imagery and doggerel lines offended all aesthetic considerations; because the characters had no flesh and blood; because it was just not poetry. The twentieth-century reaction, on the other hand, has disclosed an audience more willing to take Melville on his own terms. It has recognized certain serious limitations of the poem, but has been ready to explore the many profound problems facing mankind as they are set down in tough, effective lines of poetry. This reaction is critical rather than popular; at no time is it likely that *Clarel* will be read by a large group of people. But whereas the nineteenth century was willing to push Melville back into an obscurity that the poem should have freed him from, the modern scholar, with certain exceptions, feels a kinship to Melville through *Clarel* that no other single work of his provides. All of this means that Melville was correct in his judgment, for the poem appears to be designed for the devoted Melville reader alone.

Comments made in the early part of this study on the condition of Melville's mind in the three decades prior to the writing of *Clarel* were not intended as a psychological analysis of an artist at work. Arvin, Chase, Sedgwick, and many others have covered this ground well. They were intended, rather, to underscore the summary and all-inclusive nature of *Clarel*, which could have been written only at this time of Melville's life, and which included the seeking, the titan drives, the ambiguities, the withdrawals, and the bafflement of a lifetime. A reading of the poem against a background of all the other works—written before and after—discloses the real relationship among Clarel and Redburn, White-Jacket, Ishmael, and all the seekers; between Derwent and the Reverend Falsgrave; among Agath, Benito Cereno, Israel Potter, Daniel Orme, and the Dansker; among Mortmain, Ungar, Ahab, Pierre, and Taji;

between Ruth and Lucy; among Rolfe, Jack Chase, Marnoo, and Bulkington. There are so many like characters and parallel themes and situations that the poem appears to be Melville's comprehensive survey of his own life and works. In a word, it is the author's spiritual autobiography.

In this connection, too much cannot be made of the decision by Melville to use the material of his 1856 trip to the Holy Land. For between 1855 and 1857, more than at any other time of his life, he seemed to hang in a precarious balance of mental health: any action at that time was to have a vital bearing on his future. The tension eased considerably during the years after his return, in the quiet surroundings of the Custom House and in a transformation of his personal anxieties to national concern over the Civil War. But the strain of those two years remained a conscious memory and a continuing threat for Melville, so that years later it inspired and informed the sensitivity of Clarel, who also struggles throughout his Palestine journey. The finest elements of the poem reflect this period of spiritual dryness and intellectual uncertainty as an autobiographical echo, at the same time that they develop the poet's mature judgments on man in the universe and society. There seems little doubt that the rantings of Mortmain and Ungar, and Agath's subdued memories of defeat, mirror Melville's own state of mind over the lengthy period of composing *Clarel*, and particularly during his strained days before the Levant journey. The difference between the tension of the 1856 period and the final placement of Clarel on the Via Crucis in 1876 lies in Melville's recognition of the physical laws of the universe as immutable and of the therapeutic control that art performed in his life.

Any proper evaluation of *Clarel* must begin with its aesthetic limitations and then go into a closer study of the poem. The enormous length and the constricted lines make this difficult, even for the devoted Melville reader. At first glance, the cramped style suggests that the genius which inspired the Elizabethan imagery and the soaring, imaginative passages of the 1850s had run dry. If this did happen, as Matthiessen and Van Wyck Brooks believe,[3] in no way was Melville crippled thereby as an artist; and if he was conscious of such a loss, the knowledge only spurred him to studied variations in his art form. Whereas he had burst into print through *Typee* without apprentice study or experience, his poetry resulted from meticulous study of other poets' work and of the subtleties of prosody and language. This accounts for the deliberate choice of form for *Clarel* and for other poems, cited above, in which Melville consciously shifted from the early, voluptuous, spontaneous style to one of controlled restriction. He believed that the unattractive subject matter, moral, and tone of his material necessitated an arid style, which would probably drive away a majority of readers but would express the thought and mood of his age. If the usual embellishments were missing, those who remained to read the poem would be caught up in the argument of faith and doubt that preempted all other problems in the nineteenth century.

> But wherefore this? such theme why start?
> Because if here in many a place
> The rhyme—much like the knight indeed—
> Abjure brave ornament, 'twill plead
> Just reason, and appeal for grace.
>
> [I, iv, p. 18]

There can be no doubt that the iambic tetrameter and prosaic vocabulary, the delineation of faceless pilgrims, the severe logic explored in Platonic dialogues, and the exclusion of all emotion and easy solutions were deliberately set out by the poet to reflect the dead-end condition of a romantic age.

There are stylistic merits of the poem that should not be overlooked, despite Melville's intention to "Abjure brave ornament." The effective use of a sustained or a cluster image as a unifying device tightens the poem considerably: choking dust, thousands of stones, and contrasting sea figures produce an atmosphere of barrenness fitting to the pursuit of lost faith. Images of the cross, birds, death, stars, and light pervade the Holy Land and thoughts of the pilgrims and impress upon the reader the tragedy of modern man. Melville's eye for symbolic colors and his ear for identifying dialogue complete this one overwhelming effect of futility. The sterile imagery, in turn, is patterned into the structure of the poem, which constitutes an allegory in itself; that is, the pilgrims perform their daily actions as though they were involved in the normal behavior of linear growth and change, when, in fact, their movement is circular. The first three sections of Jerusalem, The Wilderness, and Mar Saba infuse the weary pilgrims with a hope for rest and peace in Bethlehem—the fourth section—that cannot be fulfilled; for Bethlehem is the spiritually bankrupt site of Christ's birth, and nothing more than another stopover on the way back to the wreck of Jerusalem they had left ten days before. During this test of physical and spiritual strength, certain incidents highlight their frustration and pain, such as the deaths of Nehemiah and Mortmain, but they, too, are absorbed into a total effect of bewildering movement without meaning in a burnt-out world.

In this wasteland, the Catholic Church appears as a beacon of hope, offering to the pilgrims and the reader transcendent values at the most and emotional consolation at the least. This peculiar emphasis contradicts statements Melville made throughout his life on the efficacy of the Church, to the point that Mason, Sedgwick, Zeik, and others infer from the poem a deep sympathy in the poet for the institutional Church. But in no way does *Clarel* evidence a minimum acceptance of Catholic dogma or of the need for sacramental participation as a means for gaining sanctifying grace. Nor does Melville impute to the Roman Church, or to its members, a sanctity lacking in other churches. He does praise her as a warm haven for "the poor drifting sea-weed of the universe." But this is admiration for the Church's psychology, not for her theology. He singles out the Church for her permanence in a world of transient, shifting forms. Little can be made of this, however, for toward the end of his life Melville looked for symbols of endurance everywhere. Such awe in the face of a symbol in no way argues Melville a secret Roman Catholic. There is not the slightest hint of commitment in Clarel or the other major figures, nor is there a sense of loss implied by the narrator in their failure to do so.

His concept of man's alien condition prevented Melville from sharing the Church's sanguine expectation of man's redemption. Whereas the Church founds its beliefs on Christ's sacrifice manifest in the Eucharist and the theological virtues of faith, hope, and charity, Melville saw his age—and possibly all other eras—as bankrupt in faith, bereft of hope, and ignorant of love. He read history as a series of man-made events leading ever downward to decadence, as episodes in time that demonstrated the inevitable contradiction and ambiguity that await every person. Thus he has Pierre shattering his life in an attempt to prove this history false, just as Celio, Mortmain, and Ungar insist upon discovering for themselves, and acting upon the underside of human nature and of nature itself, regardless of the risk. But perfectibility lies outside human action and understanding, or it is a contradiction of nature; as a concept offered by social scientists and theologians, it only adds a dimension to human frustration and pain. Man's natural condition is Ishmael's, one permanently attached to coffins. Promethean rebellions offer no lasting amelioration in such a state, and innocence is powerless before evil. Attempts to circumvent this natural condition in a pursuit of peace, or an escape from sorrow, end either in greater woe or in madness. There is no way out, as he told Sophia Hawthorne: " 'We can't help ourselves.' For tho' we know what we ought to be; & what it would be very sweet and beautiful to be; yet we can't be it."[4]

All of the characters of *Clarel* express, in one way or another, an aspect of this essential belief. Nevertheless, with this clearly demonstrated in the poem Melville still remained an agnostic in his own disbelief, unconvinced by his own arguments or perhaps not sure that he disbelieved. This accounts for the enigmatic Epilogue. In it, Melville steps out of the role of the narrator he carefully followed throughout the poem to console Clarel and the reader, and to suggest that there may be worlds of facts unknown to men who deal in facts so that the sign of the cross, the emblem of human suffering and endurance might be "the spirit above the dust." Having taken Clarel full circle—from despair to hope, back to crushing defeat—Melville still refused to leave him so:

> Then keep thy heart, though yet but ill-resigned—
> Clarel, thy heart, the issues there but mind;
> That like the crocus budding through the snow—
> That like a swimmer rising from the deep—
> That like a burning secret which doth go
> Even from the bosom that would hoard and keep;
> Emerge thou mayst from the last whelming sea,
> And prove that death but routs life into victory.
>
> [IV, xxxv, p. 523]

All parts of the poem point to this final ambivalence. Construed accordingly, *Clarel* has greater meaning for the twentieth-century realist than it ever had for the nineteenth-century optimist. The "modern predicament" of contemporary western man has entered lexicons as a factual condition peculiar to an age restless without God and yet not content with its faith in technology, a sterile state repeatedly prophesied in *Clarel.* This fractured condition was the subject matter for the broken rhythms of Emily Dickinson, who also insisted on plumbing the depths of pain; it constituted the empty heath cries of Thomas Hardy, the wasteland observations of Eliot, and the acute sense of loss in MacLeish and Faulkner. The theme of the poem is at the heart of Sartre's assertions that peace for man lies only in acceptance of his estrangement from the world of objects about him. But perhaps more than other writers in the twentieth century, Camus has adopted or paralleled Melville's "spirit of revolt," which enables the rebel to diminish his suffering in an absurd universe by an act of self-identification and assertion. Like Melville's later seekers, Camus's heroes, after Merceau, move beyond this rebellion and back into society when they discover with Rieux, at the end of *The Plague,* that heroism is not denied as a possibility for man because of the narrow periphery of existence; it is found precisely when one persists, conscious of this slim chance of relieving human suffering and aware of the unliklihood of changing a world in which pain is inevitable.

This sums up Clarel's awful apprehension and his continuance on the Via Crucis after the death of Ruth. At this point, he is the man of sorrows, although not broken like Agath. Despite his youth, he experiences the painful alienation of John Marr; like Daniel Orme, he is "an absentee from existence." He is Everyman and Sisyphus. His movement is without destination because he is cut off in his own mind from God and man. But this, paradoxically, constitutes the very substance and radiance of his life. Longings for a "joint stock-company," or the "pantheistic one-heart beat," are put behind him as romantic illusions of escape from self. In this recognition and acceptance, he asserts his worth as an integral part of elemental reality:

> Healed of my hurt, I laud the inhuman Sea—
> Yea, bless the Angels Four that there convene;
> For healed I am even by their pitiless breath
> Distilled in wholesome dew named rosmarine.[5]

Like the Druze, he casts aside lamentation and anger as unavailing emotions: all is silence in the nameless universe. Peace lies only in acceptance of all the flux and processes of life "twixt heaven and hell," as the lilac replaces the willow and wildings grow over the fallen lilac. A part of nature's endless round, man ascertains his meaning and dignity when he flows into this movement and recognizes how all things—even death—as Stein points out, are a "part of the natural cycle of human destiny."[6] This confidence in human resiliency and a faith in nature's balm provide the only measure of peace and hope for civilization. In no way does this explain the purpose of human existence. But prevailing in a world where the answer is not forthcoming is an answer in itself. It is the painful wisdom that turns a man into a hero.

Notes

Notes to Chapter I

[1] "These attacks are matters of course, and are essential to the building up of any permanent reputation—if such should ever be mine—'There's nothing in it!' cried the dunce, when he threw down the 47th problem of the 1st Book of Euclid—'There's nothing in it!'—Thus with the posed critic. But Time, which is the solver of all riddles, will solve *Mardi*." Letter to his father-in-law, Lemuel Shaw, April 23, 1849: *The Letters of Herman Melville,* ed. Merrell R. Davis and William H. Gilman (New Haven, 1960), pp. 84-85.

[2] Letter to Hawthorne, June 1, 1851: *Letters,* p. 128. An earlier letter to Evert Duyckinck, in December, 1849, registered the same complaint: *Letters,* pp. 95-96.

[3] Newton Arvin, *Herman Melville* (New York, 1950), pp. 195-96.

[4] Eleanor Melville Metcalf, *Herman Melville* (Cambridge, Mass., 1953), p. 158.

[5] Jay Leyda, *The Melville Log* (New York, 1969), p. 525. The Liverpool destination must have surprised Duyckinck for earlier in the month he thought Melville was on his way to Italy: *Log*, p. 524.

[6] Ibid., pp. 528-29.

[7] Herman Melville, *Journal of a Visit to Europe and the Levant, October 11, 1856-May 6, 1857,* ed. Howard C. Horsford (Princeton, New Jersey, 1955), p. 42.

[8] Peter Gansevoort, Melville's uncle and dear friend, expressed surprise when the extended travels were not used for the writing of a book: *Log,* p. 587.

[9] Herman Melville, *Clarel: A Poem and Pilgrimage in the Holy Land,* ed. Walter E. Bezanson (New York, 1960). Melville acceded reluctantly to Putnam's insistence that the book be published under his name: *Log*, p. 748.

[10] Bezanson, ed. *Clarel,* p. cix.

[11] See a summary of James's position on this in A. N. Kaul, *The American Vision* (New Haven, 1963), pp. 38-44.

Notes to Chapter II

[1] Charles Anderson, *Melville in the South Seas* (New York, 1939).

[2] April 16, 1852: *Letters,* pp. 149-51.

[3] *Mardi* received the most severe attack; random selection of the reviews verifies this. One reviewer (George Ripley?) seemed personally offended: "We are then presented with a tissue of conceits, fancifully strung about the personages of the tale, expressed in language that is equally intolerable for its affectation and obscurity. The story has no movement, no proportions, no ultimate end; and unless it is a huge allegory, bits of which peep out here and there—winding its unwieldy length along, like some monster of the deep, no significance or point. . . ." *Log*, p. 303.

[4] Herman Melville, *Mardi* (Evanston, Illinois, 1970), p. 426.

[5] This theme is developed throughout the novel, but particularly in Chapters 78 and 143.

[6] *Mardi,* p. 630. The conversions of Yoomy and Media are also important in the overall meaning of *Mardi,* but they are not pertinent here.

[7] *Mardi,* p. 636.

[8] Tyrus Hillway, "Taji's Quest for Certainty," *AL*, XVIII (1946), 32-33.

[9] *Mardi,* p. 654.

[10] Ibid., p. 370.

[11] Ronald Mason, *The Spirit Above the Dust* (London, 1951), p. 63.

[12] Chapters 186-187. John Seelye observes that just as Taji's "phantom of lost delight is pure illusion, so can it also be shown that Serenia, after all, is a Utopia and no more of this earth than Yillah." *Melville: The Ironic Diagram* (Evanston, Illinois, 1970), p. 41.

[13] Merrill R. Davis points out that this was actually Melville's intention: the narrator is a novice on a sight-seeing tour being conducted by others to islands of their world; in addition, he is the only one emotionally afflicted by the loss of Yillah and is, therefore, unable to participate in their deliberations: *Melville's Mardi: A Chartless Voyage* (Hamden, Conn., 1967), p. 148.

[14] Herman Melville, *Moby-Dick* (New York, 1963), I, p. 7.

[15] Ibid., II, p. 181.

[16] Sedgwick does not see Ishmael converted to a balanced view of life. He

argues that Babbalanja's escape is actually a commitment, whereas Ishmael's is only an escape, or an episode, and hardly a conclusion of his story: William Ellery Sedgwick, *Herman Melville, The Tragedy of Mind* (Cambridge, Mass., 1945), p. 125. For a different judgment on Ishmael's fate, see H. C. Brasher, "Ishmael's Tattoos," *SR*, LXXX (Winter, 1962), p. 137-54. Each year brings further argument, attesting to the designed ambivalence in the novel.

[17] *Moby-Dick,* II, p. 190.

[18] In the previous year, Melville sketched a satirical story in his Shakespeare volume. It indicates that the Miltonic "Non Serviam" was on his mind throughout this period: . . . *(Devil as a Quaker)* A formal compact—Imprimis—First—Second. The aforesaid soul, said soul &c—Duplicates—How was it about the temptation on the hill? &c Conversation upon Gabriel, Michael & Raphael—gentlemanly &c—D begs the hero to form one of a "Society of D's"—his name would be weighty &c—Leaves a letter to the D—"My dear D"— . . . Receives visits from the principal d's—"Gentlemen" &c arguments to persuade—"Would you not rather be below with kings than above with fools?" *Log*, p. 297.

[19] II, p. 366.

[20] His real motives, however, are not that clear to himself or to the reader. For example, Ishmael deals patronizingly with Elijah in the same way a father pats the head of a retarded child: his new "marriage" to Queequeeg has temporarily rid him of the hypos and restored his confidence. But not quite, for it is he who resumes the conversation when the prophet is ready to leave; and it is he who goes out of the way, actually retracing his steps, to learn the meaning of the strange prophecy. By then, Elijah can say no more to any man who will doom himself in Ahab's service: Chapter 19.

[21] I mean this in a larger social sense. It hardly explains the deeper feeling he had for Nathaniel Hawthorne: a fulfillment of the fidus-Achates union he had discussed earlier in *Mardi* and continued in the Ishmael-Queequeeg bond. The dedication of *Moby-Dick* to Hawthorne expressed this regard. In addition, of all the extant Melville letters, except for a couple to John Hoadley and Evert Duyckinck, and a few, later on in life, to Catherine Gansevoort Lansing, those to Hawthorne are the only ones in which he disclosed his intimate thoughts and feelings. Two in particular, in November 1851, after Hawthorne had volunteered to review *Moby-Dick,* declared in ecstatic language the communion he thought he shared with his new friend:

> . . . So now I can't write what I felt. But I felt pantheistic then (reading Hawthorne's letter)—your heart beat in my ribs and mine in yours, and both in God's. A sense of unspeakable security is in me this moment, on account of your having understood the book . . .
>
> Whence came you, Hawthorne? By what right do you drink from my flagon of life? And when I put it to my lips—lo, they are yours and not mine. I feel that the Godhead is broken up like the bread at the Sup-

per, and that we are the pieces. Hence this infinite fraternity of feeling. *Letters,* p. 142.

[22] This will hardly settle the controversy over Melville's sympathies in the novel Howard Vincent argues that Melville was committed equally to Ahab and Ishmael: *The Trying Out of Moby-Dick* (Chicago, 1949). Alfred Kazin reads the work as a long poem with the central interest in the development of Ishmael's sensibility: Introduction to *Moby-Dick* (Cambridge, Mass., 1956). Henry Alonzo Myers includes the novel as a tragedy in the classical tradition because of the awesome, noble presence of Ahab: "Captain Ahab's Discovery," *NEQ,* XV (1942), p. 15-34.

[23] These riotous urges Melville translated into art show him anticipating twentieth-century belief as he does in so many places. For example, Rollo May's chapter "The Daimonic in Dialogue" attempts a kind of scientific explanation of the "haunted characters," the ones that Melville intuited a century before. May regards them as closer to "normal" than Melville did and, therefore, disregards alternatives such as "hell-fire" and "predestinated madness." *Love and Will* (New York, 1969).

[24] Herman Melville, *Pierre* (New York, 1963).

[25] Arvin, *Melville,* pp. 226-27.

[26] *Pierre,* pp. 502-03. About two years before this, in a Bible recently purchased, Melville altered Verse 16, Chapter 7 of Ecclesiastes to read: "Be not righteous over much; neither make thyself overwise: why shoulds't thou [destroy thyself] be desolate?" *Log,* p. 370. Unless this was an ironic alteration, as so many of his revisions and commentaries of the Bible were, it appears that Melville had mixed feelings for Pierre's Christian mission.

[27] Sedgwick, p. 57.

[28] *Pierre,* p. 402. This introspection in his own life must have been obvious to his family and friends during the composition of *Pierre.* Sarah Morewood commented on his nervousness in a letter to George Duyckinck: "I hear that he is now engaged in a new work as frequently not to leave his room til quite dark in the evening—when he for the first time during the whole day partakes of solid food—he must therefore write under a state of morbid excitement which will soon injure his health—I laughed at him somewhat and told him that the recluse life he was leading made his city friends think that he was slightly insane—he replied that long ago he came to the same conclusion himself. . . ." *Log,* p. 441.

[29] William Braswell, *Melville's Religious Thought* (New York, 1959), p. 55.

[30] *Pierre,* p. 382.

[31] Sedgwick, p. 178.

[32] *Melville,* pp. 234-35.

[33] *Letters,* pp. 149-51.

[34] *Herman Melville* (Berkeley, California, 1951), p. 229.

[35] *Log,* p. 510. This is particularly striking because it was made by G. W. Curtis, a friend who had aided Melville more times than he knew. Curtis had advised J. H. Dix, at Putnam's, in the previous year, to be wary of any of Melville's novels: "I should decline any novel from Melville that is not extremely good." *Log,* p. 500.

[36] *Log,* p. 466.

[37] This dissatisfaction with himself carries over into later years, when Melville wrote a poem on his hopes for success and his cognizance of the breakdown between him and the readers. It also has a sense of the poet's contentment despite the failure, thus leaving an effect of ambivalence, like Yeats's "A Coat."

> Children of my happier prime,
> When One yet lived with me, and threw
> Her rainbow over life and time,
> Even Hope, my bride, and mother to you!
> O, nurtured in sweet pastoral air,
> And fed on flowers and light, and dew
> Of morning meadows—spare, Ah, spare
> Reproach; spare, and upbraid me not
> That, yielding scarce to reckless mood
> But jealous of your future lot,
> I sealed you in a fate subdued.
> Have I not saved you from the drear
> Theft and ignoring which need be
> The triumph of the insincere
> Unanimous Mediocrity?
> Rest therefore, free from all despite,
> Snugged in the arms of comfortable.

"Immolated," *Collected Poems of Herman Melville,* ed. Howard P. Vincent (Chicago, 1947), p. 371. This poem might well sum up Melville's artistic frustration during the Pittsfield period, except for the missing anger.

[38] "A Truce of God for Melville," *SR*, LXI (Autumn, 1953), p. 693.

[39] E. L. Grant Watson considers this the modern psychological problem explored in *Pierre* that makes the novel possibly Melville's best work: "Melville's *Pierre,*" *NEQ,* III (1930), p. 195-234.

[40] "Benito Cereno," *The Piazza Tales* (New York, 1963), p. 170. Benito's stare is like Mortmain's in *Clarel,* as will be seen hereafter. It appears that Benito and Mortmain failed to heed Ishmael's advice: "Look not too long in the face of fire, O man!"

[41] "Poor Man's Pudding," *Billy Budd and Other Prose Pieces* (New York, 1963), p. 301.

[42] "The Encantadas," *The Piazza Tales,* p. 235.

[43] *Israel Potter* (New York, 1963), p. 220. I do not imply any kind of victory for Israel. Melville admitted that his intention and the effect he achieved are directly the opposite: " . . . no one can complain of the gloom of my closing chapters more profoundly than myself."

[44] John Clifford, a New Bedford attorney, told Melville the story of Agatha Robinson, a Quaker woman of Falmouth, deserted by her sailor-husband after two years of marriage. Seventeen years later, Robinson returned, supported his wife and daughter, and urged them to move to Missouri with him. Upon Agatha's refusal, he married a second time, with Agatha's knowledge but without her approval. The extraordinary patience and tolerance Agatha demonstrated in the long sorrow impressed Melville as rich material for a story or a novel. He offered the plot to Hawthorne. When Hawthorne rejected the proposal, Melville said that he would get on with it himself. *Letters,* pp. 153-63. There is no evidence that Melville ever did complete the work.

[45] *Billy Budd,* p. 44.

[46] "I and My Chimney," *Billy Budd and Other Prose Pieces,* p. 289.

[47] Ibid., p. 283.

[48] Ibid., p. 300. Merton Sealts sees the chimney and the secret chamber as expressions of Melville's own fears over imminent insanity: "Herman Melville's 'I and My Chimney,' " *AL,* XIII (1941), p. 142-54. A chimney plays an important part also in Chapter 12 of *Israel Potter,* when Israel experiences the terror of encasement in the "coffin-cell of the Templars," behind a massive chimney in Squire Woodcock's house. The chimney in the novel, however, is used differently, for Israel's emergence after three days' entombment parodies the death and resurrection of Christ: " 'And I am to be buried alive here?' said Israel ruefully looking around. 'But your resurrection will soon be at hand,' smiled the Squire, 'two days at the furthest.' " (p. 88).

[49] *Letters,* p. 132.

[50] *Letters,* pp. 124-25.

[51] Werner Berthoff considers the last hundred pages of *Moby-Dick* as the first indication of the author's uncertainty, a condition that reappeared in all of the succeeding works. The "freedom of view and personal unconstraint" that marked Melville's genius before this shifted to cautious allegory, withdrawal, and resignation as themes and expression. *The Example of Melville* (Princeton, New Jersey, 1962), pp. 45-7, 61 ff.

[52] John Berstein, *Pacifism and Rebellion in the Writings of Herman Melville* (The

Hague, 1964), pp. 159-60. Paul Brodtkorb reads the ending as more positive than I have stated, with the final scene centered on Frank as "potential saviour" presenting the existential moment, beyond which "lies the naught." "*The Confidence-Man*: The Con-Man as Hero," *Studies in the Novel*, I (1969), p. 421-35. Merlin Bowen, in the same Special Issue on Melville, sees Melville's positive stance expressed earlier in the development of Pitch: "In this general darkness Pitch remains the one bright spot. . . . He represents, in his skeptical intelligence, his warm and generous humanity, his guarded hopefulness, his dogged self-respect, and his capacity for a just and disinterested anger, all that is still sound in a flawed creation." "Tactics of Indirection in Melville's *The Confidence-Man*," *Studies*, p. 418.

[53] "*The Piazza*," *The Piazza Tales*, p. 18.

[54] Herman Melville, *The Confidence-Man* (New York, 1963), p. 180.

[55] Lawrance Thompson believes that Melville could not accept a Godless world or would not admit to himself the possibility of God's absolute withdrawal: "By contrast, one might fear that Melville's concept of the Calvinistic God might gradually have become so repulsive that he might have moved through doubt and skepticism to a denial of the existence of God. This final step he never took." *Melville's Quarrel with God* (Princeton, 1952), p. 3.

Notes to Chapter III

[1] See a letter from Augusta Melville to Peter Gansevoort, September 24, 1856: *Log*, p. 522. His mother also wrote to Peter Gansevoort, in late November, 1856, shortly after Melville's departure for England: ". . . I hope Herman will feel content to remain away for six months at least for he has sadly overworked his strength—& requires recreation, freedom from care, from writing, & the little petty cares, & annoyances, of the farm which are ever recurring & are so distasteful to him." *Log*, p. 533.

[2] Howard, *Melville*, p. 233.

[3] *Log*, p. 498. The whole Pittsfield period remains clouded, but there is surely a connection between Melville's bad health and the general seclusion on the farm. These can be connected as well with the failure of *Moby-Dick* and *Pierre* so that anything after 1852 can be traced to earlier crushed hopes. This is hinted at by Luther Mansfield, "Glimpses of Herman Melville's Life in Pittsfield, 1850-51," *AL*, IX (1938), p. 26-48.

[4] *Log*, p. 502. The parallels between Melville's bad back and the old chimney, and between Dr. Holmes and Master Scribe, have been noted by most Melville scholars.

[5] F. O. Matthiessen, *American Renaissance* (New York, 1941), p. 491.

[6] *Log,* p. 517.

[7] Melville's awareness of their disfavor accounts in part for the alienation theme of "Bartleby, the Scrivener." Written in 1853, the story clearly poses a dichotomy of success and failure in society's terms, but slyly leaves the lawyer unsure of himself after Bartleby's eviction and death. It may be that Lemuel Shaw, Jr., or even Judge Shaw himself, was Melville's model for the lawyer.

[8] *Log,* p. 521.

[9] Letter of Louis McLane to James Buchanan, May 4, 1846: *Log,* p. 213.

[10] *Letters,* p. 83. Melville's insight here, very much like Dostoevsky's, anticipates beliefs held by different psychologists in the twentieth century; that is, many sick souls are spiritually far in advance of "happier" or "healthy" souls. See E. L. Grant Watson, "Melville's Pierre," *NEQ,* III (1930), 216. R. D. Laing ascribes to these sick persons better mental or spiritual health than the average man, but only because his judgment assumes that society itself is sick: *Politics of Experience* (New York, 1967); *Divided Self* (New York, 1969). Karl Menninger would consider the madness Melville describes a fourth order of "dyscontrol"; that is, an "experimental try" at life which is merely an extension of the everyday coping devices of man to maintain a healthy condition: *The Vital Balance* (New York, 1963).

[11] Metcalf, p. 158.

[12] *The Times of Melville and Whitman* (New York, 1947), pp. 166-67. Melville notes continuing trouble with his eyes and sleeplessness in the *Levant Journal* but no incidents of vertigo.

[13] *Log,* p. 508.

[14] Braswell, pp. 108-09. This dilemma over God is essentially the thesis in Lawrance Thompson's book, cited earlier.

[15] *The English Notebooks of Nathaniel Hawthorne,* ed. Randall Stewart (New York, 1941), pp. 422-23.

[16] Ibid., p. 435.

[17] Herman Melville, *Journal of a Visit to London and the Continent, 1849-1850,* ed. Eleanor Melville Metcalf (Cambridge, Mass., 1948), pp. 9-10.

[18] *Levant Journal,* p. 89. Hereafter, I will note page numbers of the *Journal* in parenthesis, following the passage quoted.

[19] Barthold George Niebuhr published his history of Rome in three volumes between 1811 and 1832. It is considered by some scholars as the inauguration of modern scientific historical method. David Friedrich Strauss published his *Life of Jesus* in 1835-1836. Like Niebuhr he treated the Gospel stories as history.

Melville associated both with higher criticism and the move to accept Christ and Scripture only on a natural level.

[20] Between the time that Melville returned from the Middle East and the publication of *Clarel* in 1876, very few events occurred of significance to this discussion, for the obvious reason that Melville retired as a professional writer. His life during this time, therefore, will be only sketched briefly, except for those events that have relevance to *Battle-Pieces* and to the writing of *Clarel.*

[21] Merton Sealts suggests that at this time Melville knew his career as a writer was over. As evidence, he cites Melville's underlining in Chapman's translation of Homer's *Batrachomymachia*: "The work tnat I was born to do is done." "Melville's Reading: A Checklist of Books Owned and Borrowed," *Harvard Library Bulletin,* II, No. 2 (Spring, 1948), p. 160. I believe this was one of the many passing moods Melville suffered over his reputation and art. But I think that the author of *Billy Budd, Clarel, Battle-Pieces,* and the other poems, was conscious of his own power and of the tasks he assigned himself at the same time that he knew he would never write again for commercial purposes. He was also the one who underscored a more important line, in William Alger's *The Solitudes of Nature and of Man*: "[Beethoven] says, 'I was nigh taking my life with my own hands. *But Art held me back. I could not leave the world until I had revealed what lay within me*'." *Log,* p. 721.

[22] "From this time on, a sweetness and serenity began to spread over the man. . . . there might be hours of stormy egoism or inner defiance, but in the main there was peace." Lewis Mumford, *Herman Melville* (New York, 1929), p. 307; Van Wyck Brooks, p. 262, and Mason, pp. 210-13, support this view. Melville documents it somewhat as well. He wrote a letter to Samuel Shaw in half-jocular tone, in which he told of his neuralgia and other ills, but said that foolish ideas of not wanting to live were no longer with him because he found life too interesting to leave it. *Letters,* pp. 216-17.

[23] The poems, "Frescoes of Travel," were refused by all of the publishers contacted by Elizabeth after Melville had sailed to San Francisco with his brother, Tom. They did not appear in print until 1891 when they were included in *Timoleon* as "Fruit of Travel Long Ago."

[24] The poet was well aware of the popular belief which singled out America as the world's and God's country. The second half of the line is his comment on the War and belief: ". . . linked with man's foulest crime." The poem is "Misgivings." *Collected Poems,* p. 3. An essay on this subject can be found in Richard H. Fogle's "Melville and the Civil War," *Tulane Studies in English,* IX (1959), pp. 61-89. Melville's singular objectivity in these War poems is praised by a contemporary Southerner, Ralph E. Hitt, "Melville's Poems of Civil War Controversy," *Studies in the Literary Imagination*, II (Atlanta, Georgia, 1969), pp. 57-68.

[25] Perry Miller believes, on the contrary, that Melville in fact never really recovered from the *Mardi* reviews: *The Raven and the Whale* (New York, 1956), p. 271.

[26] *Log,* p. 677.

[27] "Supplement," *Collected Poems,* pp. 462-63.

[28] "Lee in the Capitol," *Collected Poems,* p. 146.

[29] See the letter from Maria Melville to Catherine Gansevoort, March 11, 1867: *Log,* p. 686.

[30] *Main Currents in American Thought* (New York, 1930), III, p. 14.

Notes to Chapter IV

[1] *Log,* p. 747.

[2] Jay Martin observes how every important author after Whitman's lead in autobiographical literature was "compelled to become increasingly *aware,* to move in art toward self-revelation. Necessarily, much of the result of this remained private literature." He sees Henry Adams and Emily Dickinson particularly convinced of this need, and even the outspoken Twain and Howells writing hundreds of pieces not meant for publication. *Harvests of Change* (Englewood Cliffs, New Jersey, 1967), pp. 281-82. The ambivalence in connection with *Clarel* was only a part of a life-long problem Melville had regarding the public, probably from *Mardi* on:

> You may think, in your own mind that a man is unwise,—indiscreet, to write a work of that kind, when he might have written one perhaps, calculated merely to please the general reader, & not provoke attack, however masqued in an affectation of indifference or contempt. But some of us scribblers, My Dear Sir, always have a certain something unmanageable in us, that bids us do this or that, and be done it must—hit or miss.

Letter to Richard Bentley, June 5, 1849: *Letters,* p. 86. Melville's comments to Hawthorne on fame and patronage are well known.

[3] Bezanson, ed. *Clarel,* p. xli.

[4] June 16, 1876.

[5] June 26, 1876.

[6] XXVIII (July 6, 1876), p. 9.

[7] IX (August, 1876), p. 108.

[8] XXII (August, 1876), p. 282.

[9] July 10, 1876.

[10] Bezanson, ed. *Clarel,* p. xliii. I was not able to find this review. Neither was Bezanson until he learned from Jay Leyda that it was reprinted in the Springfield (Mass.) *Republican*, September 8, 1876. My survey of the early scholarship on the poem necessarily follows closely upon Bezanson's account, in his Introduction to the Melville text.

[11] XVIII (September, 1876), pp. 391-92.

[12] CCX (October, 1876), p. 282.

[13] This accounts partially for Melville's calling in the publication, although he was probably equally discouraged by the sale of only four hundred and seventy-eight copies. John Winterich, "The Compleat Collector," *SRL*, VII (1932), p. 531.

[14] "Herman Melville," *The Review,* I (1919), pp. 276-78, 298-301. Melville's brother-in-law, John Hoadley, had advanced a similar argument in 1876 as a protest over the vicious *World* criticism. His anger possibly rose out of family loyalty. But the statement he made anticipated twentieth-century critics: "*Clarel* is not easy reading. It requires determined study, and every attention must be at it furnished (?), to relish it until several perusals. But it will grow on thoughtful reading, and will give Her [man] Melville a firm footing on a higher plane than anything he has before written." *Log,* p. 751.

[15] October 10, 1884: *Letters,* p. 117.

[16] *Herman Melville, Mariner and Mystic* (New York, 1921), pp. 356-60. Despite the casual treatment Weaver gave the poem in his biography, he edited the full text for publication in 1924. This text, again in two volumes, lacked annotated notes. Yet its service to Melville readers cannot be underestimated, considering the unavailability of the 1876 edition.

[17] *Herman Melville* (New York, 1926), p. 16.

[18] Ibid., p. 169.

[19] Mumford, p. 322.

[20] Ibid., p. 314.

[21] Herman Melville, *Representative Selections,* ed. Willard Thorpe (New York, 1938), p. xcv.

[22] *Herman Melville: Marin, Metaphysicien, et Poete* (Paris, 1939), pp. 467-90.

[23] *Renaissance,* p. 401.

[24] Ibid., p. 412.

[25] Herman Melville, *Selected Poems,* ed. F. O. Matthiessen (Norfolk, Conn., 1944), p. 7.

[26] "Herman Melville's Thought After 1851," Unpublished Dissertation (University of North Carolina, 1942).

[27] "Herman Melville's 'Clarel'," *College English*, IV (1943), p. 480.

[28] Ibid., p. 480.

[29] Ibid., p. 483.

[30] "Herman Melville's 'Clarel'," Unpublished Dissertation (Yale University, 1943). Bezanson summarized his findings in a later article: "Melville's 'Clarel': The Complex Passion," *Journal of English Literary History*, XXXI (1954), pp. 146-59. Both were preliminary to the definitive edition of *Clarel* with its comprehensive introduction and set of notes, published in 1960, as cited earlier.

[31] Herman Melville, *Selected Poems*, ed. William Plomer (London, 1943), p. 8.

[32] Sedgwick, pp. 216-17.

[33] Rudolph Von Abele believes that late in his life Melville became reconciled to the universe as it is and to man's precarious existence in it, and that the heart in Melville triumphed over the head. But neither in *Clarel*, nor in any other work, did Melville suggest that reconciliation could be found through the Catholic Church: "Melville and the Problem of Evil," *American Mercury*, LXV (1947), pp. 592-98.

[34] Brooks, p. 21. Brooks does not single out *Clarel*. He includes it as only one of the literary effects of a man whose reputation rests solely on *Moby-Dick*. These other works would not be read if the great novel had not been written: cf. p. 172.

[35] Ibid., p. 249.

[36] *Melville's Use of the Bible* (New York, 1949), p. 57.

[37] *Melville* (New York, 1949), p. 296.

[38] *Herman Melville* (New York, 1949), p. 243.

[39] Ibid., p. 256.

[40] *Melville*, p. 272.

[41] Ibid., pp. 286-87.

[42] *Herman Melville*, pp. 309-10.

[43] Mason, p. 244.

[44] Ibid., p. 242.

[45] *Melville's Quarrel,* p. 337.

[46] *Melville,* p. 284.

[47] "Melville and the Quest for God," Unpublished Dissertation (Iowa State, 1952).

[48] *Levant Journal,* p. 315.

[49] *Ishmael* (Baltimore, 1956), p. 75.

[50] Ibid., p. 315.

[51] *The Fine Hammered Steel of Herman Melville* (Urbana, Illinois, 1957), p. 10.

[52] Ibid., p. 11.

[53] Ibid., p. 15.

[54] Ibid., p. 27.

[55] "*Clarel*: An Investigation of Spiritual Crisis," Unpublished Dissertation (Catholic University, 1958), p. lxvi.

[56] Ibid., p. 201.

[57] "The Traditional Element in Herman Melville's Thought with Special Attention to *Clarel,*" Unpublished Dissertation (Georgetown University, 1959).

[58] Bezanson, ed. *Clarel,* p. lxvi.

[59] Ibid., p. cix.

[60] *The Long Encounter* (Chicago, 1960), p. 253.

[61] Ibid., p. 282.

[62] "Melville's *Clarel*: Doubt and Belief," *Tulane Studies in English* (1960), pp. 101-16.

[63] *Pacifism and Rebellion in the Writings of Herman Melville* (The Hague, 1964), pp. 188-201.

[64] *Melville: The Ironic Diagram* (Evanston, Illinois, 1970), pp. 136-45. The lines of *Moby-Dick* are from II, p. 264.

[65] *Tortured Synthesis: The Meaning of Melville's* Clarel (New York, 1971).

[66] "Herman Melville's *Clarel*: An Existentialist Gospel," PMLA, LXXXIII (1971), pp. 375-87.

[67] *Melville's Drive to Humanism* (Lafayette, Indiana, 1971), p. 278.

[68] They include H. P. Marshall, "Herman Melville," *The London Mercury,* VI (November, 1924 to April, 1925), pp. 56-70; Percy H. Boynton, *More Contemporary Americans* (Chicago, 1927); Henry S. Canby, *Classic Americans* (New York, 1932).

Notes to Chapter V

[1] *Clarel* is written in four major parts, with each section made up of many cantos: I, "Jerusalem," 44 cantos; II, "The Wilderness," 39 cantos; III, "Mar Saba," 39 cantos; and IV, "Bethlehem," 35 cantos.

[2] Textual references throughout this study will be to book, canto, and page number of Bezanson's text. Those readers who are familiar with *Clarel* may wish to skip to the next chapter since the next pages do little more than retell the plot. This approach seems correct, for my own experience indicates that few students of American literature have actually read the poem. If this is true, an outline of the poem will provide necessary background for an understanding of the critical discussions that follow.

[3] Melville intended such usage for he introduced Part IV with specific allusion to the Magi legend:

> Three mitered kings—Amerrian,
> Apelius, and Damazon—
> . . . .
> Thence, prompted by the vision yet
> To find the new-born Lord nor err,
> Westward their pious feet they set—
> With gold and frankincense and myrrh.
>
> [IV, 1, p. 403]

Clarel, Rolfe, and Vine are the modern Magi. Unlike them, Derwent has no genuine religious mission: he is clearly a tourist.

[4] Melville wrote an Epilogue to the poem. Because it adds nothing to the story I have not included it in this narrative. The Epilogue will be discussed in the succeeding chapters where Melville's thought is examined.

Notes to Chapter VI

[1] *Collected Poems,* p. 231.

[2] "Greek Architecture," *Collected Poems,* p. 248. This is the whole poem.

[3] "The Differences in Melville's Poetry," *PMLA*, LXX (Sep., 1955), p. 621.

[4] "Melville's Struggle With the Angel," *MLQ*, I (June, 1940), p. 206.

[5] R. P. Blackmur, "The Craft of Herman Melville: A Putative Statement," *The Expense of Greatness* (New York, 1940), p. 165. In *Melville,* Lewis Mumford's judgment on Melville's craft is equally harsh, p. 322.

[6] Newton Arvin, "Melville's Shorter Poems," *Partisan Review*, XVI (1949), p. 1034.

[7] "Melville the Poet," *Kenyon Review,* VIII (Spring, 1962), p. 208.

[8] Sedgwick, p. 199.

[9] Warren, p. 210.

[10] *Collected Poems,* p. 57.

[11] Ibid., "In a Garret," p. 228. This is the whole poem.

[12] "C—'s Lament," *Collected Poems,* pp. 232-33.

[13] "Shelley's Vision," *Collected Poems,* p. 233.

[14] Melville alluded to the Bible in all of his writing, but never as much as in *Clarel:* six hundred allusions, as compared with the next highest number, two hundred and fifty in *Moby-Dick:* Wright, p. 9.

[15] Arvin, "Shorter Poems," p. 1037.

[16] Significant in this connection is James Mark Purcell's listing of 180 new words Melville added to the English language, with not a single word coming from *Clarel.* However, this may be simply yet another example of a critic failing to include *Clarel* in a specialized canvas of Melville's works: "Melville's Contributions to English," *PMLA,* LVI (1941), pp. 797-80.

[17] Mason points out, in another connection, that when Melville suffered his greatest bewilderments he found intricate and ambiguous symbols corresponding to his own dilemmas; when he enjoyed serenity, he used simple allegory. *Spirit Above the Dust,* p. 259.

[18] *Levant Journal,* p. 137.

[19] *Daily Missal,* Maryknoll edition (N. Y., 1960), p. 116.

[20] Alan Liebowitz sees the image of the crag throughout Melville's work as the transcendent force against which the hero must test himself: Pierre and the Memnon Stone (his Terror Stone); John Paul Jones, in *Israel Potter,* and the crag of Ailsa, from which he retreats in fear; Babbalanja and the rock of Pella; Taji and his cliff to scale; Ahab and the jaws of the whale, which constitute a rock of horror for him. *Progress into Silence* (Bloomington, Indiana, 1970), pp. 178-79.

[21] *Clarel,* lxxxi.

[22] As I have noted, Melville achieves an effect of sterility through barren images. The images themselves, however, are often used as symbols and thus operate on two levels. This is particularly evident in the poet's use of death imagery.

[23] Wright, p. 30.

[24] *Mardi,* p. 339.

[25] Earlier in life, Melville told Sophia Hawthorne that he was "going to build a real towered-house, an actual tower." Metcalf, p. 92. The sad fact is that, unlike Hawthorne, he never did build the tower.

[26] "Isaiah," 60: 1-4, *The Jerusalem Bible* (New York, 1966).

[27] Ibid., I: 20-21.

[28] The wreck symbol can be found in any number of Melville's poems. See "The Haglets," "The Aeolian Harp" (actually uses Agath's same line, "Wreck ho, a wreck."), "Far Off-Shore," "The Berg," and "Off Cape Colonna."

[29] These symbols are led up to directly in the poem. Only once is there a complete incongruity, i.e., where the poet seeks a different effect and introduces an element out of context. This occurs when the pilgrims overlook Sodom. Mortmain lectures them in a kind of Dantesque cataloguing of sin. The group is stunned and cannot comment; but two spirits, hovering above them, interpret Mortmain's jeremiad in words echoing Milton's *Paradise Lost* (II, xxxvi, p. 265). Nowhere else in the poem is the supernatural brought to visible life nor the imagery so obviously contradictory.

[30] Edward Rosenberry's study of Melville as a comic author ignores *Clarel* completely: *Melville and the Comic Spirit* (Cambridge, 1955). Constance Rourke refuses comment on *Clarel:* "With the writing of his one great work Melville was finished." Rourke's point is that after *Moby-Dick* his imaginative force—which produced his comic effect—was dead: *American Humor* (New York, 1931), p. 160.

[31] The Book of Ezra and Nehemia pp. 582-600.

[32] "Book of Ruth," I: 17, pp. 339-40.

[33] See above, p. 232.

[34] The final lines of "Monody" also play with the vine metaphor but differently because of the winter-kill of death:

> Glazed now with ice the cloistral vine
> That hid the shyest grape.

I have no doubt that the short, poignant elegy was written for Hawthorne. *Collected Poems*, pp. 228-29.

[35] On December 14, 1849, Melville wrote a letter to Evert Duychinck in which he touched upon the same subject: "But we that write & print have all our books predestinated—& for me, I shall write such things as the Great Publisher of Mankind ordained ages before he published 'The World'—this planet, I mean—. . . . What a madness & anguish it is, that an author can never—under no conceivable circumstances—be at all frank with his readers.—" *Letters*, p. 96.

[36] Wells, "Herman Melville's *Clarel*," pp. 480-81.

Notes to Chapter VII

[1] In both novels, particularly *Omoo*, Melville is also severe on Protestant missionaries.

[2] James Baird suggests that if Melville had seen more of Catholic practical wisdom in the handling of the established customs of primitive societies, he would have come to an admiration of the Church, even where he could not accept its dogma: *Ishmael*, p. 100.

[3] Chapters 105-121.

[4] Chapter 187.

[5] The Encantadas, "Rodondo Rock," *The Piazza Tales*.

[6] *White-Jacket* (New York, 1963), pp. 210-11. Melville felt this uncharitable act deeply, for about thirty years later he cites the same abuse in *Clarel*, when the monks at Mar Saba refuse burial inside their walls to Mortmain (III, xxxii, p. 400).

[7] In another poem, Melville remarked on the durability of the Church and the Papacy:

> Since wag his tongue at Popes who may
> The Popedom deeds endure his say.

"At the Hostelry," *Collected Poems*, p. 316.

[8] In the ninth section of the "Marquis de Grandvin" poems Melville recounts an experience of his Italian tour of 1857 that impressed him. He tells how the noisy throng came to complete silence in reverential reception of the Host which was processed before them: *Collected Poems*, p. 366. Melville used the same experience in *Clarel* (II, i, p. 143) to demonstrate the rigidity of the old Presbyterian.

[9] "The Devotion of the Flowers to Our Lady: To Our Queen," *Collected Poems,* p. 312.

[10] *Melville's Use of the Bible,* p. 6. Braswell generally concurs with this statement, pp. 12-16.

[11] Ibid., p. 7.

[12] Melville had a high regard for Matthew Arnold. In this sympathy for certain features of the Catholic Church, he shared the views expressed by Arnold, viz., the misery and bondage of the world are relieved by the influence of Jesus; the Church's endurance since Christ and its unity in the face of the many sects have a strong appeal; the Puritan churches have no beauty compared with the charm and grace—or poetry—of the church that satisfies the imagination; long after all the other Puritan churches cease to exist, the Catholic Church will prevail: *Mixed Essays, Irish Essays and Others* (New York, 1883), pp. 73-106. Irving Babbitt sees it simply as *de rigeur* for Romanticists to be drawn to the Roman Catholic Church because of the aesthetic appeal of the rites and ceremonies. *Rousseau and Romanticism* (Boston, 1919), p. 263.

[13] *Pierre*, p. 295.

[14] Ibid., p. 289.

[15] Ibid., p. 297.

[16] See Chapters I and 5 particularly.

[17] "The New Rosicrucians," *Collected Poems,* p. 297.

[18] In this passage, Rolfe lectures Derwent on a god of joy and attempts a parallel between Pan and Christ. He concludes that man rejects both.

[19] Both Mother Denis Mahoney and Zeik consider more important the death of Mortmain as a symbol of hope for Melville. Their conclusion seems to import to Melville's intent more than the text of the poem allows: Mother Denis, p. 27; Zeik, p. 165.

[20] Bowen, pp. 14-15. Bowen's title of "The Long Encounter" sums up Melville's life-long encounter between faith and reason.

[21] *Melville,* p. 281.

[22] *Moby-Dick,* I, p. 51.

Notes to Chapter VIII

[1] Thorpe considers *Clarel,* as I do, a culmination of all of Melville's works. He suggests that an understanding of the poem presumes full reading of the Melville canon: p. lxxxix.

[2] *Letters,* pp. 256-57.

[3] Reading *Billy Budd* as a "testament of acceptance" is obviously a point of view. Many critics see it instead as a last statement of despair. For example, see Richard Chase, "Dissent on 'Billy Budd'," *PR,* XV (November, 1948), 1212-1218; Joseph Schiffman, "Final Stage, Irony: A Reexamination of 'Billy Budd' Criticism," *AL,* XXII (1950), 128-36. A summary of the many views appears in the Introduction of the "definitive" edition edited by Harrison Hayford and Merton M. Sealts, Jr. (Chicago, 1962).

[4] Chase breaks down all of Melville's heroes into these two categories of Ishmael and Prometheus. *Melville,* p. 251.

[5] W. H. Auden praises such a hero whose goal is never in sight: ". . . but the religious hero cannot demand happiness, except the happiness of the commitment itself, of love for love's sake. It does not follow that he must necessarily expect misery though. Since few desire misery and not happiness or pleasure that are his temptation; it is more correct to say that whatever he does not expect is temptation." *The Enchaféd Flood* (New York, 1950), p. 98.

[6] Baird considers this the true mark of the primitivist, *Ishmael,* p. 34. Melville expressed this same religious independence, earlier in *White-Jacket:* "Our own hearts are our best prayer-rooms, and the chaplains who can help us most are ourselves." p. 197.

[7] Billy Budd learns this fact of life, too. It accounts for his acceptance of Vere's unjust action: there is no other way out.

[8] Mumford, p. 310.

[9] Melville believed that such innocence invariably leads to disaster or fails to make a contribution to society. This theme runs throughout the poems, "On the Slain Collegians" particularly, and also "Apathy and Enthusiasm," "The March into Virginia," and "Ball's Bluff." The theme is really another variant of the conflict of head and heart.

[10] Charles Olson gives a good account of the actual incident that Melville drew on for this narration: the sinking of the *Essex,* Captain George Pollard, Jr., and the subsequent acts of cannibalization in the three open whaleboats. *Call me Ishmael* (New York, 1947), pp. 3-7.

[11] Fogle presses this further: he sees Nehemiah and Pip as mad in the same way, although their madness is the wisdom of the gods. "Melville's *Clarel,*" 106.

[12] *Tragedy of Mind,* p. 205.

[13] Ibid., p. 207.

[14] *Melville,* p. 252.

[15] Stern, p. 27.

[16] *Herman Melville,* p. 23.

[17] Chapter 40.

[18] "The Ravaged Villa," *Collected Poems*, p. 222.

[19] Stuart Woodruff, "Melville and His Chimney," *PMLA,* LXXV (June, 1960), 288.

[20] Surgeon Cuticle's amputation of the sailor's leg, in *White-Jacket,* ironically attests to the advances made in medicine. See Ishmael's comment in "Brit" on "baby man" and his bragging of his science and skill: *Moby-Dick,* Chapter 53.

[21] *Billy Budd and Other Pieces,* p. 245.

[22] *Israel Potter,* p. 62.

[23] See the "geological hammer" that Anna carries in "I and My Chimney." Like Margoth's tool, hers is destructive in that she would use it to aid her mother in knocking down the chimney.

[24] Chase, *Melville,* p. 243. Tyrus Hillway presents a series of essays on this subject: "Melville and the Spirit of Science," *SAQ,* XLVIII (January, 1949), 77-88; "Melville's Geological Science," *AL,* XXI (May, 1949), 232-37: "Melville's Use of Two Psuedo-Sciences," *Modern Language Notes*, LXIV (March, 1950), 145-50; "Melville as Critic of Science," *Modern Language Notes*, LXV (June, 1950), 411-14; "Melville as Amateur Zoologist," *MLQ*, XII (June, 1951), 159-64.

[25] "The New Zealot to the Sun," *Collected Poems,* p. 227. In connection with this poem and science itself, see the suggestion by William Bysshe Stein that this is specifically a comment on John William Draper, a spokesman for science as a new religion. *The Poetry of Melville's Late Years* (Albany, New York, 1970), p. 90.

[26] "The Paradise of Bachelors," *Billy Budd and Other Prose Pieces,* p. 169.

[27] "At the Hostelry," *Collected Poems,* p. 313.

[28] Melville jotted this in the margin of his copy of Schopenhauer's *Studies in Pessimism.*

[29] Stern, pp. 10-21.

[30] *Letters,* p. 147. The same teasing contradiction appears a short time after in "The Piazza," as I have already indicated.

[31] *Moby-Dick,* II, p. 117.

[32] Ibid., I, p. 7.

[33] Woodruff, 291. Late in his life—January 22, 1885—Melville wrote to James Billson concerning his distaste for the rosy view of the nineteenth century: "As to his (James Thompson) pessimism, altho neither pessimist nor optimist myself, nevertheless I relish it in the verse if for nothing else than as a counterpoise to the exorbitant hopefulness, juvenile & shallow, that makes such a bluster in these days—at least, in some quarters." *Letters,* p. 277.

[34] Herman Melville. *The Piazza Tales*, ed. Egbert S. Oliver (Chicago, 1948), p. 247.

[35] *Melville's Use of the Bible,* p. 23.

[36] *Moby-Dick,* I, p. 143-44.

[37] "Old Counsel," *Collected Poems,* p. 199.

[38] *The Confidence-Man,* p. 99.

Notes to Chapter IX

[1] Lloyd Morris, *The Rebellious Puritan* (New York, 1927), p. 248. Chase holds an even stronger view, i.e., Melville viewed all women—wife, mother—with terror: *Melville,* p. 21. Mumford regards sexual love as a threat to Melville throughout his life and works; Mumford emphasizes this in his comments on *Pierre,* pp. 145-52.

[2] "John Marr," *Collected Poems,* p. 159.

[3] "Rip Van Winkle," *Collected Poems,* p. 284.

[4] "The Rusty Man," *Collected Poems,* p. 377.

[5] Bezanson adds Agath to this trio and demonstrates how each of them constitutes a step in Melville's own spiritual growth: "Herman Melville's *Clarel,*" p. 256.

[6] This is another example of Melville's continuing concern over median ethics vis-à-vis the tenets of the Sermon on the Mount.

[7] Melville noted in the *Levant Journal* a dinner table group: "the young Parisian, the fair young lady, the French judge with black cap on (Sentencing cap)." p. 188. The judge did not become Mortmain, but the sentencing ritual cap carries over to Mortmain, whose castigations include overt and tacit sentencing of the human race.

[8] Seelye likens Mortmain to Orme in his section on those Melville heroes for whom death "is a final act of self-assertion," pp. 155-66.

[9] *Moby-Dick,* I, p. 18.

[10] *The Piazza Tales,* p. 130.

[11] Whereas Mortmain has no hope in man, the fact of his remaining on the mountain in the hope of receiving a sign from God demonstrates that he still has confidence in God. At this point he is very much like Ahab in that he faces up to whatever comes along, on its own terms. In his role of prophet of doom, however, he functions like Elijah, who attempts to warn Ishmael of the fate awaiting the *Pequod.* Both prophets, in turn, are modeled on Elijah the Tishbite: "Suddenly into the evil court of Ahab came Elijah, prophesied violent drought, and then retreated to live by the brook Cherith." Cherith is actually mentioned in connection with Mortmain (II, xxxiv, p. 259).

[12] All of Melville's titans in one way or another ask the question that Ahab puts to Starbuck just before the chase: "What is it, what nameless, inscrutable, unearthly thing is it; what cozening, hidden lord and master, and cruel, remorseless emperor commands me; that against all natural lovings and longings, I so keep pushing, and crowding, and jamming myself on all the time; recklessly making me ready to do what in my own proper, natural heart, I durst not so much as dare? Is Ahab, Ahab? Is it I, God, or who, that lifts this arm?" *Moby-Dick,* II, p. 330.

[13] Thorp, p. xcl. Maurice Friedman notes the similar handling of this faith-despair dichotomy or laradox in *Clarel* and in Yeats's "A Second Coming." *Problematic Rebel* (New York, 1963), p. 84.

[14] Matthiessen, *Renaissance,* pp. 442-43. See my remarks on this subject in the second chapter.

[15] Stone, p. 101.

[16] It could be argued, on the other hand, that Vere thwarts the democratic will.

[17] Mason, p. 58.

[18] Reginald E. Watters, "Melville's Sociality," *AL*, XVII (1945), p. 38.

[19] *Hammered Steel,* p. 12.

[20] Jarl's tattoo of the crucifixion holds the same meaning: *Mardi,* Chapter 45.

[21] This is not to say that measured reality was the sum of earthly objects and experience for Melville. Imagination for him demonstrates man's greater, creative conquest of nature, and repeatedly indicates the earth-rooted source for all such flights. It accounts for all the significant art, philosophy, and religion of the world, out of which are spun the myths that constitute an ethos of the people. The "droppings on the Madonna's breast" may well have sprung from the superstition of peasants, but the image and belief are no different than the "creative love"

Wherefrom the faun and cherub grew,
With genii good and Oberon

[IV, xvii, p. 467]

Melville does not object to the amaranth that Vine pines for provided it complements the thorn he physically presses upon himself. The imagination that Vine uses to sing the flower and address the tree is, paradoxically, the very function that might give him reason to live.

[22] Melville's introduction of Vine, earlier in the poem, contains this same ambivalence:

no sackclothed man;
Howbeit, in sort Carthusian
Though born a Sybarite.

[I, xxix, p. 95]

Later, his allusion to the Cenci portrait is even more pointed:

He wore that nameless look
About the mouth—so hard to brook—
Which in the Cenci portrait shows,
Lost in each copy, oil or print . . .

[III, vii, p. 301]

Hawthorne's theme of Miriam as the incarnate Beatrice Cenci, in *The Marble Faun,* is the key to Melville's use of Hawthorne as the model for Vine. The implicit accusation of some dark secret hidden by Vine-Hawthorne is discussed by Julian Hawthorne: see *Log,* (782-83). Almost every major Melville scholar has commented on this Hawthorne-Vine identity, although almost nothing has been suggested concerning the homosexual attraction.

[23] "At the Hostelry," *Collected Poems*, p. 329.

[24] Bezanson, "Herman Melville's *Clarel,*" pp. 171, 175; Chase, p. 248; Griffith, p. 53; Zeik, p. 187.

[25] "The Marquis De Grandvin" (Sketch), *Billy Budd and Other Pieces*, p. 351.

[26] See Melville's comic-serious poem "Herba Santa." The final stanza could be written specifically for Djalea.

Forbear, my soul! and in thine Eastern chamber
Rehearse the dream that brings the long release:
Through jasmine sweet and talismanic amber
Inhaling Herba Santa in the passive Pipe of Peace.

Collected Poems, p. 238.

[27] Bowen, pp. 121-23.

[28] *Mardi,* p. 367. As I indicated in the review of scholarship on *Clarel,* the complementary work of Stanley Brodwin and Joseph Knapp explores with perception Melville's existentialist posture.

[29] "Rammon," *Collected Poems,* p. 411.

[30] "Supplement," *Collected Poems,* p. 465.

[31] "The Coming Storm," *Collected Poems,* p. 94.

[32] "Lee in the Capitol," *Collected Poems,* pp. 145-46.

[33] *Moby-Dick,* II, 190.

[34] *Melville's Use of the Bible,* p. 172.

[35] *Herman Melville,* p. 184.

[36] "Commemoration of a Naval Victory," *Collected Poems,* p. 115.

[37] Braswell, p. 30.

[38] "Pontoosuce," *Collected Poems,* p. 395. My point throughout has been that *Clarel* binds together or sums up all of Melville's thoughts and feelings of a lifetime. This poem functions in similar fashion but in a miniature form. It was written sometime in the 1850s, after many visits to Pontoosuc Lake, an idyllic place Melville called "Pontoosuce": he entitled the poem "The Lake." The interweaving of life and death through images of trees, grass, roots, and water, and the metaphysical inquiry into rebirth in the poem indicated that such musings, like those in *Clarel,* were not peculiar to Melville's later years.

[39] Ibid., p. 397.

[40] R. W. B. Lewis, *The American Adam* (Chicago, 1955), p. 132.

Notes to Chapter X

[1] The few obituaries at his death were either vague about the author's life and works or were curious over this oblivion. The statement in the *New York Times* was typical:

> . . . when a visiting British author a few years ago inquired at a gathering in New York of distinctly literary Americans what had become of HERMAN MELVILLE not only was there not one who was able to tell him, but there was scarcely one among them who had ever heard of the man concerning whom he inquired, albeit that man was then living within a half mile of the place of the conversation.

Cf. *Log,* p. 787.

A notice in *The Press* also commented on this obscurity:

> There died yesterday at his quiet home in this city a man who, although he had done almost no literary work during the last sixteen years, was once one of the most popular writers in the United States.
>
> Herman Melville probably reached the height of his fame about 1852, his first novel having been printed about 1847. . . . Of late years Mr. Melville—probably because he had ceased literary activity—had fallen into a literary decline, as the result of which his books are now little known. Probably, if the truth were known, even his own generation has long thought him dead, so quiet have been the later years of his life.

Cf. *Log*, p. 836; similar statements can be found on pp. 826-27.

[2] Jay Martin cites such "private literature" as widespread among nineteenth-century idealists, who found their ideals "less and less usable as a guide to action." He traces this self-revelation tendency in America to three intellectual strains: personal introspection of the Puritans; Scottish common sense philosophy; and Transcendentalism. *Harvest of Change,* pp. 280-82.

[3] Matthiessen sees *Israel Potter* as the first, convincing sign of the lost power; see above, p. 39. Brooks considers *Moby-Dick* as the last and only evidence of great talent at work; see above, p. 238.

[4] January 8, 1852, *Letters,* p. 147.

[5] "Pebbles," *Collected Poems*, p. 206.

[6] *The Poetry of Melville's Late Years,* p. 192.

Bibliography

I. PRIMARY SOURCES

Collected Poems of Herman Melville, ed. Howard P. Vincent. Chicago. Hendricks House, Packard & Co. 1947.

Family Correspondence of Herman Melville, 1830-1904, ed. Victor Paltsits. New York. The New York Public Library. 1929.

MELVILLE, HERMAN. *The Apple-Tree Table and Other Sketches.* Prınceton. Princeton University Press. 1922.

MELVILLE, HERMAN. *Clarel: A Poem and Pilgrimage in the Holy Land,* ed. Walter E. Bezanson. New York. Hendricks House. 1960.

MELVILLE, HERMAN. *Journal of A Visit to Europe and the Levant, October 11, 1856-May 6, 1857,* ed. Howard C. Horsford. Princeton. Princeton University Press. 1955.

MELVILLE, HERMAN. *Journal of A Visit to London and the Continent, 1849-1850,* ed. Eleanor Melville Metcalf. Cambridge, Massachusetts. Harvard University Press. 1948.

MELVILLE, HERMAN. *Mardi*, ed. Harrison Hayford et al. Evanston, Illinois. Northwestern University Press. 1970.

MELVILLE, HERMAN. *Representative Selections,* ed. Willard Thorp. New York. The American Book Company. 1938.

MELVILLE, HERMAN. *Selected Poems,* ed. William Plomer. London. 1943.

MELVILLE, HERMAN. *The Piazza Tales,* ed. Egbert S. Oliver. Chicago. Hendricks House. 1948.

Selected poems of Herman Melville, ed. F. O. Matthiessen. Norfolk, Connecticut. New Directions. 1944.

The Letters of Herman Melville, ed. Marrell R. Davis and William H. Gilman. New Haven, Connecticut. Yale University Press. 1960.

The Works of Herman Melville (The Standard Edition of Constable reissued 16 vols.). New York. Russell and Russell. 1963.

II. SECONDARY SOURCES

A. Books

ADAM, KARL. *The Spirit of Catholicism*. New York. Macmillan. 1937.

ANDERSON, CHARLES R. *Melville in the South Seas*. New York. Columbia University Press. 1939.

ARNOLD, E. VERNON. *Roman Stoicism.* New York. Macmillan. 1924.

ARNOLD, MATTHEW. *Mixes Essays, Irish Essays and Others.* New York. Macmillan. 1883.

ARVIN, NEWTON. *Herman Melville.* New York. William Sloan Associates. 1950.

AUDEN, W. H. *The Enchaféd Flood.* New York. Random House. 1950.

BABBITT, IRVING. *Rousseau and Romanticism.* Boston. Houghton Miflin. 1919.

BAIRD, JAMES. *Ishmael.* Baltimore. Johns Hopkins Press. 1956.

BERNSTEIN, JOHN. *Pacifism and Rebellion in the Writings of Herman Melville.* The Hague: Mouton. 1964.

BERTHOFF, WERNER. *The Example of Melville*. Princeton, New Jersey. Princeton University Press. 1962.

BLACKMUR, R. P. *The Expense of Greatness.* New York, Arrow Editions. 1940.

BOWEN, MERLIN. *The Long Encounter.* Chicago. University of Chicago Press. 1960.

BRASWELL, WILLIAM. *Melville's Religious Thought.* New York. Pageant. 1959.

BROOKS, VAN WYCK. *The Times of Melville and Whitman.* New York. E. P. Dutton. 1947.

BROWNE, RAY B. *Melville's Drive to Humanism.* Lafayette, Indiana. Purdue University Studies. 1971.

CANBY, HENRY S. *Classic Americans.* New York. Harcourt Brace. 1932.

CARPENTER, FREDERICK I. *American Literature and the Dream.* New York. Philosophical Library. 1955.

CHASE, RICHARD. *Herman Melville.* New York. Macmillan. 1949.

CHURCH, R. W. *The Oxford Movement.* New York. Macmillan. 1937.

CURL, VEGA. *Pasteboard Masks.* Cambridge, Massachusetts. Harvard University Press. 1931.

D'ARCY, MARTIN. *The Nature of Belief.* London. Sheed and Ward. 1931.

DAVIS, MERRELL R. *Melville's 'Mardi': A Chartless Voyage.* Hamden, Connecticut. Archon Books. 1967.

FEIDELSON, CHARLES. *Symbolism and American Literature.* Chicago. University of Chicago Press. 1953.

FOGEL, RICHARD H. *Melville's Shorter Tales.* Norman. University of Oklahoma Press. 1960.

FRIEDMAN, MAURICE. *The Problematic Rebel.* New York. Random House. 1963.

FREEMAN, JOHN. *Herman Melville.* New York. Macmillan. 1926.

FRIEDRICH, GERHARD. *In Pursuit of Moby-Dick.* Wallingford, Pennsylvania. Pendle Hill. 1958.

GABRIEL, RALPH H. *The Course of American Democratic Thought.* New York. Ronald Press. 1940.

GALE, ROBERT L. *Plots and Characters in the Fiction and Narrative Poetry of Herman Melville.* Hamden, Connecticut. Archon Books. 1969.

GEIST, STANLEY. *Herman Melville: The Tragic Vision and the Heroic Ideal.* Cambridge, Massachusetts. Harvard University Press. 1939.

The American Notebooks of Nathaniel Hawthorne, ed. Randall Stewart. New Haven. Yale University Press. 1932.

The English Notebooks of Nathaniel Hawthorne, ed. Randall Stewart. New York. Oxford. 1941.

HOWARD, LEON. *Herman Melville.* Berkeley. University of California Press. 1951.

The Holy Bible. The Jerusalem Bible. Garden City, New York. Doubleday. 1966.

KAUL, A. N. *The American Vision.* New Haven, Connecticut. Yale University Press. 1963.

KENNEY, ALICE. *The Ganesvoorts of Albany.* Syracuse. Syracuse University Press. 1969.

KNAPP, JOSEPH G. *Tortured Synthesis: The Meaning of Melville's 'Clarel'.* New York. Philosophical Library. 1971.

LAWRENCE, D. H. *Studies in Classic American Literature.* London. Thomas Seltzer. 1923.

LEVIN, HARRY. *The Power of Blackness.* New York. Vintage. 1960.

LEWIS, R. W. B. *The American Adam.* Chicago. University of Chicago Press. 1955.

LEYDA, JAY. *The Melville Log.* New York. Harcourt Brace. 1951.

Literary History of the United States, ed. Robert Spiller, et al. New York. Macmillan. 1949.

MARTIN, JAY. *Harvests of Change.* Englewood Cliffs, New Jersey. Prentice-Hall. 1967.

MASON, RONALD. *The Spirit Above the Dust.* London. John Lehman. 1951.

MATTHIESSEN, F. O. *American Renaissance.* New York. Oxford. 1941.

METCALF, ELEANOR MELVILLE. *Herman Melville.* Cambridge, Massachusetts. Harvard University Press. 1953.

MILLER, PERRY. *The Raven and the Whale.* New York. Harcourt Brace. 1956.

MORRIS, LLOYD. *The Rebellious Puritan.* New York. Harcourt Brace. 1927.

MUMFORD, LEWIS. *Herman Melville.* New York. Literary Guild of America. 1929.

MYERS, HENRY ALONZO. *Tragedy: A View of Life.* Ithaca. Cornell University Press. 1956.

OLSON, CHARLES. *Call Me Ishmael.* New York. Grove Press. 1947.

PARRINGTON, VERNON. *Main Currents in American Thought.* New York. Harcourt Brace. 1930.

PERCIVAL, M. O. *A Reading of 'Moby-Dick'.* Chicago. University of Chicago Press. 1950.

POMMER, HENRY F. *Milton and Melville.* Pittsburgh. University of Pittsburgh Press. 1950.

POULET, GEORGES. *Studies in Human Time,* Tr. Elliot Coleman. Baltimore. Johns Hopkins Press. 1956.

ROSENBERRY, EDWARD H. *Melville and the Comic Spirit.* Cambridge, Massachusetts. Harvard University Press. 1955.

ROURKE, CONSTANCE. *American Humor.* New York. Harcourt Brace. 1931.

ROYCE, JOSIAH. *Herbert Spencer.* New York. Fox, Duffield. 1904.

ROYCE, JOSIAH. *The Spirit of Modern Philosophy.* New York. Houghton Miflin. 1897.

SCHNEIDER, HERBERT A. *A History of American Philosophy.* New York. Columbia University Press. 1946.

SEDGWICK, WILLIAM ELLERY. *Herman Melville, The Tragedy of*

Mind. Cambridge, Massachusetts. Harvard University Press. 1945.

SEELYE, JOHN. *Melville: The Ironic Diagram.* Evanston, Illinois. Northwestern University. 1970.

SIMON, JEAN.. *Herman Melville: Marin, Metaphyscien, et Poete.* Paris. Boivin and Cie. 1939.

STEIN, WILLIAM BYSSHE. *The Poetry of Melville's Late Years.* Albany, New York. State University of New York Press. 1970.

STERN, MILTON. *The Fine Hammered Steel of Herman Melville.* Urbana. University of Illinois Press. 1957.

STONE, GEOFFREY. *Melville.* New York. Sheed and Ward. 1949.

STOVALL, FLOYD. *American Idealism.* Norman, Oklahoma. Oklahoma University Press. 1943.

SULLIVAN, J. W. N. *Aspects of Science,* 2nd series. New York. Knopf. 1926.

THOMPSON, LAWRANCE. *Melville's Quarrel with God.* Princeton. Princeton University Press. 1952.

TOWNSEND, H. G. *Philosophical Ideas in the United States.* New York. American Book Company. 1934.

VINCENT, HOWARD P. *The Trying-Out of Moby-Dick.* Boston. Houghton Miflin. 1949.

WEAVER, RAYMOND. *Herman Melville, Mariner and Mystic.* New York. George H. Doran. 1921.

WELLS, HENRY W. *The American Way of Poetry.* New York. Columbia University Press. 1943.

WINTERS, YVOR. *In Defense of Reason.* Denver. University of Colorado Press. 1947.

WRIGHT, NATHALIA. *Melville's Use of the Bible.* Durham. Duke University Press. 1949.

B. Articles

ARVIN, NEWTON. "Melville's Shorter Poems," *PR,* XVI (1949), 1034-36.

AUDEN, W. H. "The Christian Tragic Hero," *New York Times Book Review* (December 16, 1945), 1, 21.

AULT, NELSON A. "The Sea Imagery in Herman Melville's 'Clarel'," *Research Studies of the Students' College of Washington,* XXVII (June, 1959), 72-84.

BARRETT, LAWRENCE. "The Differences in Melville's Poetry," *PMLA,* LXX (September, 1955), 606-23.

BELL, MILLICENT. "Pierre Bayle and *Moby-Dick,*" *PMLA,* LXVI (September, 1951), 626-48.

BEWLEY, MARIUS. "A Truce of God for Melville," *SR*, LXI (Autumn, 1953), 682-700.

BEZANSON, WALTER E. "Melville's 'Clarel' The Complex Passion," *Journal of English Literary History,* XXI (1954), 146-59.

BEZANSON, WALTER E. "Melville's Reading of Arnold's Poetry," *PMLA,* LXIX (June, 1954), 365-91.

BOWEN, MERLIN. "Tactics of Indirection in Melville's *The Confidence-Man,*" *Studies in the Novel,* I (1969), 401-20.

BRASHER, H. C. "Ishmael's Tattoos," *SR, LXXX* (Winter, 1962), 137-54.

BRASWELL, WILLIAM. "Melville As a Critic of Emerson," *AL*, IX Fame," *AL,* V (1934), 360-64.

BRASWELL, WILLIAM, "Melville As a Critic of Emerson," *AL*, IX (1937), 317-334.

BRASWELL, WILLIAM. "Melville's Use of Seneca," *AL*, XII (1940), 98-105.

BRODTKORB, PAUL. "The Confidence-Man: The Con-Man as Hero," *Studies in the Novel,* I (1969), 421-35.

BRODWIN, STANLEY. "Herman Melville's *Clarel*: An Existentialist Gospel," *PMLA* (1971), 378-87.

CHASE, RICHARD. "An Approach to Melville," *PR,* XVI (May-June, 1947), 285-95.

CHASE, RICHARD. "Dissent on 'Billy Budd'," *PR,* XVI (November, 1948), 1212-18.

DIX, WILLIAM S. "Melville and Evil," *Rice Institute Pamphlet,* XXXV (July, 1948), 81-107.

FAST, HOWARD. "American Literature and the Democratic Tradition," *English Journal,* XXXVI (1947), 55-60.

FOGLE, RICHARD H. "Melville and the Civil War," *Tulane Studies in English,* IX (1959), 61-89.

FOGLE, RICHARD H. "Melville's *Clarel:* Doubt and Belief," *Tulane Studies in English*, X (1960), 101-16.

GIOVANNI, G. "Melville's 'Pierre' and Dante's 'Inferno'," *PMLA,* LXIV (March, 1949), 70-78.

GROSS, JOHN J. "Melville, Dostoevsky, and the People," *Pacific Spectator,* X (Spring, 1956), 160-70.

HILLWAY, TYRUS. "Pierre, the Fool of Virtue," *AL,* XXI (1949), 201-11.

HILLWAY, TYRUS. "Taji's Quest for Certainty," *AL,* XVIII (1946), 27-34.

HILLWAY, TYRUS. "Melville and the Spirit of Science," *SAQ,* XLVIII (January, 1949), 77-88.

HILLWAY, TYRUS. "Melville's Geological Science," *AL,* XXI (May, 1949), 232-37.

HILLWAY, TYRUS. "Melville's Use of Two Pseudo-Sciences," *MLN,* LXIV (March, 1950), 145-50.

HILLWAY, TYRUS. "Melville as Critic of Science," *MLN,* LXV (June, 1950), 411-14.

HILLWAY, TYRUS. "Melville as Amateur Zoologist," *MLQ*, XII (June, 1951), 159-64.

HITT, RALPH E. "Melville's Poems of Civil War Controversy," *Studies in the Literary Imagination,* II (1969), 57-68.

HOMANS, GEORGE. "The Dark Angel," *NEQ*, V (October, 1932), 699-730.

HOLLIS, SOPHIE. " 'Moby-Dick': A Religious Interpretation," *Catholic World,* CLXIII (1949), 158-62.

HOWARD, LEON. "Melville's Struggle with the Angel," *MLQ*, I (June, 1940), 195-206.

HUBBEN, WILLIAM. "Ahab, the Whaling Quaker," *Religion in Life* (Summer, 1949), 364.

LARABEE, S. A. "Melville Against the World," *SAQ*, XXXIV (October, 1935), 410-18.

MANSFIELD, LUTHER. "Glimpses of Herman Melville's Life in Pittsfield, 1850-51," *AL*, IX (1938), 26-48.

MARSHAL, H. P. "Herman Melville," *The London Mercury,* VI (November, 1924 to April, 1925), 56-70.

MATHER, FRANK J. "Herman Melville," *Weekly Review,* I (August 9, 1919), 276-78; (August 16, 1919), 298-300.

MATHEWS, J. CHESLEY. "Melville's Reading of Dante," *Furman Studies,* VI (Fall, 1958), 1-8.

MILLER, JAMES E. "Hawthorne and Melville: The Unpardonable Sin," *PMLA,* LXX (March, 1955), 91-114.

MILLER, PERRY. "Melville and Transcendentalism," *VQR*, XXIX (Autumn, 1953), 556-75.

MORRIS, LLOYD. "Melville: Promethean," *Open Court,* XLI (September, 1931), 513-26; (October, 1931), 621-35.

MYERS, HENRY ALONZO. "Captain Ahab's Discovery," *NEQ*, XV (March, 1942), 15-34.

O'CONNOR, WILLIAM VAN. "Melville on the Nature of Hope," *UKCR,* XXII (1955), 123-40.

OLIVER, EGBERT S. " 'Cock-a-Doodle-Do!' and Transcendental Hocus Pocus," *NEQ,* XXI (June, 1942), 204-16.

OPITS, E. A. "Herman Melville, An American Seer," *Contemporary Review,* No. 2 (December, 1946), 348-53.

PARKES, HENRY B. "Poe, Hawthorne, Melville, An Essay on Sociological Criticism," *PR,* XVI (February, 1949), 157-65.

POMMER, HENRY F. "Melville as Critic of Christianity," *Friends Intelligencer,* CII (1945), 121-23.

PURCELL, JAMES MARK. "Melville's Contributions to English," *PMLA,* LVI (1941), 797-808.

RAHV, PHILIP. "The Dark Lady of Salem," *PR*, VII (1941), 362-81.

RUSSELL, W. C. "A Claim for American Literature," *North American Review,* CLIV (1892), 138-49.

SALT, H. S. "Herman Melville," *The Universal Review,* IV (May, 1889), 78.

SALT, H. S. "Imperial Cockneydom," *Scottish Art Review,* II (1889), 186-90.

SCHIFFMAN, JOSEPH. "Final Stage, Irony: A Reexamination of 'Billy Budd' Criticism," *AL*, XXII (1950), 128-36.

SEALTS, MERTON. "Herman Melville's 'I and My Chimney'," *AL*, XIII (1941), 142-54.

SEALTS, MERTON. "Melville's Reading: A Check List of Books Owned and Borrowed," *Harvard Library Bulletin,* II (Spring, 1948), 141-63; (Autumn, 1948), 378-92; III (Winter, 1949), 119-30; (Spring, 1949), 268-77; (Autumn, 1949), 407-21; IV (Winter, 1950), 98-109; VI (Spring, 1952), 239-47.

SHORT, R. W. "Melville As Symbolist," *UKCR,* XV (Autumn, 1949), 38-49.

STEIN, WILLIAM B. "Melville's Poetry: Its Symbols of Individuation," *L&P*, VII (May, 1957), 21-26.

STEWART, RANDALL. "Melville and Hawthorne," *SAQ,* LI (1952), 436-66.

STODDARD, RICHARD H. "Herman Melville," *New York Mail and Express* (October 8, 1891), 5.

SULLIVAN, J. N. W. "Herman Melville," *Times Literary Supplement,* No. 1123 (July 26, 1923), 493-94.

THORP, WILLARD. "Herman Melville's Silent Years," *University Review,* III (1937), 254-62.

VAN VECHTEN, CARL. "The Later Work of Herman Melville," *Double Dealer,* II (1922), 9-20.

VON ABELE, RUDOLPH. "Melville and the Problem of Evil," *American Mercury,* LXV (1947), 592-93.

WAGENKNECHT, EDWARD. "Our Contemporary Melville," *English Journal, XXXIX* (March, 1950), 121-28.

WAINGER, B. M. "Herman Melville: A Study in Disillusion," *Union College Bulletin,* XXV (January, 1932), 35-62.

WARREN, ROBERT PENN. "Melville the Poet," *KR,* VIII (Spring, 1946), 208-23.

WATSON, E. L. G. "Melville's 'Pierre'," *NEQ,* III (April, 1930), 195-234.

WATSON, E. L. G. "Melville's Treatment of Acceptance," *NEQ,* VI (June, 1933), 319-27.

WATTERS, REGINALD E. "Melville's Isolatoes," *PMLA,* LX (1945), 1138-48.

WATTERS, REGINALD E. "Melville's Metaphysics of Evil," *UTQ,* IX (1940), 170-82.

WATTERS, REGINALD E. "Melville's Sociality," *AL,* XVII (1945), 33-49.

WEBER, WALTER. "Some Characteristic Symbols in Herman Melville's Works," *ES*, (1949), 30.

WELLS, HENRY W. "An Unobtrusive Democrat, Herman Melville," *SAQ,* XLIII (January, 1944), 46-51.

WELLS, HENRY W. "Herman Melville's 'Clarel'," *College English,* IV (1943), 478-83.

WEST, RAY B. "Primitivism in Melville," *Pr. S,* XXX (Winter, 1956), 369-85.

WILLIAMS, STANLEY. "Melville," *Eight American Authors,* ed. Floyd Stovall, New York, Modern Language Association (1956), 207-70.

WINTERICH, JOHN T. "The Compleat Collector," *SRL,* VII (1932), 531.

WOODRUFF, STUART. "Melville and His Chimney," *PMLA,* LXXV (June, 1969), 283-92.

C. Reviews of *Clarel* at Time of Publication

Academy, CV (October, 1876).

Galaxy, XXII (August, 1876).

Independent, XXVIII (July 6, 1876).

Library Table (August 1, 1876).

Lippincott's Magazine, XVIII (September, 1876).

New York Daily Tribune (June 16, 1876).

New York Times (July 10, 1876).

Westminster Review, CV (October, 1876).

World (June 1876).

D. Selected Unpublished Materials

BENNETT, JOHN F. "Melville's Humanitarian Thought." Unpublished Doctoral Dissertation. University of Wisconsin. 1956.

BEZANSON, WALTER E. "Herman Melville's 'Clarel'." Unpublished Doctoral Dissertation. Yale University. 1943.

GRIFFITH, FRANK. "Melville and the Quest for God." Unpublished Doctoral Dissertation. Iowa State University. 1952.

HAYFORD, HARRISON. "Melville and Hawthorne." Unpublished Doctoral Dissertation. Yale University. 1945.

HETHERINGTON, HUGH. "The Reputation of Herman Melville in America." Unpublished Doctoral Dissertation. University of Michigan. 1933.

KIMPEL, BERNARD. "Herman Melville's Thought After 1851." Unpublished Doctoral Dissertation. University of North Carolina. 1942.

MAHONEY, MOTHER M. DENIS. " 'Clarel': An Investigation of Spiritual Crisis." Unpublished Doctoral Dissertation. Catholic University. 1957.

ZEIK, MICHAEL. "The Traditional Element in Herman Melville's Thought with Special Attention to 'Clarel'." Unpublished Doctoral Dissertation. Georgetown University. 1958.

Index